THE BRITISH CONSERVATIVE GOVERNMENT AND THE EUROPEAN EXCHANGE RATE MECHANISM, 1979–1994

HELEN THOMPSON

PINTER

First published 1996 by
Pinter, A Cassell Imprint
Wellington House, 125 Strand, London WC2R 0BB
215 Park Avenue South, New York, NY 10003

© Helen Thompson 1996

British Library Cataloguing in Publication Data
A catalogue record for this book is available from the British Library

Library of Congress Cataloging-in-Publication Data
Thompson, Helen, 1967–
    The British conservative government and the European exchange rate
mechanism, 1979–1994/Helen Thompson.
    p. cm.
    Includes bibliographical references and index.
    ISBN 1–85567–379–7
        1. Monetary policy–Great Britain.   2. Great Britain–Politics and
government–1979–   3. European Monetary System (Organization)
I. Title.
HG939.5.T49   1996
332.4'56'09104–dc20   95–25348
                                                                          CIP

Printed and bound in Great Britain by Biddles Limited, Guildford and Kings Lynn

Contents

CONTENTS

List of Figures

Abbreviations

CAP	Common Agricultural Policy
CBI	Confederation of British Industry
CEE	Council of Economic Experts
DHSS	Department of Health and Social Security
DTI	Department of Trade and Industry
EC	European Community
ECOFIN	Economic and Financial Affairs Council of the EC
Ecu	European Currency Unit
EEC	European Economic Community
ERM	Exchange Rate Mechanism
EMF	European Monetary Federation
EMI	European Monetary Institute
EMS	European Monetary System
EMU	Economic and Monetary Union
ESCB	European System of Central Banks
EU	European Union
FCO	Foreign and Commonwealth Office
FRN	Floating Rate Notes
GATT	General Agreement on Tariffs and Trade
GDP	Gross Domestic Product
GNP	Gross National Product
G5	Group of 5
G6	Group of 6
G7	Group of 7
IGC	Inter-Governmental Conference
IoD	Institute of Directors
IMF	International Monetary Fund
MAFF	Ministry of Agriculture, Fisheries and Food
MTFS	Medium Term Financial Strategy
NATO	North Atlantic Treaty Organization
NEC	National Executive Committee (of the Labour Party)
NEDC	National Economic Development Council
OECD	Organization for Economic Co-operation and Development
PSBR	Public Sector Borrowing Requirement
RPR	Rassemblement pour la République
SEA	Single European Act
TESSA	Tax Exempt Special Savings Accounts
TUC	Trade Union Congress

Dramatis Personæ

BALLADUR, Edouard, French Prime Minister, 1993–95.

BECKETT, Terence: Director-General CBI from 1980–87.

BRITTAN, Leon: British member of the European Commission.

BUTLER, Michael: Chairman of the City European Committee.

BURNS, Terence: Chief Economic Adviser to the Treasury, 1979–91;
Permanent Secretary to the Treasury from 1991.

CALLAGHAN, James: British Prime Minister until 1979.

CARRINGTON, Peter (Lord): British Foreign Secretary 1979–82.

CHIRAC, Jacques: French Prime Minister, 1986–88.

CLARKE, Kenneth: British Chancellor of the Exchequer from 1993.

COUZENS, Kenneth: Second Permanent Secretary at the Treasury until 1982.

DELORS, Jacques: French Finance Minister and then President of the European
Commission.

GISCARD d'ESTAING, Valéry: French President until 1981.

DULSENBERG, Wim: President of the Dutch central bank.

GEORGE, Eddie: Governor of the Bank of England from 1993.

GRIFFITHS, Brian: Head of the British Policy Unit.

HEALEY, Dennis: British Chancellor of the Exchequer until 1979.

HEATH, Edward: British Conservative Prime Minister, 1970–74.

HESELTINE, Michael: Member of the British Cabinet until 1986 and after
1990.

HOWE, Geoffrey: British Chancellor of the Exchequer, 1979–83; British Foreign
Secretary, 1983–1989; British Deputy Prime Minister, 1989–90.

HURD, Douglas: British Foreign Secretary, 1989–95.

INGHAM, Bernard: Press Secretary to Margaret Thatcher, 1979–90.

KINNOCK, Neil: Leader of the Labour Party, 1983–92.

KOHL, Helmut: German Chancellor from 1982.

LAMASSOURE, Alain: French European Affairs Minister in Edouard Balladur's
government.

LAMFALUSSY, Alexander: Head of the European Monetary Institute.

LAMONT, Norman: Chancellor of the Exchequer, 1990–93

LAROSIERE, Jacques de: President of the Bank of France until 1993.

LAWSON, Nigel: Financial Secretary at the Treasury, 1979–81; British Chancellor of the Exchequer, 1983–89.

LEIGH-PEMBERTON, Robin: Governor of the Bank of England, 1983–93.

LITTLER, Geoffrey: Second Permanent Secretary at the Treasury, 1983–88.

LUBBERS, Ruud: Dutch Prime Minister from 1982.

MACMAHON, Kit: Deputy Governor of the Bank of England until 1985.

MAJOR, John: British Foreign Secretary, 1989; Chancellor of the Exchequer 1989–1990; Prime Minister from 1990.

MIDDLETON, Peter: Permanent Secretary to the Treasury, 1983–91.

MITTERRAND, François: President of France, 1981–95.

NIEHANS, Jurg: Swiss economist adviser to Margaret Thatcher.

OTTO-POHL, Karl: President of the Bundesbank until 1991.

PORTILLO, Michael: Member of the British Cabinet under John Major's premiership.

POWELL, Charles: Private Secretary on Foreign Affairs to the British Prime Minister.

REAGAN, Ronald, American President, 1981–88.

RICHARDSON, Gordon: Governor of the Bank of England until 1983.

RIDLEY, Nicholas: Member of the British Cabinet until 1990.

RUDING, Onno: Dutch Finance Minister.

SANTER, Jacques: President of the European Commission from 1995.

SCHLESINGER, Helmut: President of the Bundesbank from 1991.

SCHMIDT, Helmut: West German Chancellor until 1982.

STOLTENBERG, Gerhard: West German Finance Minister, 1982–89

THATCHER, Margaret: British Prime Minister, 1979–90.

THORN, Gaston: President of the European Commission, 1981–85

TUGENDHAT, Christopher: British member of the European Commission.

WAIGEL, Theo: German Finance Minister from 1989.

WALTERS, Alan: Personal Economic Adviser to Margaret Thatcher.

WASS, Douglas: Permanent Secretary to the Treasury until 1983.

WHITELAW, William: Member of the British Cabinet until 1987.

Preface

This book has a simple objective – to explain the policy of the British Conservative government towards the European Exchange Rate Mechanism (ERM) from the time it entered office in 1979 until 1994. Quite evidently, it is a story which differs dramatically from that of any other European Union (EU) state and the ERM. Not only was Britain the only member state to opt out of the system at its creation in 1978, but in the ensuing years the question of whether sterling should climb aboard was the subject of a bitter internal struggle within the Thatcher governments. Even after Britain finally joined the ERM in October 1990, the Conservative government, now under John Major's leadership, uniquely chose to bide its time at the Maastricht summit over whether to participate in a European single currency. Then, nine months later, Major and his Chancellor were forced, along with the Italian government, to suspend sterling's membership of the ERM. From beginning to end the British Conservative government has chosen to approach monetary integration in a fundamentally different way to its European partners.

To some, no doubt, the development of British policy can simply be explained in terms of an almost pathological anti-Europeanism. Britain has been first a bystander and then a late passenger on the European integration boat, from the European Coal and Steel Community to Maastricht. From critics and supporters of British policy alike comes the oft-expressed notion that British 'awkwardness,' is simply a question of the country's unique historical attachment to its national identity and sovereignty, as if France and Germany willingly sell out their national interests to Euro-idealism. Certainly a state whose Prime Minister could remark in 1954 that 'only the English-speaking peoples count; that together they can rule the world',[1] fully deserves all the contempt for its ignorance and insularity in which it is often held. Nonetheless, racism and xenophobia ultimately only explain history if and when they infiltrate how those who wield power perceive their interests. Post-imperial self-righteousness and arrogance have regularly deluded British policy-makers, including those deliberating about the ERM, but to explain particular policy developments is to understand how this self-deception has been translated into a broader and more encompassing set of political interests. At the heart of this book, therefore, is an attempt to explain the idiosyncracy of the British ERM story from a firm conception of the interests and subsequent dilemmas of successive Conservative politicians, the specifics of which are elucidated in the Introduction.

Written as a piece of contemporary history, this study is methodologically imperfect. It is largely based on a combination of print media sources and my interviews with relevant policy-makers. The main published sources were: a systematic examination of all coverage of the ERM membership issue in the *Financial Times*, *The Times* and *The Economist*; the general accounts of government economic policy from 1979 given by major commentators; academic studies of the ERM and discussion of the Conservative governments; the relevant reports and minutes of evidence of the House of Commons and House of Lords select committees; the reports of international economic organizations such as the OECD; and biographies and memoirs of political actors, particularly those of Nigel Lawson and Margaret Thatcher. Of these sources the Lawson and Thatcher memoirs are probably the most problematic. Whilst both authors present their accounts as the authoritative record of the Thatcher governments, at times they offer directly contradictory analysis of ERM policy and related issues. In this book, therefore, neither memoirs are taken at face value. Nonetheless, an important distinction is drawn between them. Whilst Lawson's and Thatcher's interpretation of events can be jointly criticized, Lawson offers a depth of detail about day-to-day policy-making on the issue and a general consistency strikingly absent in Thatcher's account. The former Prime Minister's memoirs are generally top heavy on glamorous overseas trips, and often ahistorical on ERM membership.[2] Consequently, I have regularly drawn upon Lawson's account of internal government meetings, at least as a starting point for discussion, even if particular elements are subsequently challenged. By contrast, Thatcher's memoirs are for the most part used only as an account of her own struggle with Lawson and as a potential insight into her motives at different times.

Between 1992 and 1995 I interviewed 29 people, mostly British civil servants and Bank of England officials. With one exception, which involved written correspondence, the interviews were carried out in person. All the interviews were conducted on a non-attributable basis. Given the ongoing sensitivity of the issue, this was insisted upon by all interviewees. Where possible the approximate institutional position of the interviewee quoted or referred to is cited, but protecting anonymity sometimes even makes this information impossible. Obviously, this approach is fraught with difficulty. I have, inevitably, made my own judgements about competing subjective memories and claims, and the reader is in no position to assess for him or herself the particular credibility of any source. However, as a broad rule, no information from any particular interviewee has been used unless there is some other reason for believing it to be true. At the same time it was possible to make reasonable judgements about the validity of particular information offered through cross-referencing or 'triangulating' evidence, comparing claims with other interviewees responses, documentary sources and media coverage. For example, the claim in Chapter 1 that Geoffrey Howe came to support membership as early as 1981–82 was based on evidence to this effect by three interviewees, one of whom was a personal friend of Howe but opposed to ERM membership, another who was also a personal friend and a supporter of membership, and a third who opposed membership and had generally clashed with Howe.

I very much hope that one day somebody with access to official papers will write a more complete history. I am certain that I am guilty of errors of fact, misjudgements and omissions (the record of the discussions about ERM entry which took place in 1981 and the start of 1982 is most clearly incomplete). To have attempted to reconstruct the development of the Conservative government's policy towards the ERM at this point in time was not intended as hubris or to overstep the limits of scholarly endeavour. I am acutely aware of the strengths of the historical method and the perils of half-informed judgements. It is simply to say that I was confident that there were enough presently available sources, in one guise or another, to draw some reasonable conclusions about a subject with such immense implications for Britain's economic and political future. What follows is in many ways an unedifying, albeit at times entertaining, story of a set of politicians, who for reasons of their own, found it difficult to resolve a fundamental question of whether or not Britain's currency should be tied to those of its EU partners. Out of that legacy they, or a new Labour government, will decide over the next few years on Britain's monetary future in relation to the rest of the world economy. To have some reasonable sense of how we arrived at this position will, if history is anything to go by, change nothing, but to my mind it is preferable to merely intellectually acquiescing to the absurdities that so often pass for serious commentary on the subject in this country.

To say that I have accumulated extreme debts in writing this book is an inadequate reflection of reality. Quite simply, there is little in this enterprise which can be separated from my dependence on others from before I even began. My first debt is to Patrick Dunleavy, my doctoral thesis supervisor at the London School of Economics. Although I fear at times I exasperated him with my less than coherent thinking and writing, his patience, kindness and criticism made it possible for me to progress both as a doctoral student and in revising the study for publication. Whatever the inadequacies of this book, they would have been far greater without his help. At the LSE I must also thank Brian Barry, Alan Beattie, George Jones and John Barnes for their encouragement and perceptive suggestions. I am also happy to acknowledge the financial assistance of the William Robson Memorial Fund in preparing this manuscript for publication. A very special debt of gratitude goes to Claire Wilkinson for her generous help in facilitating the interviews, unfailingly sorting out what no doubt seemed like an endless series of problems and enduring an awful lot of my less than amenable moods.

My sincere thanks to the various people who allowed me to interview them. For reasons of confidentiality I cannot thank them personally, but I am very grateful for their time, courtesy and quite often candour.

Through writing this book I have become deeply aware of how much I learned from being taught British politics, as an undergraduate, by Jim Bulpitt at the University of Warwick. His stubborn commitment to the analysis of history and politics as they have happened, rather than for the convenience of our own ideological mythologies, has been an example from which I hope I have profited.

My thanks also go to Stanley Hening from the Department of European Studies at the University of Central Lancashire who generously gave me considerable freedom and the resources to complete my doctorate as swiftly as I could manage. Whilst my actions undoubtedly suggested otherwise, my gratitude, albeit redundant, is deep and enduring.

To those who helped academically with their encouragement and advice, I would like to thank Robert Elgie, Andrew Gamble, Dave Good, Steve Griggs, Peter Hennessy, Bob Hepple, Christopher Hood, William Keegan, Hans-Dieter Klingemann, Paul Taggart and Etain Tannam. I would also like to thank Veronica Higgs at Cassell for her unfailing help.

I am grateful to Peters, Fraser and Dunlop for the permission to quote from *The View from No. 11* by Nigel Lawson.

Needless to say, I alone am responsible for what follows and the errors which no doubt remain.

As this book has progressed from doctoral thesis to manuscript, its physical production has over the last two years been made difficult by my somewhat trying personal circumstances. Left to my own devices, I would simply have ground to a halt. To those who made it possible for me to continue, I am acutely grateful. To my parents, Barbara and Christopher Thompson, who, as always, leaped to my aid with care and generosity; to Alice Thompson for unselfishly giving me so much of her time up and down the country when there were infinitely more pleasurable things to do than sit at a word processor; to Julian Reindorp who typed much of my doctoral thesis with interest and enthusiasm way beyond the call of friendship; and to Kate Abernethy, whose professional skill, and good humour, saved me when I was rapidly running out of options just as the end was in sight.

My final debt is to Thanasis D. Sfikas who, although we now live separate lives, continues to inspire. In his completeness and his lucidity, he remains the most extraordinary person I have ever known. By far the greatest pleasure, and the greatest sadness, in writing this book has been the knowledge that in the end it would be dedicated to him.

Helen Thompson
Cambridge
May 1995

NOTES

1 Quoted in A. Milward, (1992) *The European Rescue of the Nation-State*, London: Routledge, p. 432.

2 For example, on p. 723, Thatcher comments that 'until now [October 1990], the ERM had never been a rigid system . . . With the publication of the Delors Report, however, the Europeans began to regard the ERM as part of the move towards locking currencies, leading to a single currency. Accordingly, devaluations were more frowned upon than they had been. But they still occurred . . . It was only when my successor went along with the objective of EMU as spelled out in the Maastricht Treaty and made it clear that sterling would enter the narrow band of the ERM that the pressure never to revalue "growed and growed" until it became an overriding dogma.' In reality, there were no effective realignments of currencies within the ERM from 1987 (before the Delors Report) to 1992. During this period, the ERM states were absolutely committed to maintaining parities even when this was costly and the ERM operated as a 'rigid system'.

For Thanasis, in whom there was an invincible summer

Introduction

Trying to understand the development of any particular set of policies or decisions made by British governments raises some fundamental problems of analysis. Can decision-making be separated from the idea of the state? Is the policy process driven by politicians, bureaucrats or interest groups? Do politicians have collective interests, and, if so, are they defined by electoral, party or ideological considerations? What are the environmental and structural constraints on elite actors pursuing their own interests? Most importantly, if we are to do more than tell a story, then we must provide some answers to the questions of who are the principal actors in decision-making and how the interests of those actors are to be conceptualized.

Whilst it would have been possible to apply a conventional theoretical approach to this study – for example, using a rational choice, new institutionalist or neo-Marxist perspective – I believe that any of these methods would distort rather than add to our understanding of the matter in hand. The traditional rational choice models of economic policy-making, namely the variants of the political business cycle, have little to say about governments' interests in relation to the means by which their electoral ends are reached, and are too focused on narrow economic options to accommodate the EU dimension to the ERM issue. A new institutionalist approach, focusing on the major organizational locations of British government and their enduring rules, would fly in the face of the most casual empirical observation that shifts in policy towards the ERM did not develop either gradually or in response to long-run adaptions in the positions of institutional actors. Meanwhile, any neo-Marxist analysis would rely on accepting the dubious assumption that there is a necessary relationship between ministerial decision-making and an accumulation strategy. If the story of ERM membership

1

is indeed the story of a major fault line in Conservative government in the 1980s and 1990s, it would surely be a mistake to assume a priori that the development of policy can be explained in terms of the strategic project of 'Thatcherism'.

Given the limited utility of established modes of analysis, this study is based on a particular series of assumptions about British and EU politics and political economy as they relate to the substance of the ERM issue. The remainder of this Introduction articulates the nature of these assumptions as an analytical framework, and what this means in terms of the practical organization of the book. Of course, the particular assumptions outlined are open to criticism from those with a different theoretical disposition, but ultimately their value can only be judged by the quality of the explanation they produce of how the Conservative government's ERM policy developed.

The first assumption of this study is that the crucial British political actors on the ERM stage were the Prime Minister, the Chancellor and the Foreign Secretary. Through much of the general academic literature on British economic policy, the image of an all-powerful Treasury, assisted by the Bank of England, looms large.[1] But in the only comprehensive empirical analysis of decision-making on economic policy issues, Bruce-Gardyne and Lawson concluded, 'what is striking about our case histories is the chequered record of Treasury achievement.'[2] In general, as the history of the first Wilson government testifies to, it is the Prime Minister and Chancellor who have dominated economic policy-making, particularly on issues of monetary and exchange rate management. They are generally autonomous both from the preferences of the Treasury and the Bank of England and from their Cabinet colleagues, who tend to be involved only on issues of public expenditure.[3]

Nevertheless, on an issue like the ERM, it is reasonable to expect that the decisive EU policy actors will also exercise influence. During Britain's applications for EEC entry and the early years of membership, both commentators and participants in the policy-making process believed that the Foreign Office dominated successive Foreign Secretaries.[4] However, there are several reasons for believing that the Prime Minister, Foreign Secretary and Chancellor were always going to be firmly in control of the ERM issue in EU policy terms. Whilst ministers had very limited electoral interests in the 1960s applications for EEC membership, since then European policy has become significant electorally, both directly and indirectly, and ministers have clearly defined interests independent of the Foreign Office. Unsurprisingly, in this context commentators have perceived a shift in EU policy authority towards the Prime Minister.[5] At the same time, even in the 1960s the Foreign Office was not influential in international economic issues. On non-devaluation, which was directly relevant to the applications for EC membership, the Foreign Office exercised no influence at all. When the Labour government finally decided to devalue in 1967, the Foreign Office was not involved at any stage of the decision-making process.[6] In sum, this book places the Prime Minister, Chancellor and Foreign Secretary at the centre of analysis. It is the interests and interactions of these three ministers which define the space in which the other institutions of the core executive operate.[7]

The second assumption of this book is that the behaviour of these actors is best analysed through at least starting with some notion of rationality. This is not to suggest that human behaviour is always rational, motivated by a clear-sighted and fully informed set of preferences, and exercised so as to maximize benefits net of costs – given constraints. Quite obviously, human beings are often deluded and foolish, and pursue contradictory ends. But this does not mean that it is either empirically tenable, or analytically useful, to say simply that their behaviour is random and purposeless. Even if ultimately unsuccessful in achieving their ends, political actors clearly do identify interests for themselves, which then direct their behaviour. Those interests may well not be based on perfect information, nor will actors necessarily strive to do other than 'satisfice' them, but it is not unreasonable to assume that they will also seek to calculate and pursue them in a generally consistent manner.[8] For this particular study, therefore, I am assuming that the set of motivations brought to bear on the ERM question by the Prime Minister, Chancellor and Foreign Secretary in 1979 were still the same in 1994. What is important is to understand the context and the constraints under which those motivations were played out at any particular time. The question which that raises, of course, is just what might be the interests of politicians in office on a matter like the ERM.

The third assumption of this book is that ministers making decisions on the ERM will have three broad interests, relating to economic policy, policy towards the EU and their capital accumulation priorities. Of these three factors primacy is given to ministers' economic policy interests, and that interest is understood to be first and foremost to maximize the chance of re-election. This supposition is justified on several grounds. First, the attempt to win power through the electoral system is what distinguishes parties from other political organizations. It would, therefore, seem reasonable to define the interests of their elite actors in relation to that activity. Second, the nature of the British political system intensifies what is the logical preference of any set of ministers to hold on to power. Since there are no alternative sources of power to controlling the House of Commons, such as an effective second chamber or regional government, governments which do not secure re-election are left with nothing.[9] Third, it is widely accepted that macro-economic outcomes and considerations are very significant determinants of general elections.[10] With the electorate so sensitive to a government's economic performance, it would be very odd if ministers did not prioritize the electoral consequences of economic policy options. Fourth, by allowing the Prime Minister to select the date of a general election, the British political system gives full scope to managing economic policy in an electoral cycle.

However, as Dunleavy recognizes, accepting the primacy of electoral interests does not mean that governments will exclusively pursue preference-accommodating policies or strategies. Rather, it is quite logically and empirically reasonable to believe that ministers can use their political power to shape preferences to their own advantage.[11] Indeed, governments have considerable scope to pursue electoral objectives in economic policy beyond preference accommodation. As Grant and Nath argue, voters' view of the relative importance of different economic issues changes over time, and governments can engineer that change by affecting voters' perception of what is and is not possible regarding certain economic variables. In this view politicians attempt to ensure that they are judged on the main economic variable which they said was important on entering office.[12]

At the same time preference accommodation may have adverse electoral consequences for a governing party. Voters perceptions' of politicians are by no means solely dependent on their assessment of the relationship between their own policy preferences, however those preferences are shaped, and a government's policy performance. By and large the electorate's perception of a government's general competence is also important. Governments are likely to suffer electorally if they pursue policies which cause serious public divisions either in ministerial ranks or within their parliamentary party. Whatever their views on actual policy, voters tend to react against muddle and conflict. Moreover, a government's electoral interests will deter them from policies which are likely to be difficult to implement effectively. Such problems will tend to arise when a government has adversarial relations with those institutions or groups on which it relies to execute particular policies. Once more the electorate may well react against any impression of weak government, whatever its underlying policy preferences. Certain policies may, therefore, be ruled out neither on ideological grounds nor because they fail to accommodate sufficient preferences on the immediate policy issue.

In this context it is assumed that ministers do not have fixed interests in economic policy. Instead, their behaviour has to be analysed within the context of a range of considerations defined by the electoral cycle.

First, ministers want to provide material benefits to sufficient voters, particularly in the run-up to a general election. Alternatively, they may look to strengthen the economic position of their political constituencies *vis-à-vis* other social and geographic groups. Second, ministers seek to deliver particular policy benefits on which they have, or can at least plausibly claim to have, a comparative advantage over opposition parties. Third, they have an interest in delivering an economic policy package to the electorate which can be sold effectively by the rhetorical political language they have adopted. Fourth, ministers are interested in pursuing policies which they can implement effectively, and which do not create problems of party management. Finally, ministers' economic policy interests are not independent from their position in other policy areas.

Even in assuming a collective electoral interest for ministers, it is still possible to account for divisions between them. At a simple level, ministers will disagree over the best short- and long-term means to achieve re-election, whether it be the electorate's likely response to particular policy outcomes or issues of general credibility. More profound conflict will occur over fundamental ideas as to how the macro-economy works, or assessments of Britain's position in the international economic and political system. Different beliefs about underlying economic relationships and structures, for example, will lead to different judgements about the relationships of both individual and the combination of policies to electoral ends. This is not to suggest that all conflict between ministers can be simply reduced to a dispute over electoral strategy without regard to ideological disagreement. But it is to say that how ministers resolve conflict over specific policy decisions cannot be analysed without considering the relevant electoral environment.

Having conceptualized ministers' economic policy interests in terms of re-election, this study gives primacy to domestic politics in understanding their EU policy interests.[13] As Milward has so persuasively shown, empirical investigation has laid bare the paucity of functionalism and neo-functionalism as explanations of integration within Western Europe. To understand the EU is first and foremost to understand national policy choices, conditioned by domestic politics, and the relationship between those choices and what can be achieved through inter-governmentalism and integration.[14] Moreover, what is true for any member state in terms of domestic politics is particularly true for a British government. Obviously, EU policy offers ministers potential electoral benefits in terms of leadership and controlling resources. But the adversarial nature of British party conflict and long-standing political ambivalence towards EU membership means that opposition parties can potentially reap high rewards from any misjudgement in policy. At the same time, with EU membership serving as a cross-cutting party cleavage, governments' freedom of manoeuvre is often constrained by their own party if they want to avoid a problem of party management. Consequently, ministers have a strong interest in whether their overall stance strikes a pro- or anti-European tone. In this context, the interests of the Prime Minister, Chancellor and Foreign Secretary in regard to the ERM cannot be separated from either their objectives over the full range of EU policy issues or domestic political management.

Pluralists and elite theorists would no doubt argue that any attempt to conceptualize a framework of interests for ministers on the ERM could stop here. For example, in his essentially pluralist analysis of British economic policy-making, Grant sees no reason why ministers should be constrained by the interests of capital, nor any empirical evidence that they are, arguing that capital in Britain is generally weak in relation to the state.[15] However, simply to stress capital's weakness in terms of representation ignores the interactive relationship which exists between the interests of ministers and those of capital. If the aim of macro-economic policy is to deliver particular outcomes in a real economy organized around capital, then ministers have an interest in the general performance of capital. At the same time, since ministers can affect the process of accumulation, they may develop an interest in the growth of particular forms of accumulation.[16]

Certainly, selective intervention in the accumulation process offers ministers in general, and the Prime Minister and Chancellor in particular, opportunities to pursue preference-shaping strategies. Of the four broad strategies identified by Dunleavy, two are directly relevant. First, ministers can identify social locations or geographical areas where their support is concentrated, and then systematically facilitate their growth. By contrast, growth in locations preponderantly supporting opposition parties can be discouraged. Second, even if the size of particular social groups is not altered, ministers may intervene to alter their relevant social and economic position in order to strengthen their party's support among a target category. Ministers can accrue electoral benefit by increasing the perception of advantage of particular social and economic groups *vis-à-vis* other such groups.[17] To achieve these ends, ministers can give financial assistance to investment in particular sectors of the economy through R&D partnerships and direct subsidies and grants. Alternatively, ministers can assist selective sectors through the regulatory framework which is applied for business operations, or they can create incentives for investment in particular geographical areas through special tax breaks and infrastructure expenditure. Such policies can clearly add both to the absolute and relative prosperity of the groups who are dependent upon the economic performance of a geographical area or sector of the economy.

It is ministers own attitude towards accumulation which is likely to determine the impact of capital interests on policy outcomes. In this respect, ministers' interests will vary according to circumstance. The potential electoral gains of preference-shaping in the medium term will be measured against the short-term costs in terms of time and resources. Ministers may choose not to intervene, or opt for limited intervention, or they may try to develop a systematic accumulation strategy to ensure a steady flow of material benefits to a potential electoral base.

Consequently, if ministers do not have priorities in terms of capital accumulation, then they are unlikely to be constrained in economic policy by the effects of different outcomes on particular sites of accumulation. By contrast, ministers who possess a fairly systematic accumulation strategy for particular groups of capital are more likely to consider the preferences of those capital groups in their policy choices. The pursuit of a particular intervention strategy may act as a self-imposed constraint on economic policy. This does not mean that ministers' interests in regard to the former will necessarily triumph over the latter, but that intervention strategies will create an additional cost-benefit analysis. Ministers face incentives to pursue particular policies, and will embrace costs when they decide on policies which are detrimental to their favoured sites of accumulation. In this context, ministers' own interests in capital accumulation have to be understood within their overall electoral interests.

The organization of this book reflects the analytical framework outlined above. Chapters 1 to 5 each begin with an examination of the operation of the ERM during a particular period. This provides a clear yardstick for assessing the costs and benefits to the British government of membership and non-membership at that time. The narrative then chronologically traces the development of policy, with particular emphasis given to those periods when ERM membership was actively discussed within the Prime Minister-Chancellor-Foreign Secretary triangle.

In considering these long periods of decision-making about whether to join the ERM, the aim is to reconstruct the choices facing the Prime Minister, Chancellor and Foreign Secretary at any one time, given their interests, and then to describe how the issue eventually played out. Within this context the specific objectives are threefold. First, I seek to assess the costs and benefits of ERM membership in economic and EU policy, given the preferences of the principal ministerial actors and the government's overall electoral position. In terms of economic policy, the analysis considers the effects of membership on ministers' ability to pursue their monetary, exchange rate and fiscal objectives. In regard to

EU policy, the analysis identifies the impact of ERM policy on ministers' ability to bargain within the Union, given their domestic considerations and overall EU objectives. Second, I outline and examine the likely effects of ERM entry on particular capital groups, and the efforts of those groups to influence policy within the context of ministers' own capital accumulation priorities. Third, I identify and explain the positions taken by, and the interactions between, the Prime Minister, the Chancellor and the Foreign Secretary, and consider the views held by officials at the Treasury, the Foreign Office and the Bank of England. In the process, I analyse the terms and assumptions in which these actors saw the ERM, and the whole question of exchange rate management.

Chapter 6, describing Britain's short-lived membership of the ERM and subsequent withdrawal, is organized somewhat differently. The first part of the chapter examines sterling's participation in the ERM from October 1990 to the crisis months of the summer of 1992. At this point, the choices facing British ministers are reconstructed in terms of their economic and EU policy interests and capital accumulation priorities; this is followed by a discussion of the events leading to Black Wednesday and sterling's exit from the system. The second half of the chapter examines how British ministers handled Britain's renewed non-membership of the ERM in the same terms as those identified above. The final chapter then draws some conclusions about British policy from 1979 to 1994.

NOTES

1 See P. Anderson, (1964) 'The Origins of the Present Crisis', *New Left Review*, 23; T. Nairn, (1979) 'The Future of Britain's Crisis', *New Left Review*, 113; F. Longstreth, (1979) 'The City, Industry and the State', in C. Crouch (ed.), *State and Economy in Contemporary Capitalism*, London: Croom Helm; G. Ingham, (1984) *Capitalism Divided: The City and Industry in British Social Development*, London: Macmillan; A. Ham, (1984) *Treasury Rules: Recurrent Themes in British Economic Policy*, London: Quartet; S. Pollard, (1982) *The Wasting of the British Economy: British Economic Policy 1945 to the Present*, London: Croom Helm; C. Thain, (1985) 'The Education of the Treasury: The Medium Term Financial Strategy', *Public Administration*, 63 (3); H. Heclo and A. Wildavsky, (1977) *The Private Government of Public Money: Community and Policy Inside British Politics*, London: Macmillan; D. Coates, (1980) *Labour in Power*, London: Longman; W. Keegan and R. Pennant-Rea, (1979) *Who Runs the Economy: Control and Influence in British Economic Policy*, London: Maurice Temple-Smith; P. Mosely, (1984) *The Making of Economic Policy*, Brighton: Harvester Press.

2 J. Bruce-Gardyne and N. Lawson, (1970) *The Power Game: An Examination of Decision-Making in Government*, London: Macmillan, p. 162.

3 See Bruce-Gardyne and Lawson, *The Power Game*, for a more detailed discussion.

4 See Bruce-Gardyne and Lawson, *The Power Game*; G. Edwards, (1992) 'Central Government', in S. George (ed.), *Britain and the European Community: The Politics of Semi-Detachment*, Oxford: Clarendon Press.

5 See D. Vital, (1968) *The Making of British Foreign Policy*, London: Allen & Unwin; G. Edwards, 'Central Government'; S. Jenkins and A. Sloman, (1985) *With Respect Ambassador: An Inquiry into the Foreign Office*, London: BBC.

6 W. Wallace, (1975) *The Foreign Policy Process in Britain*, London: Royal Institute of International Affairs, pp. 169–73.

7 For a discussion of the idea of the core executive, see P. Dunleavy and R. Rhodes, (1990) 'Core Executive Studies in Britain', *Public Administration*, 68, (Spring) pp. 3–28.

8 This understanding of rationality is derived from Simon's idea of 'bounded reality'. See H. Simon, (1957) *Administrative Behaviour*, New York: Free Press. For a discussion of its application to British politics, see J. Bulpitt, (1988) 'Rational Politicians and Conservative Statecraft in the Open Polity', in P. Byrd (ed.), *British Foreign Policy Under Thatcher*, Oxford: Philip Allan.

9 Bulpitt, 'Rational Politicians and Conservative Statecraft', pp. 187–88.

10 See, for example, D. Sanders, (1991) 'Government Popularity and the Next Election', *Political Quarterly*, 62, pp. 235–61.

11 P. Dunleavy, (1991) *Democracy, Bureaucracy and Public Choice: Economic Explanations in Political Science*, Brighton: Harvester Wheatsheaf.

12 W. Grant and S. Nath, (1984) *The Politics of Economic Policymaking*, Oxford: Blackwell, p. 141.

13 For analyses of the EU and member states centred on domestic politics, see S. Bulmer, (1983) 'Domestic Politics and European Community Policy-Making', *Journal of Common Market Studies*, 21 (4), pp. 349–63; S. George, (1994) *An Awkward Partner: Britain in the European Community*, 2nd edn., Oxford: Oxford University Press; George (ed.), *Britain and the European Community*; S. Bulmer and W. Patterson, (1987) *The Federal Republic of Germany and the European Community*, London: Allen & Unwin.

14 A. Milward, (1992) *The European Rescue of the Nation-State*, London: Routledge.

15 W. Grant with J. Sargent, (1987) *Business and Politics in Britain*, London: Macmillan, p. 26.

16 The term 'accumulation' is used in this context not out of the mistaken belief that capitalism is completely dependent on capital accumulation, but as a convenient shorthand for the complex processes of investment and regulation which determine economic performance.

17 Dunleavy, *Democracy, Bureaucracy and Public Choice*, p. 120.

1

The ERM, the EC Budget and Monetarism: 1979–1983

Occasionally words must serve to veil the facts. But this must happen in such a way that no one must become aware of it; or, if it should be noticed, excuses must be at hand, to be produced immediately.
Machiavelli, *Instructions to Raffaello Girolami*

THE ERM: A DIRTY FLOAT

The ERM was born out of disillusionment among the EC states with the floating exchange rate regime which followed the collapse of Bretton Woods. By 1978 floating was producing not only diverging currencies but a licence for states to inflate at will, with three significant effects. First, floating made a nonsense of many of the trade, industrial and, particularly, farming policies of the Community, which were based on some unanimity of interests. Second, intra-Community trade was threatened. In principle, floating should have been beneficial because most intra-Community trade was in manufactured goods, producing a competition of labour costs that made it essential that exchange rates offset those cost differentials. However, floating was not achieving this result, and instead rates were overshooting – namely moving in the opposite direction to inflation – and creating demands for protectionist policies. Finally, floating was making demand management difficult. Those states with weak currencies who attempted to expand in an inflationary environment came under sustained deflationary pressure in the foreign exchange markets. Meanwhile, states with stronger currencies found that trying to stimulate demand in export-oriented sectors was ineffective as the investment climate was being primarily determined by the international monetary environment and not by individual macro-economic policies.

This general disillusionment was most keenly felt by the West German Chancellor, Helmut Schmidt. His particular anxiety was that the downward float of the dollar was strengthening the Deutschmark against other European currencies, leaving German goods uncompetitive and the Deutschmark increasingly functioning as an international reserve asset. In political terms, Schmidt saw a European monetary system as an act of self-assertion by Europe against the Carter administration, which he considered too weak to provide leadership out of the world economic malaise and unresponsive to Europe's interests, particularly in security matters. Schmidt found a significant ally in President Giscard d'Estaing of France. Giscard was keenly aware of the costs to French farmers of the disruption to the Common Agricultural Policy (CAP), and believed that French industry would only become a world competitor when some anti-inflationary discipline was injected into the French economy. Moreover, if Germany was to reflate its economy as Giscard wished, it needed, he calculated, to be offered the carrot of monetary stability.

It was from this coalition of German and French interests that the political impetus for a European monetary system was born. Having decided to act, Schmidt and Giscard looked to bring the British government into their deliberations and established a triumvirate team for discussions. However, the British representative, Kenneth Couzens, a senior Treasury official responsible for international finance, quickly became isolated from his French and German colleagues, who simply developed their own proposal for a new European system of pegged exchange rates, which Schmidt and Giscard then presented to the Bremen European Council in July 1978.[1]

The proposal elicited a mixed response from the British Prime Minister, James Callaghan, and his Chancellor, Dennis Healey. While neither relished the prospect of isolation from the other EC states, they were worried that Britain would not be able to maintain a parity within the proposed system without bearing costs, given sterling's status as a petro-currency, its fundamental weakness in relation to the Deutschmark and its track record in fixed exchange rate systems. Within the Labour Cabinet, the parliamentary party, the NEC and the TUC there was significant opposition to joining any system which might be deflationary or appear to subordinate British interests to those of Germany. Callaghan and Healey sought to keep their options open as long as possible, but the opposition came to a head at the Labour Party conference in October 1978 where a barrage of anti-membership motions were forwarded. Confronted with this awkward reality, Callaghan turned decisively against participating in the new initiative.[2]

In December 1978 in the aftermath of the European Council in Brussels, the EC states formally agreed to launch a European Monetary System (EMS) with an Exchange Rate Mechanism (ERM) as the centrepiece of the system. Whilst all nine EC states were to be members of the EMS, Britain alone would not participate in the ERM. The start of the system was delayed by a French effort to raise farm prices and finally came into operation in March 1979. The aims of the EMS were

11

threefold: first, and most importantly in the short term, to facilitate trade by creating a zone of monetary stability in the EC; second, to co-ordinate the monetary and exchange rate policies of member states towards the rest of the world; and, third, to prepare the way for the birth of a European Monetary Federation (EMF) and the use of the European Currency Unit (Ecu) as a reserve currency.[3]

The ERM itself was designed to try to combine some of the advantages of a fixed exchange rate system with those of flexibility. Each member agreed a central rate for its currency in terms of a weighted composite basket currency known as the Ecu. These central rates were organized in a parity grid and each participant undertook to defend their currency within a 2.25 per cent band of the parity, or a 6 per cent band for the Italian lira. Pressure on the parities was measured through a divergence indicator. If a single currency varied by more than 75 per cent of its permitted divergence from the system as measured by its Ecu exchange rate, corrective action had to be taken, whether it be by central bank intervention or policy adjustment. In the event of sustained pressure, the parity rates could be realigned relatively easily by col-lective agreement.

If the ERM states did not want to contemplate frequent realign-ments, then the system was going to exert a counter-inflationary discipline on economies which expanded too rapidly in relation to their partners. A unilaterally expanding state, sucking in imports, would eventually be faced with either a balance of payments deficit or rising inflation. Consequently, the state's currency would fall towards the bottom of its ERM band. Under its membership obligations, that government would either have to intervene to buy its currency, deflate its fiscal policy to restrain the demand for imports or raise interest rates to attract capital. States with currencies appreciating towards the top of their band would have to sell their currencies or cut interest rates to keep their currency down.

The consequence for weak currency states might be that they had to deflate when the domestic economy needed to expand. For strong currency states there would be a cost in fuelling their money supply through intervention, and in renouncing the counter-inflationary weapon of an appreciating exchange rate. However, if the provisions for easy realignments were utilized, as certainly Schmidt and Giscard envisaged them to be, there would be no reason why the ERM should perform as a traditional fixed-rate system at all. Instead, it would operate as a 'dirty float'. The chief aim would be to allow the exchange rate to offset some differential in inflation without letting currencies move in the opposite direction to inflation, as frequently occurred under free floating.[4]

The ERM 1979–83

For most of the duration of the first Thatcher government the ERM operated as a 'dirty float' without any currency permanently dominating the system. In 1979–80 balance of payment differentials were the primary determinants of currency movements, initially leaving the lira as the strongest currency. By contrast, the Deutschmark was often relatively weak due to a large German external deficit in the wake of the second oil price shock. Member states sought to maintain their currency parities primarily by monetary policy adjustment, making no effort to co-ordinate fiscal policy, and accepting realignments when parities came under serious pressure. Indeed, the first realignment occurred in September 1979, just six months after the system's birth, when the Danish krone was devalued and the Deutschmark revalued. Two months later, the krone was devalued again. Clearly showing their preoccupation with reducing exchange rate volatility, at the start of 1980 France and Germany agreed between themselves to postpone both the creation of any EMF and the use of the Ecu as a reserve asset.[5] By the first anniversary of the system's birth in March 1980, the ERM states were heralding their success, with the European Commission reporting that in a generally poor economic environment the ERM was cutting exchange rate instability between EC states by two-thirds.[6]

However, in the summer of 1981 the ERM came under its first serious threat, as the meteoric rise of the dollar – the result of the Reagan administration's tight monetary policy and benign neglect of the American currency – reached fresh heights.[7] With the Deutschmark bearing the brunt of the dollar's rise, the Bundesbank was forced to raise its interest rates, leaving the other ERM states to follow suit as their currencies weakened against the Deutschmark. Whilst 1980 had passed without any realignments, 1981 saw the devaluation of the lira twice and the franc, together with the revaluations of the Deutschmark and the Dutch guilder. With high interest rates and exchange rate instability threatening the fragile recovery of the EC economies from recession, in the latter half of 1981 the ERM states started expressing interest in developing the system further. In November 1981 the French Finance Minister, Jacques Delors, set out proposals for extending the use of the Ecu and defining an 'agreed zone' across the Atlantic in which the dollar would be maintained in a stable relation to other currencies within that zone. But agreement in practice proved difficult, particularly on the vexed question of a joint approach to the dollar, and the ERM remained in a state of some flux.[8] By the end of 1982, the French franc, the lira, the krone and the Belgian and Luxembourg franc had all been devalued and the Deutschmark and guilder revalued again. Unsurprisingly, amidst these circumstances, inflation rates remained generally high among the ERM states, with the difference between the low inflation states around Germany and others such as France and Italy accelerating. Unlike a typical fixed exchange rate system, the ERM was not producing inflation convergence. Rather, with all the realignments occurring in the same direction as inflation it was simply operating as a dirty float to prevent overshooting.[9]

CONSTRUCTIVE EUROPEANISM AND MONETARY TARGETS: MAY–OCTOBER 1979

The Conservative party first became involved with the ERM issue in the aftermath of the Bremen summit in July 1978. Condemning Callaghan for standing outside the EC mainstream, Thatcher declared in the House of Commons that the British people were shocked to find themselves 'relegated to the European second division', having been 'the victors in Europe'.[10] But for all Thatcher's rhetorical denunciations of the Labour government, the Conservative Party had given little thought to the matter itself. Only in November did a policy emerge, when Geoffrey Howe, the Shadow Chancellor, persuaded his colleagues to support the principle of the proposed ERM as a possible way forward.[11] When, on 6 December, Callaghan announced in the House of Commons that Britain would not be joining the ERM, Thatcher responded that 'This is a sad day for Europe'. Labour was, according to Thatcher, content to have 'Britain classified among the poorest and least influential countries' in the EC.[12] Again, however, Thatcher's rhetoric masked ambivalence: at no stage did she or any other member of the opposition front bench promise that a Conservative government would reverse the decision. Indeed, the 1979 general election Conservative manifesto did not mention the subject at all.[13]

After the Conservative general election victory in May 1979, the new Chancellor, Geoffrey Howe, announced that Britain's non-membership of the ERM would be reviewed, and a decision taken by September as to whether to join the system.[14] In many ways this was a paradoxical decision, because there was such a clear conflict between ministers' apparent economic policy agenda and the demands of ERM membership. In May 1979 Conservative ministers were publicly committed to reducing inflation as their fundamental macro-economic objective, by controlling the growth of the money supply, as measured by the monetary aggregate sterling M3 (£M3). This is a broadly defined monetary aggregate consisting of cash and current and deposit bank accounts, of which the two main components are bank lending and the Public Sector Borrowing Requirement (PSBR). The PSBR, the government promised, would be reduced by cuts in public expenditure, and bank lending would be controlled by interest rate policy. In theory, therefore, Thatcher and Howe wanted to direct both monetary and fiscal policy at inflation. What they renounced on the counter-inflationary front was any kind of incomes policy, reverting instead to free collective bargaining.

In practice, the government's policy, as manifested in the June 1979 budget, was more ambivalent. In terms of monetary policy, Howe honoured the counter-inflationary commitment by tightening the £M3 range inherited from Labour and increasing interest rates by 2 per cent. He further reduced the volume of public spending in 1979–80 by £1.5 billion and set cash limits on expenditure to squeeze out another £1 billion. However, other aspects of policy were decidedly inflationary. A 3 per cent cut in the standard rate of income tax and a reduction in the top tax rate from 83 to 60 per cent in the budget increased demand in the economy. The income tax cut was then financed by increasing VAT from 7 to 15 per cent, adding 4 per cent to inflation over the next year. At the same time Howe cut subsidies to nationalized industries, who responded by raising their prices, boosting inflation by another 2.5 per cent. To finally compound the inflationary pressure, Thatcher and Howe decided to implement the Clegg Commission recommendation on public sector pay awards, leading to an increase of 25 per cent in the sector's wage bill and triggering a large rise in private sector claims.

The one area which operated as an unambiguous counter-inflationary bias was the exchange rate itself. With Thatcher and Howe leaving the currency to the market, sterling swiftly appreciated, responding both to its new status as a petro-currency and to high interest rates. Given that sterling rose well beyond the 2.25 per cent range allowed to ERM currencies, Thatcher's and Howe's hands-off approach was completely incompatible with ERM membership. They simply could not have effectively pursued monetary targets inside the ERM. The central bank intervention necessary to keep a currency within a fixed range means that money will enter and leave circulation according to the requirements of that objective. When a currency appreciates, the central bank has to sell the currency and so add to the national money supply, whatever the consequences for monetary growth. In 1977, for example, the Labour government had tried to hold sterling below a rate of $1.70 to $1.75 whilst operating money supply targets. But the Bank of England's foreign exchange market operations meant that £M3 over-shot its target, forcing the government to abandon the sterling ceiling.

The potential conflict in policy objectives which the ERM review raised was intensified by the policy instrument which Thatcher and Howe had chosen to limit money supply growth. With bank lending an important component, £M3 could be controlled primarily either by interest rates or by some form of qualitative credit controls. Rationing credit in some manner would perhaps have made it possible to reach some accommodation between strict monetary targets and ERM membership. But Thatcher and Howe chose to rely on interest rates, categorically preventing any simultaneous pursuit of both policies. During July 1979, Howe lifted some exchange controls and then, in October, all remaining controls except those pertaining to Rhodesia. As a result, the corset which set a limit on the growth of banks' interest-bearing liabilities became redundant, as banks could now by-pass the controls by lending to British customers from overseas subsidiaries. In sum, whilst the ERM states used interest rates as the exclusive policy instrument of membership, Thatcher and Howe were using interest rates as virtually the exclusive instrument of a monetary policy directed at a money supply target.

At the same time there was no incentive for the government to review ERM policy in terms of their attitude towards capital accumulation. Although both the manufacturing sector and the City were declining relative to international competition, Conservative ministers showed no real interest in any project to galvanize either of them. Instead, ministers hoped to improve the competitiveness of manufacturing industry by withdrawing subsidies and regional aid from the sector. Meanwhile business groups were not putting any pressure on ministers to join the ERM. Although manufacturing industry would probably have benefited more from membership than the prevailing policy, in so much as inside the ERM sterling and interest rates would have been lower, the CBI was opposed to ERM entry. It retained the view, which it had expressed in 1978, that membership would run the risk of leaving sterling overvalued and overall policy deflationary.[15] In the City, views on the best long-term approach to the ERM question were more mixed.[16] But even those institutions which in principle favoured membership judged that the time was not opportune to join because of the volatile monetary environment produced by the falling dollar. Notwithstanding the problems that high interest rates and sterling's volatility caused some City firms, particularly those which were themselves dependent on borrowing or relied on manufacturing clients, no voices for ERM membership were heard from this quarter in 1979.[17]

Given the absence of any economic incentive for ERM membership, the rationale for the policy review initiated in May 1979 lay firmly in the government's European policy hopes. On taking office, the new ministers signalled both a willingness to link the troublesome issue of Britain's budget contributions to other outstanding matters in Community politics and a general desire to be more *communitaire* than the outgoing Labour government. By August Conservative ministers had made significant concessions to their EC partners over farm price rises, Community authority over industry subsidies, nuclear energy research and pollution and had implicitly accepted that the EC states should have some special rights in regard to North Sea oil. On the ERM issue itself, in June Howe agreed to contribute 20 per cent of Britain's gold and dollar reserves to the European Monetary Co-operation Fund in exchange for Ecus.[18] The next month, the Chancellor dropped the Labour government's claim for an automatic interest rate subsidy if Britain were to join the system and accepted that this would depend on economic conditions on entry.[19]

This evidence suggests that ministers were at this stage at least considering the possibility of using ERM entry to secure a deal on Britain's budget contributions. The problem with this strategy was that once sterling started to appreciate none of the other EC states were particularly keen for Britain to join the ERM, believing that sterling's strength, especially as a petro-currency, would disrupt the mechanism. France, the most reluctant to compromise over the budget, now positively wanted Britain to stay out. To make matters even less promising, the German government, who ministers desperately needed as an ally on the budget, was most interested in gaining concessions over access to North Sea oil after the second oil price shock.[20] Ultimately, by allowing, and indeed welcoming, an appreciating exchange rate as a counter-inflationary weapon, ministers made their incentive to consider ERM membership redundant.

Within this context it is not surprising that the policy review turned into a low–key affair with Foreign Office officials making most of the running. Senior Foreign Office officials believed, as they had done in 1978, that membership made sense on economic and political grounds:

> We just thought that the Treasury was wrong on their own grounds but that is not an easy battle to fight … A lot of us felt that we were making a perfectly serious economic and financial analysis, but it happened to be different from what was certainly the majority view in the Treasury.[21]

In the view of another diplomat, 'we would have had less of a battle over the budget if we had been more accommodating on the ERM'.[22] Similarly, a member of the European Secretariat at the Cabinet Office reflected: 'Had we been a full participant in the ERM our general standing could have made our task on the budget that much easier … It would have reduced the antagonism.'[23] Whatever the merits of their case, the Foreign Office officials made little headway with Lord Carrington, the Foreign Secretary, who saw Rhodesia as the fundamental problem facing the department, and was neither interested nor well-versed in economic issues.[24]

Meanwhile Howe was not inclined to develop the interest he had shown in opposition any further, and received no encouragement to do so from Treasury officials. In 1978 the Treasury had been rigorously opposed to ERM membership for several reasons, and remained so. From the beginning Treasury officials 'had considerable doubt as to whether it [the ERM] would survive,'[25] and did not want Britain to participate in a mechanism which could be construed as anti-dollar. Even within a viable system, they considered that sterling's status as a petro-currency and the likely dominance of German interests, leaving sterling overvalued, would provide an inappropriate policy mix.[26] At the same time the Treasury dismissed the idea that the matter should be linked to European policy, and challenged the Foreign Office's competence on the issue:

> Although it [the FCO] has consistently had some very bright people on the economic side, who understand the issue as well as anybody else, the Foreign Office is perceived both in Number 10 and the Treasury and elsewhere in Whitehall as sort of stepping outside of its own parish if it gets involved in financial and monetary discussions. And it is always quite difficult for the Foreign Office to influence that, although they have had people who understand the issue just as clearly in economic terms as anybody else. It's part of the Whitehall one-upmanship. In the same way, the Foreign Office will tend to say to people, 'Oh, you don't understand the foreigner' and so on. The Treasury will always say to the Foreign Office: 'You don't really understand finance, you're amateurs dabbling in this game. We're the real professionals.'[27]

Lacking support from the politicians, the Foreign Office would have looked in vain to the Bank of England to support its economic case. Although Gordon Richardson, the Governor of the Bank, publicly expressed cautious support for the objectives of the ERM in June 1979, he was at this time far from committed to membership.[28] According to one Foreign Office official, Richardson was not prepared to 'put its [the Bank's] head very far above the parapet on the issue'.[29]

In this light on 22 July the government let it be known that a final decision as to whether to join the ERM was being postponed until October or November. But when in mid-September rumours took hold in the foreign exchange markets that sterling would enter the ERM by the end of the month, officials told the press that Britain would remain outside the system.[30] The next month, Thatcher held a meeting with Richardson, Howe and other Cabinet officials to discuss the matter. Quickly agreeing that membership was not appropriate, they devised a formula to say that Britain would join the system when the 'time was right'.[31] Clearly, whatever limited advantages the ERM might provide on Britain's budget contributions, economic policy objectives had priority.

SCHMIDT AND THE EC BUDGET: MARCH 1980

Nonetheless, five months later the ERM issue surfaced again, when, on 5 March 1980, Chancellor Schmidt promised Thatcher that membership could increase Britain's chance of securing a satisfactory budget deal.[32] Schmidt believed that sterling's participation in the ERM would balance the system and reduce the pressure on the Deutschmark as a reserve asset.[33] After her meeting with Schmidt, Thatcher signalled her willingness to reconsider the issue, even though sterling was continuing to rise steeply and Howe and the Treasury were busy putting the finishing touches to the Medium Term Financial Strategy (MTFS). The MTFS, presented in the budget that month, aimed to control inflation over four financial years; the rate of monetary growth, measured by £M3, would be progressively reduced through cutting the PSBR. The strategy was attempting to concentrate both monetary and fiscal policy on inflation, which had risen from 10.3 per cent in May 1979 to 19.8 per cent in March 1980, largely as a result of the 1979 budget. Monetary policy, the MTFS specified, would be set according to £M3 growth, and fiscal policy would remain tight, with any further cuts in taxation left to the future. With no mention of an exchange rate objective, the MTFS as a monetary strategy was deeply incompatible with ERM membership. At the same time, with sterling already appreciating and Britain having the most favourable external deficit in the EC, sterling would probably have come under further upward pressure once inside the ERM. If, as a result, sterling was revalued, despite being an inflationary currency, then the other ERM states would have had to accept the kind of overshooting which was contrary to the entire rationale of the system as it was then operating.

Given Thatcher's and Howe's commitment to the MTFS, there would have needed to have been an overwhelming case in terms of European policy benefits for Schmidt's offer to have been seriously considered. Certainly, ministers were in a difficult position on the budget dispute. At the Dublin summit in December 1979 Thatcher's insistence on 'our money back' had diminished the chances of any early settlement, and afterwards the French press reported that France no longer cared whether Britain stayed in or left the Community. Although Schmidt had been fairly sympathetic to Britain's case in 1979, by the start of 1980 he felt that increased German security expenditure in the wake of the Afghanistan crisis placed the negotiations in a different perspective. Now Thatcher faced another European summit at the end of March without the prospect of any budget agreement. Her weak bargaining position was further exacerbated by domestic politics. By 1980 Labour was starting to commit itself to withdrawal from the EC, and with the economic advantages of membership at their lowest since 1973, some Conservatives feared that Labour could reap considerable electoral advantage from its new stance.[34]

Nevertheless, there was still no clear trade-off between ERM membership and a budget solution. Germany wanted concessions on a common energy policy, as well as on the ERM, in return for its support, whilst France and others still feared that sterling's participation would disrupt the system. Moreover, France saw progress on the budget as inexorably linked to a common lamb policy; meanwhile, Denmark and Holland wanted an early agreement on a common fisheries policy.[35] The dilemma for the British government, therefore, was that there was neither a guarantee that membership would resolve the budget issue nor any real domestic incentive to be seen as more *communitaire*.

In this context, it is not surprising that there is scant evidence that either Thatcher or Howe ever seriously contemplated accepting Schmidt's proposal. Not only did Thatcher generally not like trade-off bargaining on EC issues, she increasingly believed that the budget issue should be resolved on its own merits. As one exasperated Foreign Office official remarked, 'it was a constant difficulty to try to persuade her to see things that way ... She would say that was typical Foreign Office stuff'.[36] At the same time Thatcher recognized, as she told French television on 10 March, that sterling's performance – inexorably bound up with the government's monetary policy – gave rise 'to very considerable difficulty' in joining the ERM.[37]

Unsurprisingly, when Thatcher chaired another high-level meeting to discuss the issue, she insisted that 'domestic monetary policy must remain paramount'.[38] The only new support for ERM entry came from Richardson and other senior Bank officials. They were not interested in the budget question, but now supported entry for the exact opposite reason from which Thatcher and Howe were opposed: Richardson and these officials disliked the strict targets of the MTFS, and believed that ERM membership would result in a welcome devaluation of sterling, restoring industrial competitiveness and making intra-European trade easier.[39] Richardson's view was by no means a unanimous one at the Bank of England; officials in the domestic monetary division, for example, remained opposed to joining a system which would have eroded the active role which they enjoyed under the existing discretionary monetary regime.[40] Nevertheless, with Richardson now an ERM supporter, the Bank had effectively set its stall for the debate which was to follow in subsequent years. As one Bank official put it, on an issue like ERM, 'in a way all that matters is what the Governor says'.[41]

By the end of the month, Thatcher and Howe were re-articulating their opposition to membership in public. Howe told a German financial magazine that the time was not ripe for membership because of sterling's volatility, Britain's high inflation and the possibility of further capital outflows following exchange control abolition.[42] Meanwhile Thatcher was preparing to turn the European policy dimension to the issue on its head. On 18 March Thatcher told the House of Commons that Britain might withhold part of its EC payments if a satisfactory budget agreement was not reached.[43] Such an action would have breached the Treaty of Rome, but France had recently successfully violated EC law in banning British lamb imports, making the British threat more credible than it might otherwise have been.[44] Far from using ERM membership as part of a bargaining strategy in the Community, Thatcher was now determined to present the Conservative government as the resolute defender of British national interests and remove Labour's possibly dangerous charge of pro-Europeanism. Ten days later, after another summit with Schmidt, Thatcher declared that control of the money supply must have priority in British economic policy, and the episode was brought to an end.[45]

SLAMMING THE DOOR: JUNE 1981–JUNE 1983

For the next 15 months the ERM issue remained dormant, only to resurface in June 1981. At that time Nigel Lawson, then Financial Secretary and third minister in line at the Treasury, tried to open the issue with Howe. Lawson believed that membership was likely to operate as a more successful counter-inflationary monetary discipline than the monetary targets, which were by now proving extremely difficult to achieve and might prove even more troublesome in the run-up to the general election.[46]

In July and August the press reported that the government was considering ERM membership again.[47] However, at this stage there is no evidence that Lawson's views were having any impact on either Howe or Thatcher. On 14 September Lawson joined the Cabinet as Secretary of State for Energy and was effectively excluded from the policy debate which was to come.[48] Leaving a final memo to Howe on the subject, he wrote:

[We are] receiving increasing evidence of the weakness of £M3 as a reliable proxy for underlying monetary conditions, without any greater confidence being able to be attached to any of the other monetary aggregates. This clearly strengthens the case for moving over to an exchange rate discipline.[49]

Howe appeared to remain unconvinced, claiming to the press that sterling's depreciation during 1981 did not alter its petro-currency status, and that the other ERM states did not wish Britain to join.[50]

It was in October 1981 that the question Lawson had raised about ERM membership as a possible counter-inflationary monetary discipline was given real impetus. Whilst the two previous reviews of policy were driven by European factors, the discussions which took place at the end of 1981 and the start of 1982 were firmly rooted in economic policy considerations. On 16 September and 1 October Howe raised interest rates to defend sterling from downward pressure in the foreign exchange markets. The decision represented both a clear indication of how far policy had departed from the MTFS and the pertinence of Lawson's question about whether ERM membership was the best way to use the exchange rate as a monetary discipline.

Crucially, whilst the MTFS was clearly incompatible with ERM membership, Thatcher and Howe were now pursuing an economic policy which could not only be easily adjusted to ERM entry but which in many ways would have positively benefited from sterling's participation in the system. In November 1980 the Prime Minister and Chancellor had taken their first step away from the MTFS when they cut interest rates from 16 to 14 per cent, despite the fact that £M3 was rising rapidly. The cut came after the CBI had promised the government a 'bare knuckle fight' over sterling's appreciation, and ICI had announced a third-quarter loss. It was a recognition that the strength of sterling was badly damaging industrial competitiveness and deepening the recession. Thatcher proceeded to commission the Swiss economist Jurg Niehans to investigate the cause of sterling's appreciation. He concluded that sterling's rise was largely due to excessively high interest rates and that sterling's status as a petro-currency was responsible for only 20 per cent of the appreciation. If monetary policy was too tight, Niehans judged, then the strict pursuit of the £M3 targets was the problem.

The Niehans Report inspired the 1981 budget. The budget combined planned cuts in public expenditure and an increase in income tax with a 2 per cent cut in interest rates to 12 per cent. Despite the furore which the budget caused among those who saw it only as a mad deflationary squeeze that would deepen the recession, the aim was quite clearly to use monetary policy to bring sterling down to stimulate growth, whilst switching the emphasis of the counter-inflationary strategy to fiscal policy. Thatcher and Howe were now effectively accepting that, contrary to the theory of the MTFS, the exchange rate did matter as a determinant of economic policy, and in the aftermath of the budget sterling began to fall.

But, by the third quarter of 1981, ministers reckoned that sterling was falling too steeply, reacting not only to the lower level of British interest rates but to the strength of the dollar. After Bank of England intervention failed to protect sterling, Howe raised interest rates from 12 to 14 per cent on 16 September and by a further 2 per cent on 1 October, despite the risk of creating a secondary recession. Only when sterling stabilized did Howe reverse the increases in four half of one per cent stages between 14 October and 22 January. After October 1981, it was evident, despite claims to the contrary, that Thatcher and Howe were using a fairly narrow exchange rate target rather than a £M3 target as the basis of monetary policy. Between October 1981 and October 1982 sterling averaged 88 to 92 on its effective index against other currencies, and changes in interest rates clearly occurred within the context of sterling's performance and not the £M3 targets.[51] The Prime Minister and Chancellor's new policy reflected both their acceptance that the exchange rate was important and their inability to run a successful policy around £M3. The money supply targets were simply never met, and by the end of 1981, ministers could no longer offer the distorting effects of the corset abolition and a civil service strike as credible excuses. Although Howe and the Treasury examined other possible monetary targets such as money GDP (GDP in current prices) and M0 (cash plus banks deposits with the Bank of England) as different methods of monetary control, they did not elevate them to the status previously held by £M3.

Since the experiment with monetarism was effectively over, ERM membership was obviously much more compatible with ministers' apparent economic objectives than in 1979 and 1980. First, and most fundamentally, Thatcher and Howe were committed to the general aim of exchange rate stability. Whilst Thatcher and Howe were pursuing an exchange rate target based on sterling's effective index – which included its performance against non-ERM currencies – ERM membership would not have required a significant shift in policy. Second, the Prime Minister and Chancellor had accepted in the 1981 budget that monetary and fiscal policy could be used for different purposes. In assigning the former to the exchange rate and the latter to controlling domestic expansion, they formulated policy in the way most compatible with ERM membership. Third, in the autumn of 1981 sterling was falling against the dollar in the same way as the ERM currencies were, and British ministers had responded in a similar way to their Community counterparts. Rather than Britain having singular interests as a petro-currency state, the new situation revealed certain shared interests between Britain and the ERM states. At the same time ERM membership offered ministers actual positive benefits in achieving their monetary objectives. It was likely that sterling would have become established as a strong ERM currency because of the importance of balance of payment differentials in determining currency movements within the system at this time. Against the background of the interest rate hike in September and October 1981, membership was, therefore, likely to mean that sterling could be defended at a chosen rate with lower interest rates and with reserve intervention by the Bank supported by other ERM states.

The benefits of ERM membership as a counter-inflationary monetary discipline were matched by a potential pay-off for ministers in terms of those sectors of the economy which they wished to support. After leaving manufacturing industry to itself in 1979 and 1980, ministers were now pursuing a more interventionist policy. In the first quarter of 1981 the government gave financial assistance to British Leyland and ICL, respectively. When Patrick Jenkin took over from Keith Joseph at the Department of Trade and Industry in September 1981, he developed a fairly positive industrial policy, if never naming it as such. It involved actively promoting rationalization and re-industrialization in declining industries, help for small firms with loans, and support for innovation in sunrise high technology industries such as fibre optics and telecommunications. Although the CBI remained opposed to entry, if ERM membership could deliver a measure of exchange rate stability and lower interest rates, manufacturing industry stood to benefit. At the beginning of October sterling was lower than at any time since the Conservatives came to office. Whilst some – the chemical industry, for example – wanted sterling to go lower, there was considerable consensus in industry that the exchange rate was tolerable.[52] At any rate, even if industrialists did want a cheaper pound, Thatcher and Howe were not prepared to allow sterling to fall – at least in the short term – and membership would have reduced the risk of a new appreciation in sterling.

Only in terms of European policy objectives was there little case for ERM entry. Sterling's depreciation and the desire of the ERM states in 1981 to develop the system did mean that Britain's non-membership of the ERM was a more salient issue within the Community than in 1979–80. In June the Commission President, Gaston Thorn, publicly called for Britain to enter the system to help strengthen the EC zone against the dollar.[53] Three months afterwards the British Commissioner, Christopher Tugendhat, made a similar call.[54] More importantly, the other member states were now seriously interested in British entry. In September Delors publicly reversed France's stance on the issue.[55] This was shortly followed by a statement from the Bundesbank chief, Karl Otto-Pöhl, that British entry would not only protect sterling but was necessary for the system to develop.[56]

However, whilst ERM membership potentially offered ministers greater bargaining leverage within the Community than in 1979 and 1980, Thatcher, in particular, was not interested in relinking the issue with Britain's budget contributions. In May 1980 Thatcher had agreed to a temporary two-year budget agreement, and three months later Britain assumed the EC presidency. At the same time British electoral politics was being transformed by the rise of the Alliance. The Conservatives now faced two opposition parties: one strongly committed to the EC at the same time as public opinion seemed to be shifting back towards maintaining EC membership, and the other committed to withdrawal from the EC, which remained the majority view of the electorate. Consequently, although ministers saw the presidency as an opportunity to create general goodwill, they appeared content to avoid a final budget settlement to position themselves politically as the defender of Britain's national interests within the Community.[57]

Howe and the ERM

Against this backdrop, it was Howe who gave real impetus to a new ERM debate. Whilst Lawson, Thatcher and Howe have all claimed in their memoirs that Howe remained opposed to membership at this time, and indeed for the remainder of his tenure as Chancellor, there is considerable evidence that, by autumn 1981, Howe was seriously interested in ERM entry.[58] According to one official personally close to Howe:

> It was the overvaluation of the pound in 1980 and 1981 and
> Geoffrey Howe's experiences outside the ERM, when he had to
> put interest rates from 12 per cent, in the autumn just before
> the party conference, to 16 per cent in order to protect the
> pound as the pound had started to decline. Why they wanted to
> do that I don't know because the pound was still far too high. It
> was that that convinced him that stability of exchange rates was
> an aim that was worth pursuing in the ERM.[59]

Certainly, Howe felt the issue was salient enough to tell the House of Commons on 11 November:

> The EMS question is a serious one which deserves careful
> consideration. Difficult questions are involved. As we have one
> of the major international currencies and because of our self-
> sufficiency in oil, the effects of world events on sterling tend to
> be diametrically opposite to their effects on other EMS
> currencies. However, with some prospect of increased stability

in the price of oil, it is right that the question should be kept under constant review.[60]

If Howe continued to oppose membership, as he and others claim, it begs the question of why ERM membership remained on the agenda after Lawson's departure to Energy.

Indeed, by December a certain public momentum appeared to be developing towards membership. On 7 December the *Financial Times* reported that the Cabinet was 'inching towards membership in the spring', although the final decision was yet to be made. A senior minister, previously opposed to membership, told the *Financial Times* that membership was now 'probable'.[61] Inside the circles of decision-making, there is evidence that even more far-reaching decisions were now being made. According to one Treasury insider, in January 1982 Treasury ministers and officials were working on the basis of a fixed date for entry: 'we were ten days away from joining'.[62]

Assuming this is true, the situation represented a complicated set of relations within and between ministerial and official ranks. Howe must have been involved in any provisional decision which was taken, but the role of his senior officials is less clear. Certainly, Douglas Wass, the Permanent Secretary at the Treasury, dropped his earlier opposition to membership without becoming an active ERM supporter some time before he retired at the start of 1983. He had concluded that the system was durable, the provisions for realignments were being used, and that without strict monetary targets, British policy was no longer fundamentally incompatible with ERM membership. Nonetheless, he did not believe 'we were losing much by not being in'.[63] Meanwhile, the other two most senior Treasury officials, Kenneth Couzens and Terence Burns, the Chief Economic Adviser, remained firmly opposed to membership, as did lower-level policy staff. The Treasury's overseas finance division, which was most directly concerned with the issue, maintained a comprehensive critique of membership, still believing that sterling was a petro-currency, membership would be deflationary, devaluation was probably necessary in the future, and that another target would become a hostage to fortune.[64]

At the same time it is evident that Treasury officials did not want to admit that a policy compatible with ERM membership was already being pursued. The Bank of England was not allowed in its press releases on interest rate changes even to mention the exchange rate as a supporting reason for any action.[65] Eleven years later one Treasury official declared that the policy pursued from autumn 1981 was not centred on the exchange rate but involved 'looking at all the dials' from monetary aggregates to the exchange rate.[66] Even to itself, the Treasury was reluctant to admit the failure of monetary targeting. In the words of one senior official: '[Even by 1983], I don't think the exchange rate had become the dominant factor. There was still a great deal of lip service being paid to £M3, and the MTFS was still the article of faith.'[67] It was a case, as another official reflected, of very much wanting to believe that the monetary targets 'would come right in the end'.[68]

For its part, the Foreign Office still supported ERM entry, particularly given Britain's EC Presidency, but remained in a weak position to push its case. Howe and the Treasury still claimed the ERM as their exclusive domain, and appear to have kept the Foreign Office away from their thinking. As one Foreign Office official recalled: 'I never saw any sign that the Treasury or the Prime Minister were seriously interested in making a move.'[69] The Treasury's attitude fitted in with a sustained pattern of behaviour. According to one Foreign Office official, when Britain joined the EC the Treasury considered that nobody outside their ranks should have any view on matters affecting the Treasury: 'It was always the Treasury which was reluctant to share their thoughts with the Permanent Representative at the Foreign Office; that was still persisting in the early 1980s.'[70] Neither, given that, in the words of one official, 'the Treasury regarded the Bank as their usurer', was the Foreign Office in a position to make a strong alliance with Richardson at the Bank.[71]

At the same time any effort to secure Thatcher's support for membership was likely to be weakened by the Foreign Office's intervention. By 1981 Foreign Office officials believed that Thatcher 'tended to discount Foreign Office advice completely'.[72] In 1980 Thatcher had 'resented the feeling she was being pushed around by the Foreign Office' to settle on Rhodesia, and became guarded in her relations with the department.[73] In the words of one Foreign Office official:

> There is no doubt that the Foreign Office were a kind of bunch of demons who were trying to sell Britain down the river at all occasions and with great enthusiasm. She became extremely attached to and respected the advice of individual senior Foreign Office people ... I can think of a whole number of individuals whose advice she profoundly respected. I don't say she took it always. But she respected them and liked them and recognized that these were people of quality. But once they became submerged in the 'Foreign Office', they became highly suspect and basically insidious agents for foreign powers.[74]

Consequently, whatever manoeuvrings were going on around them, the Foreign Office believed that there was little chance of successfully pressing their case and were preoccupied with finding a solution to the budget without linking it to the ERM: '[Our attitude was] let's not waste too much time trying to persuade the Treasury and the Prime

Minister that we ought to be in this thing. Let's go on with the [EC] budget and leave it till later.'[75]

Yet whatever provisional decisions were made in early January 1982, presumably by Howe, Thatcher soon put paid to any foreseeable prospect of ERM entry. On 22 January 1982 Thatcher held a full Prime Ministerial meeting on the issue, attended by herself, Howe, Lord Carrington, Douglas Wass, Alan Walters, (the Prime Minister's personal economic adviser), Gordon Richardson and his deputy, Kit MacMahon. By common consent among those who have commented on the meeting, Richardson and MacMahon expressed strong support for ERM entry. They believed that stability for sterling was important in itself, and that the ERM provided the best framework for using the exchange rate as a monetary discipline.[76] But for his part, Lord Carrington was simply not interested. According to one source:

> I think that the Foreign Office was pretty keen. I'm not sure
> that Peter Carrington was keen. The Foreign Office was
> claiming that if we joined the ERM, the budget issue would be
> resolved ... We'd find that the French and Germans were much
> more amenable to all Britain's suggestions and so on, a big list
> of wonderful results. I remember Peter Carrington said: 'And
> that's what my advisers tell me, but I don't believe a word of
> it.'[77]

Meanwhile, although Thatcher, Howe and Lawson – who admits that he did not know about the meeting until sometime afterwards – all claim that Howe spoke against membership,[78] this does not tally either with apparent prior developments or the recollection of one participant that Howe argued the case for entry with 'modest enthusiasm'.[79] Revealingly, another source recalled that after Thatcher left office she told him that Howe had 'started hankering after membership as early as 1982'.[80]

For the Prime Minister's part, her behaviour suggests that she saw that the issue had reached a new intensity within the government. Throughout the autumn Thatcher had received minutes from Walters on the issue and was briefed for the 22 January meeting by him. Walters was well known as a fierce opponent of pegged exchange rates in general and of the ERM in particular, believing that it overvalued currencies, required exchange controls to work and was inflationary because high inflation states ended up with lower real interest rates than low inflation states.[81] As for Thatcher's contribution to the discussion itself, she herself offers a quite restrained reflection:

> I said that I was not convinced that there would be solid
> advantage in joining the ERM. I did not believe that in practice

it would provide an effective discipline on our economic management. Rather, it removed our freedom of manoeuvre. I accepted, however, that when our inflation and interest rates moved much closer to those of West Germany the case for joining would be more powerful. For the time being, we would maintain our existing position on the issue.[82]

However, others suggest that the meeting was conducted in rather more heated tones. One participant recalled that 'she destroyed the Bank's case'.[83] In the words of another: 'She really slammed the door seven or eight times. The arguments were very much in her mind as to why we should not join . . . The door was slammed and that was it.'[84] It has to be asked, if it was simply a case of rebutting the Governor and Deputy Governor of the Bank of England, as in March 1980, and not a dispute with her Chancellor, why Thatcher would have responded in such a manner.

Thatcher's continuing opposition to the ERM can perhaps best be understood in two terms. First, membership would have constituted a very public repudiation of the previous £M3 policy, and Thatcher wanted to be seen as the resolute leader who was 'not for turning'. Although she and Howe were already pursuing an exchange rate policy, she did not have any interest in proclaiming the fact, given the political significance attached to the MTFS. This government was after all supposed to be distinguished from its predecessors by its willingness to stick to an articulated economic plan, whatever the short-term cost. So, in these terms, a disguised exchange rate target was more beneficial than joining the ERM.

Second, Thatcher's claim for freedom of manoeuvre outside the ERM made some sense in terms of the Conservatives' electoral position. The autumn of 1981 represented the lowest point in the government's political fortunes between 1979 and 1983. On the economic front, the rise in interest rates risked a secondary recession, inflation was predicted to rise again, unemployment was heading towards the three million mark and the PSBR was way above target for the year. Correspondingly, between September and December 1981 there was a steep fall in the government's already weak position in the opinion polls, culminating in a nadir of less than 20 per cent in December. During this period the party also lost two by-elections in Croydon and Crosby to the Alliance, and commentators were concluding that the Conservatives were heading for a huge electoral defeat. By the time Thatcher decided not to enter the ERM, the government was recovering some ground but still stood below 25 per cent in the opinion polls.[85]

In trying to reverse the situation and win the election, ministers faced conflicting imperatives. On the one hand, they needed to reduce inflation, since their credibility was fundamentally tied to inflation rather than unemployment, which they were successfully blaming on external forces. On the other hand, ministers wanted to stimulate some kind of recovery through manufacturing industry with tangible benefits for voters. The crucial question was, therefore, whether the Prime Minister and Chancellor could afford to tighten fiscal policy again if inflation was to rise. If they were not prepared to raise taxes or cut expenditure, then some other policy instrument would have to be assigned to the task. With an incomes policy and credit controls already repudiated, ERM membership would have cost Thatcher and Howe the opportunity to use an appreciation in sterling as a deflationary policy weapon. By contrast, non-membership left the two ministers with the discretion, if they wished, to use interest rates for counter-inflationary purposes within their own commitment to an exchange rate policy. At the same time non-membership preserved the long-term opportunity to devalue to try to recapture competitiveness once inflation was under control.

A Non-Issue

Nevertheless, in practice, Thatcher and Howe did not need the counter-inflationary discretion given by the Prime Minister's insistence on staying outside the ERM because inflation began to fall, declining from 12 per cent in January 1982 to 4.5 per cent by the end of the year. Consequently, the Prime Minister and Chancellor were able to pursue their effective exchange rate target for sterling and to significantly reduce interest rates without having to pursue restrictive policies elsewhere. Indeed, the bias of policy was now firmly expansionary. In July 1982 Howe abolished hire-purchase controls, boosting consumer spending, and then, in the 1982 autumn statement, he exhorted local authorities and nationalized industries to meet their capital spending targets.

In November, with inflation falling, the Chancellor initiated an internal debate about whether there was scope for a devaluation in sterling to boost competitiveness. Despite the economic stimulus provided through 1982, he did not believe that sufficient recovery was taking place, and the autumn statement forecast a zero balance of payments surplus in 1983, the huge positive contribution of oil notwithstanding. But when the foreign exchange markets learned of the debate, sterling fell steeply. Even though the Bank of England quickly spent 10 per cent of Britain's foreign exchange reserves in intervention, sterling's weakness persisted. Unwilling to countenance any further depreciation, Howe raised interest rates by 1 per cent on 26 November and a further 1 per cent on 12 January.

In deciding against the devaluation option, the Prime Minister and Chancellor were choosing not to use part of the freedom of manoeuvre that staying outside the ERM had given them. By continuing to pursue a stable exchange rate policy, backed by monetary policy, Thatcher and Howe effectively embraced the costs of membership, namely a higher rate for sterling, and the costs of non-membership in a unilateral loss of the reserves and, probably, higher interest rates. Nevertheless, there was no re-examination of the ERM issue. Following the Falklands victory in June 1982, the government was now in a strong position in the polls, and with Thatcher planning a general election for 1983, there was little incentive to make any major policy changes.[86]

Nor at the end of 1982 did ministers face any imperative in terms of their European policy to re-examine the issue. The government's EC relations reached a nadir in May 1982, when the other member states overrode Britain's veto on farm price increases – the first failure of a national veto since the 1965 Luxembourg Compromise. Afterwards, ministers looked to repair relations without reaching a deal on the budget, or reconsidering joining the ERM. Although the European Commission was becoming increasingly exasperated by Britain's non-membership, the other member states did not exert the kind of pressure for entry which they had done towards the end of 1981.[87]

To conclude, in 1979 and 1980 the Conservative government had some incentive to re-examine Britain's non-membership of the ERM to further its objectives in European policy. However, during this period joining the ERM would have put paid to ministers' economic strategy. At the same time non-membership did not impose any costs on ministers in terms of their relations with the capital groups which they wished to support. By June 1983, despite the continuing monetarist rhetoric, Thatcher and Howe were operating an economic policy similar in substance to ERM membership but at Thatcher's insistence outside the system and in tandem with a relatively isolationist EC policy.

Nonetheless, the terms of the macro-economic debate on ERM which emerged between 1979 and 1983 were highly significant. Essentially, this centred around the question of whether monetary targets or exchange rate stability were the best means of using monetary policy as a counter-inflationary discipline. It was the failure of the former policy in the shape of the MTFS which underlay the position of both those who opposed and supported membership. The opponents of ERM were in part simply unwilling to admit, or accept, the failure of the MTFS as terminal. Meanwhile ERM supporters either never really believed in the

MTFS (Gordon Richardson and other Bank of England officials) or they believed that after the failure of monetary targeting, ERM membership represented an alternative counter-inflationary monetary framework (Howe and Lawson). Lawson, for example, saw joining the ERM, as a means of pursuing exchange rate stability through a disciplined interest rate policy to reduce inflation. Similarly, Richardson argued at the Prime Ministerial meeting in January 1982 that membership would be beneficial in preventing sterling from depreciating and inflation from rising. These actors judged the advantages of membership as if sterling would be entering either a relatively fixed exchange rate system, or at least as if British monetary policy would be operated assuming this were the case, and so ignored the ERM's flexibility. They believed that what monetary targets could not deliver as a counter-inflationary monetary discipline could be achieved through exchange rate stability and ERM membership. Ironically, this view stood in direct contrast to the more flexible benefits that ERM membership actually offered currencies at this time.

Despite the prospect of a new Conservative term in office and the possibility this offered for policy renewal, it appeared likely that in the foreseeable future the ERM debate would remain within the terms of reference induced by the MTFS. By June 1983 senior officials un-committed to the MTFS had either left their post or were soon to depart. They were replaced with people for whom the MTFS represented a greater personal investment. At the Treasury Douglas Wass retired in April 1983 and Peter Middleton took over as Permanent Secretary. Wass was always sceptical about the money supply policy, whereas Middleton, despite his more junior position, was consummately in-volved with the development of the MTFS. Indeed, Thatcher supported Middleton's promotion over more likely candidates precisely because of the commitment he showed to the MTFS. At the Bank, Thatcher did not renew Gordon Richardson's term as Governor, angry at his apparent failure to achieve the MTFS monetary targets. Picked by Thatcher as a more like-minded Governor, in July 1983 Robin Leigh-Pemberton took over in Threadneedle Street. Although as Chairman of National Westminster Bank he had supported ERM entry, his lack of central banking experience meant that at least in the short term he was unlikely to either challenge Thatcher or the intellectual assumptions of the Treasury. In this context, and particularly if Howe were to leave the Chancellorship, it seemed as if Thatcher was preparing to entertain the possibility of a return to some form of monetary targets. If, as seemed probable, that were to fail, then ERM membership was likely to be discussed again as an alternative within very much the same terms as had emerged between 1981 and 1982.

NOTES

1 For good accounts of the negotiations leading to the Bremen summit, see K. Dyson, (1994) *Elusive Union: The Process of Economic and Monetary Union in Europe*, Harlow: Longman; P. Ludlow, (1982) *The Making of the EMS: A Case Study of the Politics of the EC*, London: Butterworth Scientific.

2 S. George, (1994) *An Awkward Partner: Britain in the EC*, 2nd edn., Oxford: Oxford University Press, p. 129. For a typically British perspective on the creation of the ERM see E. Dell, (1994) 'The Origins of the European Monetary System', *Contemporary European History*, 3(1), pp. 1–60.

3 *Economist*, 4 July, 1987, p. 21.

4 For a discussion of the limited aims of the original ERM, see Dyson, *Elusive Union*, Chapter 4.

5 *Financial Times*, 8 February 1980; *The Times*, 9 February 1980.

6 *Economist*, 8 March 1980, pp. 54–55.

7 For a discussion of the dollar's roller-coaster ride in the 1980s, see Y. Funabashi, (1988) *Managing the Dollar: From the Plaza to the Louvre*, Washington: Institute for International Economics; and R. Gilpin, (1987) *The Political Economy of International Relations*, Princeton: Princeton University Press, Chapter 4.

8 *Financial Times*, 25 November, 1981; *Times*, 13 November 1981; 16 February 1982.

9 For a full discussion of the ERM during these years, see H. Ungerer *et al.*, (1983) *The European Monetary System: The Experience 1979–1982*, Washington: IMF.

10 *Times*, 11 July 1978.

11 Non-attributable interview.

12 *Daily Telegraph*, 7 December 1978.

13 *Ibid.*, 20 December 1978.

14 *Financial Times*, 12 May 1979.

15 House of Commons, (1978) *Select Committee on Expenditure, First Report: Minutes of Evidence*, London: HMSO, pp. 1–2.

16 *Economist*, 2 November 1978, pp. 58–59.

17 J. Coakley and L. Harris, (1983) *The City of Capital: London's Role as a Financial Centre*, Oxford: Blackwell, pp. 204–05.

18 *Financial Times*, 22 June 1979.

19 *Ibid.*, 27 July 1979.

20 *Economist*, 23 June 1979, pp. 50–54; *Economist*, 29 September 1979, p. 55; *Financial Times*, 12 May 1979; 21 June 1979; 23 July 1979.

21 Non-attributable interview with Foreign Office official.

22 Non-attributable interview with Foreign Office official.

23 Non-attributable interview with Cabinet Office official.

24 Non-attributable interviews with Foreign Office officials.

25 Non-attributable interview with Treasury official.

26 F. Giavazzi et al. (eds), (1988) *The European Monetary System*, Cambridge: Cambridge University Press, p. 1; W. Keegan and R. Pennant-Rea, (1979) *Who Runs the Economy: Control and Influence in British Economic Policy*, London:

Maurice Temple-Smith, p. 171; George, *Awkward Partner*, p. 129; M. Crawford, (1982) 'No EMS for Britain', *Banker*, 132 (4), p. 152; House of Commons, *First Report: Minutes of Evidence*, p. 5; *Economist*, 22 April 1978, p. 90; *Economist*, 27 May, 1978, p. 55; *Economist*, 21 October 1978, pp. 58, 69; *Economist*, 28 October 1978, p. 23; *Financial Times*, 8 July 1981.

27 Non-attributable interview with Foreign Office official.

28 Non-attributable interviews with Treasury and Foreign Office officials; *Financial Times*, 15 June 1979.

29 Non-attributable interview with Foreign Office official.

30 *Financial Times*, 23 July 1979; *Financial Times*, 15 September 1979; *Financial Times*, 18 September 1979; *Times*, 24 July 1979; *Times*, 10 September 1979; *Daily Telegraph*, 18 September 1979.

31 M. Thatcher, (1993) *The Downing Street Years*, London: HarperCollins, pp. 691–92;

32 *Financial Times*, 6 March 1980; *Times*, 6 March 1980.

33 *Ibid.*

34 *Economist*, 8 December 1979, pp. 48–49; *Economist*, 19 January 1980, p. 46; *Economist*, 26 January 1980, p. 58; *Economist*, 9 February 1980, pp. 47–48; *Economist*, 8 March 1980, pp. 15–16.

35 *Financial Times*, 6 March 1980; *Financial Times*, 7 March 1980; *Financial Times*, 10 March 1980; *Financial Times*, 11 March 1980; *Financial Times*, 13 March 1980; *Financial Times*, 29 March 1980.

36 Non-attributable interview with Foreign Office official.

37 *Financial Times*, 11 March 1980.

38 Thatcher, *Downing Street Years*, p. 692.

39 W. Keegan, (1984) *Mrs Thatcher's Economic Experiment*, Harmondsworth: Penguin, pp. 141–47; *Financial Times*, 6 March 1980; *Times*, 6 March 1980.

40 Non-attributable interviews with Bank of England officials.

41 Non-attributable interview with Bank of England official.

42 *Financial Times*, 19 March 1980.

43 *Ibid.*

44 *Economist*, 8 March 1980, pp. 15–16.

45 *Financial Times*, 29 March 1980.

46 N. Lawson, (1992) *The View from No. 11: Memoirs of a Tory Radical*, London: Bantam, p. 111.

47 *Financial Times*, 8 July 1981; *Times*, 24 August 1981.

48 Lawson, *Memoirs*, p. 112.

49 *Ibid.*

50 *Financial Times*, 24 September 1981.

51 Keegan, *Economic Experiment*, p. 179.

52 *Financial Times*, 6 October 1981.

53 *Ibid.*, 18 June 1981.

54 *Ibid.*, 26 September 1981.

55 *Ibid.*, 11 November 1981.

56 *Ibid.*, 21 October 1981.

57 *Economist*, 19 December 1981, p. 32.

58 Thatcher, *Downing Street Years*, p. 693; Lawson, *Memoirs*, pp. 112–113; G. Howe, (1994) *Conflict of Loyalty*, London: Macmillan, p. 112.

59 Non-attributable interview.

60 *Hansard*, 11 November 1981, pp. 556–57.

61 *Financial Times*, 7 December 1981.

62 Non-attributable interview.

63 Non-attributable interviews.

64 *Financial Times*, 1 February 1982; *Times*, 6 October 1981.

65 Non-attributable interview with Bank of England official.

66 Non-attributable interview with Treasury official.

67 Non-attributable interview with Treasury official.

68 Non-attributable interview with Treasury official.

69 Non-attributable interview with Foreign Office official.

70 Non-attributable interview with Foreign Office official.

71 Non-attributable interviews with Foreign Office and Cabinet Office officials.

72 Non-attributable interview with Foreign Office official.

73 Non-attributable interview with Foreign Office official.

74 Non-attributable interview with Foreign Office official.

75 Non-attributable interview with Foreign Office official.

76 Lawson, *Memoirs*, p. 112; non-attributable interviews.

77 Non-attributable interview. This account of Carrington repudiating his brief is also told as a dateless anecdote in J. Bruce-Gardyne, (1986) *Ministers and Mandarins: Inside the Whitehall Village, London:* p. 61: 'Lord Carrington, equipped with a cast-iron Foreign Office presentation in favour of immediate British accession to the European ERM, and knowing that his Prime Minister would not touch it with a bargepole, read it out with due solemnity, and concluded, 'That, Prime Minister, is what I was told to say, and it seems to me a load of rubbish'.

78 Lawson, *Memoirs*, pp. 111–12; Thatcher, *Downing Street Years*, p. 693; Howe, *Conflict of Loyalty*, p. 275.

79 Non-attributable interview.

80 Non-attributable interviews.

81 A. Walters, (1990) *Sterling in Danger: The Economic Consequences of Fixed Exchange Rates*, London: Fontana, pp. 70–78, 87; non-attributable interviews.

82 Thatcher, *Downing Street Years*, p. 693.

83 Non-attributable interview.

84 Non-attributable interview with Treasury official.

85 J. Bruce-Gardyne, (1984) *Mrs Thatcher's First Thatcher Administration: The Prophets Confounded*, London: Macmillan, pp. 116–19; Keegan, *Economic Experiment*, pp. 171–73; D. Sanders, H. Ward, D. Marsh, (1987) 'Government Popularity and the Falklands War: A Reassessment', *British Journal of Political Science*, 17(3), pp. 281–86.

86 The only suggestion that the ERM issue arose at all at this time comes in Bruce-Gardyne, *First Thatcher Administration*, which simply states that the option was canvassed but Thatcher and the Treasury remained opposed.

87 *Economist*, 22 May 1982, pp. 15, 75–76; *Economist*, 25 September, 1982, p. 42; *Financial Times*, 19 January 1983; *Times*, 19 January 1983.

2

Just Saying No: 1983–1985

Caesar: So in the world: 'tis furnish'd well with men,
            And men are flesh and blood, and apprehensive;
            Yet in the number I do know but one
            That unassailable holds on his rank,
            Unshak'd of motion: and that I am he,
            Let me a little show it, even in this,
            That I was constant Cimber should be banish'd,
            And constant do remain to keep him so.
                      William Shakespeare, *Julius Caesar*

A COUNTER-INFLATIONARY ERM

If the ERM had essentially operated as a dirty float between 1979 and the beginning of 1983, then, by 1985, it was akin to a relatively fixed exchange rate system. Indeed, between March 1983 and June 1985 there were no realignments of ERM currencies. In July 1985 the lira was devalued, but it would be misleading to interpret this as a sign of fundamental weakness in the new order. Although the realignment coincided with a bout of dollar weakness, the previous achilles heel of the system, the adjustment was actually caused by the pressure of the Italian budget deficit on the lira. At the same time there were none of the acrimonious disputes over the terms of the devaluation which had characterized previous realignments.[1]

The ERM now contained a counter-inflationary bias in both monetary and fiscal terms. Monetarily, the bias operated through German leadership of the system. Rather than the relatively neutral divergent indicator demonstrating the currencies' positions within the exchange grid, the Deutschmark was now operating as an anchor currency. The Bundesbank set its monetary policy to fit its counter-inflationary objectives and the other ERM states adjusted their monetary policy accordingly. A rise in German interest rates usually meant that the other states would follow suit, so as to maintain a premium over German rates. Similarly, in terms of intervention by central banks, the emphasis shifted from obligatory intervention in the fluctuations margins, signalled by the divergent indicator, to 'intra-marginal' intervention in Deutschmarks. By using intra-marginal intervention states

36

were aiming to act before currencies came under so much pressure in the fluctuation margins that speculators possessed a one-way option on the direction of a currency's future movement.[2]

Fiscally, the ERM states were now prepared to use restrictive policies to defend parities, rather than simply resorting to devaluation when those parities came under pressure. As early as 1981, Italy and Ireland started to make more rigorous efforts to reduce their budget deficits and allowed their currencies to appreciate in real terms to reduce inflation. Then, in March 1983, the French socialist government abandoned its efforts at unilateral expansion and embarked on a policy of fiscal adjustment to reduce inflation. The socialists had come to power in 1981 under President Mitterrand's leadership committed to reducing unemployment by increasing public expenditure. However, with its competitors reducing demand to combat inflation, France soon faced a massive balance of payments crisis which put the franc under pressure. Although France devalued in October 1981 and June 1982, and the government introduced some mild deflationary measures, the franc remained weak. By March 1983 Mitterrand faced the choice of withdrawing France from the ERM and pursuing a neo-protectionist policy, or acceding to German demands for further and drastic public expenditure cuts. Despite opposition from several prominent ministers, Mitterrand chose to remain inside the ERM and devalue the franc again. With the French government committing itself to a fiscal austerity plan to reduce inflation, the German government conceded a simultaneous 5.5 per cent revaluation of the Deutschmark.[3]

The French U-turn signalled the start of a crucial new phase in the ERM's development. As Figure 2.1 indicates, the new deflationary bias in policy produced a gradual convergence in inflation among the ERM states towards German levels. Whereas in 1980 German inflation was 7.1 per cent lower than the EC average, by 1985 the differential had fallen to 3.4. Viewed as a whole, the ERM states were gaining a new long-term credibility in the counter-inflationary process through their individual and collective unwillingness to accommodate inflationary pressure through devaluation.[4]

A SLEEPING ISSUE: JUNE 1983–DECEMBER 1984

In Britain after the 1983 general election, Thatcher made Nigel Lawson Chancellor and sent Geoffrey Howe to the Foreign Office. Lawson quickly initiated a review of monetary policy. As part of the review, Geoffrey Littler, the new Second Permanent Secretary at the Treasury and Head of Overseas Finance, wrote a paper assessing the value of ERM membership as a monetary framework. Arguing that France was demonstrating that ERM membership could bring considerable benefits, he advocated joining the ERM in 1984 on condition that the oil market remained stable, the British and German economies continued to converge, progress was made on the negotiations on the EC budget, and that the dollar fell against the Deutschmark.[5] However, neither Lawson, nor Middleton (the Permanent Secretary) nor Burns (the Chief Economic Adviser) were interested in Littler's proposal. Steeped in the intellectual culture of domestic monetary policy and the MTFS, Lawson and his most senior officials instead used the review to seek an operational framework for new monetary targets. Although the ERM option was far more in tune with the implicit exchange rate policy which Thatcher and Howe had pursued from 1981 to 1983, Lawson clearly wanted to refocus policy on the money supply.

The problem for Lawson was to decide upon which money aggregate to target in the wake of the previous failure of £M3. After a debate on the respective merits of £3, M0, M2 (money available for transaction

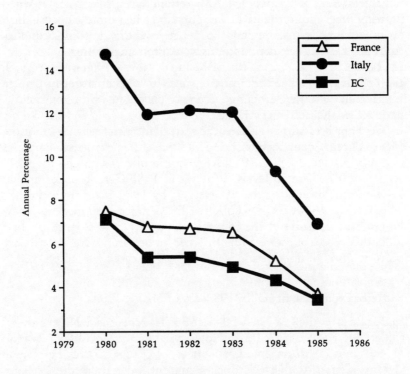

Figure 2.1: Comparative Inflation Differentials with Germany 1980-1985
(Source: Economic Outlook)

purposes), non-interest bearing M1 (cash plus non-interest bearing deposits withdrawable on demand) and monetary base control (targeting banks' reserves with the Bank of England), Lawson tentatively concluded that M0 'could have a more important part in monitoring monetary conditions.'[6] Trying to rekindle the monetarist ashes, in the 1984 budget Lawson announced five-year monetary targets for both £M3 and M0.

Yet, in practice, from July 1983 to the end of 1984 Lawson did not run monetary policy according to strict monetary targets any more than Howe had between 1981 and 1983. In the year from June 1983 he reduced interest rates and allowed sterling to depreciate. When, in July 1984, sterling began to slide more rapidly against the dollar towards $1.30, Lawson raised interest rates twice. Such action suggested that he and Thatcher were keen to loosen monetary policy to try to stimulate growth, but that they were also not prepared to ignore the exchange rate. But then, within months, the two ministers reverted again to benign neglect. When sterling fell below $1.20 in November, Lawson cut interest rates to 9.5 per cent. Apparently, the cut was driven neither by the performance of M0 nor by the exchange rate, but rather the dual desire to stimulate an economy threatened by the miners' strike and to create an environment conducive to the success of the British Telecom share issue.[7]

By the end of 1984, the financial markets were unwilling to attach much credence to the M0 target, and Lawson was unwilling to exclude other considerations from monetary policy. Yet Lawson and the Treasury were not prepared to admit to the failure. In October 1984 Lawson declared in his Mansion House Speech

> that the monetary aggregates determined interest rates, and that the exchange rates only counted if there was reason to suppose that domestic monetary indicators were misleading.[8]

However, as Lawson himself admits:

> This line was a fiction even when I uttered it, as the exchange rate played a much larger part in policy than I was prepared to admit in public. But there was genuine difficulty about any alternative presentation ... The idea of giving weight to the exchange rate as a factor in monetary policy decisions, but not having an exchange rate target, was extremely hard to put across.[9]

Yet any suggestion that the exchange rate was determining monetary policy was also a fiction, given the loosening of policy at the end of 1984. Once again monetary policy and its presentation were riddled with inconsistency.

By the end of 1984, the net result of monetary developments since the general election was a shift from a policy fairly comparable to ERM membership to one which was not. In contrast to his predecessor, Lawson was not pursuing exchange rate stability, and monetary policy was not clearly assigned to the exchange rate. Moreover, his acquiesence to the fall in sterling and a relatively loose monetary policy suggested that inflation was not his main priority. This divergence in approach between British policy and that of the ERM states was compounded by Lawson's and Thatcher's fiscal stance. Having created additional revenue through privatization, Lawson declared in the 1984 autumn statement that tax cuts of £1.5 billion should be possible in the 1985 budget and that the government's aim was now to 'really get down to the business of reforming taxation'.[10] In the remainder of 1984, the Prime Minister and Chancellor used every opportunity to celebrate the likelihood of even greater tax cuts of the magnitude of £2–3 billion. Unlike the ERM states, who saw fiscal policy primarily in counter-inflationary terms, Thatcher and Lawson now conceived fiscal measures as ends in themselves.

Yet, despite the essential incompatibility between the economic policy approach and ERM membership, towards the end of 1984 the issue tentatively began to resurface both within and outside the government. In the City, firms and individuals were becoming increasingly interested in ERM entry. In August 1984 the *Lloyds Bank Economic Bulletin* argued that the fall in sterling in the previous month could have been avoided inside the ERM.[11] Three months later a group of City bankers and economists published a report highlighting the benefits of membership, given both that inflation was converging throughout the EC and that sterling could no longer be deemed a petro-currency.[12] Meanwhile the EC states were rekindling their interest in Britain joining the ERM. At the Fontainebleau summit in May 1984 the heads of government had reached a comprehensive settlement on outstanding Community issues, including the budget question, without reference to Britain's non-membership of the ERM. But, by autumn 1984, monetary co-operation was moving to the top of the EC's new agenda, as some member states sought new ways to strengthen European economic performance in relation to the USA and Japan. As part of this reappraisal, in November the Commission and the German Finance Minister called for Britain to enter the ERM so that monetary co-operation could be improved.[13]

At the same time Lawson, Howe and Leigh-Pemberton were all, in varying ways, redefining their position on membership. Although Leigh-Pemberton came to the Bank of England as an ERM supporter, it was only in October 1984 that he first publicly articulated a view on the subject. Casting doubt on the utility of monetary aggregates, he argued that, despite 'some technical difficulties', there were 'a number of attractions' to ERM membership.[14] For Howe's part the evidence discussed in the previous chapter suggests that he had come to the Foreign Office already converted to entry, but in October 1984 the press appeared to be briefed on his views for the first time.[15] Most importantly, as the year was turning, Lawson concluded that ERM membership was seriously worth considering.[16] In his memoirs, Lawson states that his support for membership ran in a continuum from 1981, when he was Financial Secretary, to 1985, and that he did not believe that the 'right opportunity' to persuade Thatcher arose until 1985.[17] However, according to one of his officials, Lawson began his Chancellorship 'rather dispassionate' about the ERM. Only at the very end of 1984 and start of 1985 did he begin 'to see real positive merit' in entry.[18] Indeed, Lawson himself admits that problems in policy during this period contributed to his support for entry.[19]

At the start of 1985 these developments in and out of government were at best tentative, but within two weeks a massive sterling crisis would rock the government's economic policy to its foundations and precipitate a wholescale reappraisal of the ERM issue.

FLOATING TOWARDS PARITY: JANUARY–FEBRUARY 1985

As 1985 began, the dollar was rising against all currencies and sterling in particular. By the end of the first week of January, sterling was headed towards $1.15 without any floor in sight. Despite Lawson's renewed interest in exchange rate stability, he and Thatcher decided neither to intervene nor to raise interest rates. Publicly they insisted that there was no problem with sterling, since the situation was caused by the strength of the dollar and a fall in the price of oil. Neither, they argued, was there any inflationary risk, since the rise in the price of imports would be offset by lower oil prices.

On the basis of these events and a briefing from Bernard Ingham, Thatcher's chief press officer, the *Sunday Times* ran a story on 6 January that Thatcher and Lawson were determined to maintain a hands-off policy, even if sterling fell to a 1–1 parity against the dollar. In response, the foreign exchange markets sold sterling even quicker. Thatcher and Lawson were now deeply frustrated: they were indeed practising benign neglect, but they did not want the media to report policy in that way. To avoid a repetition of the *Sunday Times* story, they ensured that all future questions about sterling were referred to the Treasury.

In private neither Thatcher nor Lawson were indifferent to sterling's depreciation, but they did not want to take action to stem it. Instead, they hoped that the publication of good £M3 figures on 8 January would finally convince the markets that there was nothing fundamentally wrong with the British economy. However, when the £M3 figures were published sterling continued to fall. Once again Thatcher and Lawson were reluctant to translate their private concern into corrective action. Only when sterling fell to $1.13 and lost four pfennigs against the Deutschmark on Thursday 10 January, despite the price of oil stabilizing, did the Prime Minister and the Chancellor finally decide to discard benign neglect, and the next morning interest rates were duly *raised by one per cent to* 10.5 per cent.

The new policy was quickly undermined by Bernard Ingham. That afternoon, and in direct contradiction to the morning's events, Ingham told the lobby that foreign reserves would not be 'thrown' at sterling, and that no particular rate was being defended. With the exception of the *Observer*, the Sunday papers and the BBC all assumed that Ingham was accurately articulating government policy, and the *Sunday Times* led with the headline, 'Thatcher ready to let one pound equal one dollar'. The media stories effectively wiped out the interest rate rise and threw the government's commitment to sterling into disarray. Seeking to avert further damage, the Treasury hauled government information officers out of their beds and into Whitehall to urge financial journalists to ignore the morning's newspapers.[20]

With the Monday newspapers briefed that the Chancellor was prepared to raise interest rates again to defend sterling, and the Bank of England intervening heavily in the markets, Lawson and Thatcher hoped to avoid any further tightening of policy. Unsurprisingly, sterling continued to fall, and Lawson resorted to ordering the Bank to reactivate the Minimum Lending Rate for the day to raise rates by a further 1.5 per cent, publicly declaring that inflation was now the overriding priority. In the House of Commons Lawson went on to accept that confusion and ambiguity within the government itself was partly responsible for the crisis: 'I am afraid that there was a feeling in the markets that the government had lost their willingness and ability to control their affairs so as to maintain the downward pressure on inflation.'[21]

During the remainder of the week sterling steadied. Meanwhile Thatcher persuaded President Reagan of the need for action to hold down the dollar. On 17 January the G5 finance ministers announced an unprecedented agreement to act together through intervention to stabilize foreign exchange markets where necessary. It was the first time that the Reagan administration had recognized that the dollar's rise was an international problem. However, in the following weeks the American administration failed to match its words with actions, and it was left to the European and the Japanese central banks to co-ordinate action against the dollar. Nonetheless, at home Thatcher and Lawson remained firmly resolved to defend sterling, respectively declaring that sterling was 'far too low' and that the dollar 'was grossly overvalued'.[22] Yet sterling continued to fall. On 28 January, after oil prices weakened and speculation against sterling increased, Lawson raised interest rates a further 2 per cent to 14 per cent. He declared that speculation against sterling 'was greatly overdone', but that the government would not 'run any risk of misapprehension as to our continuing resolve to conquer inflation'.[23]

The Sterling Crisis and ERM Membership

The sterling crisis was a defining moment for the second Conservative government because it completely exposed the previous inconsistency in both the practice and presentation of monetary policy. In just over a week Lawson and Thatcher had been forced to totally reverse their approach. Having rejected the idea of 'throwing' money at sterling, the two proceeded to broker an international agreement to 'throw' money against the dollar. From benign neglect towards sterling and the inflationary consequences of its depreciation, they had placed the exchange rate and the reduction of inflation at the centre of their economic strategy. If the MTFS was designed as a particular monetary means to reduce inflation which denied the importance of the exchange rate, then the sterling crisis vividly demonstrated that this proposition was untenable. Any counter-inflationary framework could not exclude the exchange rate. After raising interest rates by 4.5 per cent very obviously to defend sterling, Lawson could no longer credibly claim monetary policy was determined by the monetary targets. In 1980–81 Howe was able to claim that the MTFS was being maintained at the same time as the policy was being abandoned to manage sterling downwards. However, in the wake of the sterling crisis no such option for covering the end of the post-1983 MTFS existed. Not only was the exchange rate central to monetary policy but it was essential that policy was presented in these terms.

The crisis imposed significant political costs on the government. First, at a conservative estimate £100 million was lost in reserve intervention.[24] Second, Britain was left with exceptionally high nominal and real interest rates. Real rates stood at almost 10 per cent, dealing a serious blow to Lawson's efforts to stimulate growth. Although the dollar rose against all currencies during January, only the British government was forced to raise interest rates (see Figure 2.2). Indeed, France and Italy both cut their rates during the same period.[25] Third, after Thatcher and Lawson had heralded tax reform and tax cuts for the

1985 budget, the crisis imposed a new fiscal constraint on the government. The foreign exchange markets suspected that Thatcher and Lawson initially wanted to take advantage of a depreciation in sterling so as to increase dollar-priced oil revenues and cut taxes. As early as 15 January, Lawson admitted that in view of the sterling crisis tax cuts were at risk and public expenditure cutbacks might be necessary.[26] At the same time the interest rate hike raised the cost of financing the national debt and limited the Chancellor's room for fiscal manoeuvre. When Lawson eventually delivered his budget in March 1985, he was reduced to announcing a series of minor supply-side measures, with the previously trumpeted tax cuts and reforms quietly forgotten.

The lessons of the sterling crisis directly related to the issues which the ERM sought to address. Primarily, the crisis rammed home the fact that no British government could afford for the foreign exchange markets to believe that it did not have an opinion on the exchange rate.

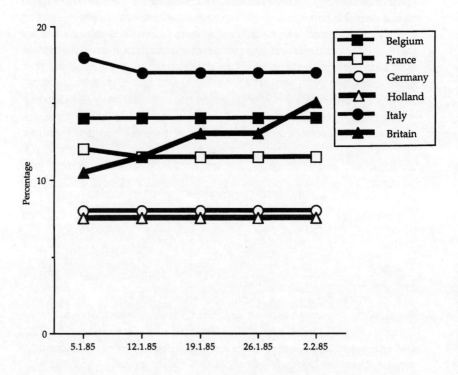

Figure 2.2: Comparative Prime Lending Rates January-February 1985
(Prime Lending Rates are British Base Rates plus one per cent)
(Source: Economist Economic and Financial Indicators, January-February 1985)

Moreover, the fiasco with Bernard Ingham's briefings demonstrated the cost of any ambiguity within the government itself. The Prime Minister, Chancellor, their officials and the Bank of England needed to speak with one voice on the subject. Indeed, the benefits of the new policy were well demonstrated in February 1985. With the Reagan administration failing to abide by the G5 agreement, the dollar continued to rise against all currencies, including sterling, and on 25 February sterling fell to a low of $1.03. Only concerted and co-ordinated intervention by the European central banks at the end of the month finally succeeded in pushing the dollar down. Yet although sterling fell to lower levels than during the January crisis, Lawson did not have to raise interest rates further because the foreign exchange markets believed in his commitment to sterling. Meanwhile, despite the Deutschmark and other ERM currencies bearing the brunt of the dollar's rise in February, their depreciation did not result in the kind of crisis which befell sterling during the previous month. The Bundesbank raised its Lombard rates by 0.5 per cent but not its base rate. Of the other ERM states, only Holland raised its base rates and then by just 1 per cent. Clearly, the ultimate arbiter of the credibility of the ERM states was not their performance against the perennially volatile dollar. By contrast, with sterling falling 6 per cent against the dollar but only 1.8 per cent against the Deutschmark, the British government had been severely punished, despite the decreasing importance of Atlantic trade to Britain.[27]

In this light the sterling crisis created a clear economic policy incentive for Thatcher and Lawson to review the ERM issue again. As early as 11 January, Lawson brought up the issue at an internal Treasury meeting. In Lawson's view, 'the case for buttressing the pound and firmly dispelling the increasing uncertainty over monetary policy was clear', but his senior officials, with the exception of Littler, remained sceptical.[28] One senior official commented: 'Nigel Lawson decided he wanted to join for reasons that none of us were terribly clear about. It was almost as though having pursued a successful policy, he wanted to pursue an unsuccessful one for a spell.'[29] The meeting concluded with an agreement that officials would examine the mechanics of ERM membership and make contingency plans to increase the foreign exchange reserves.[30]

On 28 January Thatcher and Lawson met to discuss the final interest rate rise. Thatcher told the Chancellor that Ruud Lubbers, the Dutch Prime Minister, had suggested to her that the guilder was a more stable currency than sterling because of its membership of the ERM, and that she wanted Lawson to examine whether in the present circumstances ERM entry was desirable.[31] This was good news for Robin Leigh-Pemberton, who two days later publicly stated that in his view sterling might be suffering less from speculative attacks and would be easier to defend inside the ERM.[32] On 3 February Thatcher accepted Lawson's proposal of a Prime Ministerial seminar on the issue on 13 February.[33] Lawson hoped that the seminar would reach a quick agreement in principle, with a view to entering the ERM in the summer. With the firm support of Howe and Leigh-Pemberton and some Conservative back-benchers becoming restless on the subject, Lawson appeared to be in a strong position.[34]

The Prime Ministerial meeting was attended by Thatcher, Lawson and his senior officials, Leigh-Pemberton and other Bank officials, Howe and John Redwood as Head of the Prime Minister's Policy Unit. Alan Walters, Thatcher's former economic adviser and now in the USA, was invited but did not attend. Although considering that immediate entry was inappropriate, Lawson, Howe and Leigh-Pemberton all advocated membership within the foreseeable future. For her part, Thatcher was less enthusiastic in principle and was also concerned that the exchange reserves were very low in comparison to the ERM states. Nevertheless, she agreed that once the reserves were increased, ERM membership would be reconsidered.[35]

A NEW CONSENSUS: FEBRUARY–SEPTEMBER 1985

After the meeting of 13 February, Lawson and his officials examined ways to build up the foreign exchange reserves so that a decision on ERM membership could be taken later in the year. In the months that followed, Lawson did not waver in his support for ERM entry, asking his officials to write papers on the implications of membership rather than the case for entry itself.[36] As one official commented, '[Lawson] did not require a tremendous amount of advice on all this'.[37]

By the summer of 1985 Middleton, Burns and other senior officials were all converted to membership. In part this reflected the sheer dominance of Lawson and his views within the Treasury. One of his somewhat exasperated senior officials reflected:

> If he says, I want to join the ERM, you talk about it to him, all the rest of it, but you're not going to say no, you don't think so. You've got to try and help him do it ... He was a permanent problem from then on. He basically lost interest in the way we were running economic policy and proceeded to try to run it in a different way, based primarily on the exchange rate.[38]

Certainly, in the immediate aftermath of the sterling crisis some senior Treasury figures were reluctant to give up on the monetary targets once and for all. Terry Burns, for one, wanted to try to re-anchor monetary policy around a M0 target. According to Lawson:

'They [the senior officials] felt that the government – and they personally – had invested a great deal of intellectual capital in the existing
monetary policy framework and were loath to abandon it.'[39] Nonetheless, these officials finally concluded that there were two fundamental
problems with the monetary targets. First, the targets were not providing information which was useful in making monetary decisions. One
Treasury official observed that 'there was some disillusionment with the
monetary targets because we did not understand the relationships'.[40]
According to another, 'the monetary side of things had got very
difficult, mainly because velocities were all over the show'.[41] Second, the
Treasury officials believed that their conception of monetary targets in
government policy was now too difficult to present in public:

> We came to the conclusion that there was no single definition of
> money supply which is of any utility to a policy operator. The
> only thing which you can do is to hold very firmly to the
> underlying concept of what it is you want to control, get the
> maximum input data on what you can get, with the greatest
> subtlety of definition and watch how it is changing. And then
> [you] make almost a kind of analogue judgement, rather than a
> digital calculation, to get the feel of when it is getting a bit too
> much and you can rein back, or when it's tight and ought to be
> loosened. But you can't explain that to the gentlemen of the
> press. They'll say at once, 'Don't know what you are talking
> about, no control, lost all sense of direction.' It translates that
> way.[42]

By contrast, ERM membership seemed an effective and presentable
anchor:

> Given that background, it was becoming increasingly
> attractive–seeing incidentally that the European [monetary]
> system itself was becoming more self-confident, more robust and
> giving a stronger impression to the markets. It was terribly
> tempting to say: 'Look, suppose we latched into that [the ERM]
> in the right set of circumstances and then continued our
> monetary policy, we [the Treasury] would not have this problem
> of presentation. We could go on doing monetary policy, liaising
> closely with the Bank as usual.'[43]

Another Treasury official who became converted to membership in this
period recalled:

> We had to take decisions of some sort. We could not just say,
> we'll continue to think about it. That was becoming
> increasingly untenable. The other thing that we began to think
> by 1985 was that the UK economy was getting into the

position where it *could* join the ERM. The inflation basis looked not unreasonable.[44]

At the same time, since it now appeared that ERM membership offered exchange rate stability and lower interest rates for any given inflation rate, there was a clear convergence between the benefits of joining the system and the Treasury's institutional preferences. Certainly in Lawson's view, low interest rates were now a clear policy goal for Treasury officials.[45]

Against this background, the top levels of the Treasury became uniformly pro-ERM during the first half of 1985. Only at lower levels did some scepticism remain. These opponents of membership generally fell into two groups. The first, and larger group, was of economists who remained wedded to the idea of a domestically based monetary policy around some form of monetary targets. In the view of one ERM supporter within the Treasury, 'one or two felt almost that their *métier* in life was being challenged because they saw it as giving policy to the Bundesbank'.[46] The second group was made up of administrators who, according to one official, 'just had hackles about Europe'.[47]

Meanwhile, at the Bank of England, Leigh-Pemberton and his deputy, Kit MacMahon, remained as firm on the issue as Lawson. Both reckoned that the January crisis could have been avoided inside the ERM and that it was necessary to inject some financial discipline into the government's monetary framework. When MacMahon retired, his replacement, George Blunden, initially emerged as a sceptic, but during the course of 1985 changed his view, partly in deference to the Governor.[48] Opinion lower down at the Bank of England was fairly evenly divided between strong supporters and strong opponents of membership. As in 1980 and 1981, the greatest opposition to membership came from the domestic monetary division. These officials believed that sterling was still too volatile a currency to become a stable member of the ERM, and that the convergence of British inflation towards the lowest levels in Europe might well prove to be a temporary phenomenon.[49] For one sceptic, at least, the problem was simply Britain's continuing economic divergence from the ERM states:

> Among those most directly and professionally concerned with monetary management, there was quite a degree of misgiving over the timeliness of fixing an ERM parity at the time . . . [Some of us believed] *de facto* a parity system of that sort would have a tendency to become very much a fixed-rate type of arrangement. Or at least that any departure from fixity would come to have the characteristic of failure. And [so we came] to feel that it would not be wise to get committed to it *unless* and *until* we could be reasonably confident that that would be a

discipline that we would both be able to and want to observe. What that starting point led to was self-evidently a questioning of the extent to which we could regard the optimal currency area conditions as being satisfied by the UK within the ERM economic area. [There were] two particular areas which we were immediately concerned at the lack of fulfilment of those conditions. One was the then divergence in patterns of external trade between ourselves and the Continental countries with much greater [UK] involvement and exposure to other parts of the world – dollar and Pacific area – than they had. And the other was the difference in resource endowment which was most notable in our North Sea oil resource.[50]

Nevertheless, despite the divisions within the Bank, Leigh-Pemberton and MacMahon were determined to take a higher profile supporting ERM when decisions were made than the Bank had done between 1980 and 1983.[51]

In May 1985 Lawson got the green light from Thatcher to borrow foreign currency to build up the reserves, and five months later he announced an issue of $2.5 billion floating rate notes (FRNs).[52] With this decision, Thatcher effectively allowed the Chancellor to fully reopen the ERM question. Believing that 'it would be extremely difficult to convince Thatcher', Lawson got his officials to work on assembling a specific case for membership to focus her mind.[53] At the same time Lawson was anxious to keep the Foreign Office and the European Secretariat of the Cabinet Office outside the debate.[54] In part, Lawson was simply recognizing that the continuing support of Geoffrey Howe and the Foreign Office for membership was counter-productive to the task of convincing Thatcher. In the words of one Treasury official: 'We put a lot of effort into mobilizing allies, and that included actually demobilizing the Foreign Office ... They were such an easy target for her, and poor Geoffrey Howe was an easy personal target for her.'[55] In addition, the Treasury continued to believe that the issue was their territory, and were disdainful of the perceived political nature of the Foreign Office's case for membership. One senior official remarked disparagingly that 'The Foreign Secretary sort of always wants to join organizations'.[56] Lawson himself, whilst judging that exclusion from the ERM diminished Britain's influence in the Community, saw the economic case for entry as standing 'wholly' on its own terms.[57]

When in August Howe gave Lawson a Foreign Office paper which advocated entry to the ERM within the next few months, Lawson dismissed it out of hand.[58] He wished to operate with Thatcher on a bilateral basis and succeeded in engineering a proposal from Thatcher for a Prime Ministerial seminar on the subject on 30 September.[59]

By the second half of 1985, what had emerged were clear terms of reference for a new ERM debate. When membership first became an issue of economic, as opposed to EC policy, in 1981, the debate was defined by the immense difficulties of operating the MTFS. The question in 1981–82 was whether sticking to the MTFS monetary targets or opting for exchange rate stability was the best means of using monetary policy as a counter-inflationary discipline. Those who then opposed ERM membership were unwilling finally to abandon the MTFS. Now there could be little doubt about the failure of the MTFS as either an effective or credible monetary framework. Opponents of membership did not envisage a return to a strict monetary target policy, but rather contested the viability or desirability of entry to the ERM itself.

At the same time the failure of the MTFS defined the position of those who supported membership as it had in 1981–82. Advocates of membership were explicitly claiming that because money supply targets had not worked as a counter-inflationary monetary framework, the way forward was to pursue exchange rate stability through the ERM as a similarly defined framework. It was the means used in MTFS not the policy end itself which was responsible for its failure. Lawson himself declares that membership would 'represent exactly the same' kind of 'public commitment' to an anti-inflationary stance as the MTFS had been.[60]

For ERM supporters membership would be the formal replacement of one set of monetary means to control inflation with another and, thus, not a significant shift in policy. Two senior Treasury officials reflected respectively:

> We never saw it as a fundamental shift in policy. It's just a question of how you go about the same thing.

> It became very attractive simply as a device consistent with what we wanted to do but a damn sight easier to explain.[61]

But, ironically, by 1985 the ERM was decidedly more than a collective counter-inflationary monetary framework. The ERM states considered that there were multiple causes of inflation, from rising levels of domestic demand to large wage increases and unfettered credit expansion. Consequently, they were committed to using a range of policy tools, including fiscal policy, to control inflation. Asked how Lawson perceived the relevance of fiscal policy to ERM membership, a Treasury official replied: 'In Nigel Lawson's mind, the ERM was principally a way of setting interest rates – of tying British monetary policy to well-established German credibility.'[62] This left the paradoxical situation whereby the operation of the ERM denied the underlying premise of the MTFS that inflation is fundamentally a monetary phenomenon, while Lawson and officials at the Treasury and Bank of England clung to that premise in their conversion to ERM membership.

Business and the ERM

If the sterling crisis had precipitated this fundamental review of the ERM issue within government, a similar process had occurred outside it. During 1985 a succession of business groups, economic organizations and financial commentators came out in favour of ERM entry. On 20 February for the first time the CBI's policy-making body voted by an overwhelming majority to support membership. The CBI saw both an economic and political case for entry. In economic terms, CBI members disliked the existing level of exchange rate volatility, invariably putting exchange rate stability as the first item on sensitivity analysis in investment projects. Although firms were able to hedge against exchange rates in the short term, they saw no consolation in this over the long term.[63]

The sterling crisis had brought the issue of currency volatility to a head. Previously, firms valued exchange rate stability, but were confident that it could be better achieved outside rather than inside the ERM. Now they were anxious that Britain was suffering from a uniquely damaging level of volatility. One CBI official commented on the sterling crisis: 'There was a surprising degree of unanimity, that if we were going to set up Britain on a proper basis, if British industry was going to be set up satisfactorily, we'd got to have something better than this.'[64] At the macro-level, the CBI believed that membership could achieve the convergence of British inflation towards the lowest EC levels, and thus improve Britain's trading performance in the EC. If the costs of British companies went up faster than maintaining the exchange rate in a relatively fixed parity would allow, then those companies would lose profits and decline. At the same time, the CBI hoped, the ERM would act as a counter-inflationary discipline on the government.[65] According to one CBI official, 'the CBI had no confidence in the British government's ability to manage our monetary affairs'.[66]

In political terms, the CBI's main concern was that British business would not reap all the benefits of EC membership until Britain was a member of all the Community's institutions. Kenneth Edwards, the Deputy Director-General of the CBI, told the Treasury and Civil Service Select Committee:

> We are desperately concerned that we are moving to a two-
> speed Europe situation ... We tend to be excluded from the
> internal marketing arrangements. In the case of standards, there
> is an agreement between West Germany and France about the

recognition of each other's standards over a particular band. There is also the question of the satellite broadcasting sector where the Germans and the French are getting together in the area of technical co-operation. We are outside that, as we are sitting outside the EMS ... The EMS is another example of a two-speed Europe developing ... It may be suggested that the economic arguments for entry into the ERM are finely balanced ... However, the political arguments seem to be overwhelmingly in favour.[67]

By depreciating the currency, the sterling crisis had also opened up the prospect of entry to the ERM at a rate which the CBI considered more competitive than in previous years On the day that the CBI announced its support for membership sterling stood at DM3.62. Certainly, some in the CBI remained doubtful that industry could compete at this rate.[68] Edwards admitted to the select committee that 'many companies would like to see a different parity'.[69] Yet in the view of Terence Beckett, the CBI's Director-General, 'exchange rate volatility was more serious to industry than the level of rates',[70] and throughout 1985 he 'thumped the drum very hard about ERM'.[71]

In the City the sterling crisis induced a similar reappraisal of the issue. In making their case for ERM entry, Lloyd's of London argued that sterling's volatility with the dollar was causing problems to City business, and that membership would reduce the volatility.[72] Unsurprisingly, City institutions believed that the sterling crisis had demonstrated an absence of counter-inflationary will, and that ERM membership was a discipline to keep politicians as far away from monetary policy as possible.[73] Whilst City institutions did not lobby ministers as systematically as the CBI, their views were clearly transmitted to the Bank of England to pass on to Lawson.[74]

The general support expressed in 1985 by both financial and manufacturing capital was paralleled by a plethora of economic organizations and financial commentators. In August the National Institute of Economic and Social Research predicted that membership would provide greater financial discipline.[75] The London Chamber of Commerce argued that entry was necessary to stabilize sterling and to take full benefit from EC membership.[76] In November the London Business School called for membership to reduce exchange rate volatility.[77] The same month the influential Financial Times commentator Sam Brittan came out in favour of entry. During the sterling crisis he had scathingly rejected membership on the grounds that sterling was a volatile petrocurrency, but he now argued that ERM membership was the only way of injecting some counter-inflationary credibility into policy and of restraining the Chancellor from fiscal expansion.[78]

Only the Institute of Directors (IoD) did not march to this procession for ERM entry. John Hoskyns, the Director-General, castigated the ERM as 'absolute nonsense', and charged that the pursuit of exchange rate stability only induced more damaging instability elsewhere.[79] His view was shared by the IoD's Policy Unit, if not by its less influential European Advisory Council, which tended to favour membership. But, despite the strength of Hoskyns's views, the IoD's position became compromised. In the summer of 1985 Geoffrey Howe asked Hoskyns if the IoD could write him a letter stating that in certain circumstances membership might make sense. Hoskyns agreed as a personal favour to Howe. On 30 August the IoD sent Howe its assessment of the pros and cons of membership. Howe presented to the media the part of the letter which made the potential case for membership and ignored Hoskyns's argument that membership might be unsustainable and damaging to the domestic economy.[80] On 4 September the press reported that Hoskyns believed that there were strong financial and political reasons for joining, and that business would benefit from a more stable currency framework and the future development of the Ecu.[81] To all intents and purposes, it appeared that the IoD was another passenger on the ERM bandwagon.

THATCHER'S VETO: SEPTEMBER–DECEMBER 1985

With a Prime Ministerial seminar set for 30 September the ERM debate was set to reach its climax, and it did so against a background in which ministers faced substantial incentives in terms of their economic policy, capital accumulation priorities and EC policy finally to join the ERM. In the months after the sterling crisis Thatcher and Lawson had aimed to stabilize sterling whilst reducing interest rates whenever possible. By the end of July interest rates stood at 11.5 per cent, but thereafter no further cuts were possible. On 22 September the G5 finance ministers, including Lawson, negotiated the Plaza agreement to reduce the value of the dollar by 10 per cent through co-ordinated intervention.[82] The next month Lawson announced the suspension of the £M3 target for the rest of the financial year. Although £M3 was no longer an operational guide to policy, it did retain some importance to the markets as a symbol of financial discipline. According to Lawson, the exchange rate and M0 were now the dual guide to policy. But the markets did not take M0 seriously as a target, and the absence of a formal exchange rate target left Lawson without a credible financial framework. On the fiscal front he announced in the autumn statement of 1985 a twofold increase in the target for privatization receipts over the next three years. Using this increased room for fiscal manoeuvre, Lawson promised that public expenditure would be stabilized, after having risen by 4 per cent across the two previous years, and that tax cuts would follow. Clearly, Thatcher's and Lawson's apparent economic objectives were compatible with ERM membership, at least for the immediate future; they were committed to exchange rate stability and had assigned monetary policy to that end.

Given this policy assignment, ERM membership would probably have allowed for a reduction in interest rates. With the ERM's growing collective credibility, it was possible to defend currencies at lower rates of interest than those prevailing in Britain. Throughout 1985 Britain had high nominal and real interest rates in comparison to the ERM states. As Figure 2.3 shows, in November 1985 only Italy, with its consistently below-average inflation performance, had higher nominal and real interest rates among the major ERM states. Although France had a higher inflation rate in 1985, it enjoyed lower nominal interest rates without the franc coming under pressure.[83] In overall monetary terms membership offered Thatcher and Lawson both a counter-

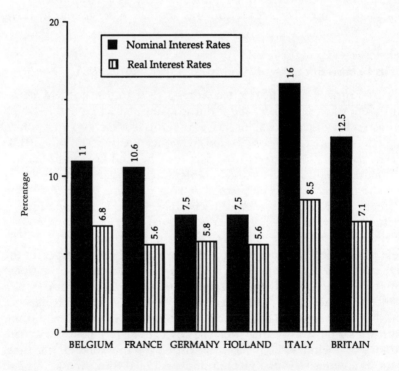

Figure 2.3: Comparative Nominal and Real Interest Rates November 1985.
(Source: Economist Economic and Financial Indicators November 30, 1985)

inflationary exchange rate control and the stimulus for growth which they wished to provide.

Whilst there were no direct fiscal benefits to membership, at least in the short term it would not have required any change in fiscal policy. In 1985 British inflation was 5.5 per cent compared to 5.8 per cent in France, 9 per cent in Italy and 5.5 per cent in the EC as a whole.[84] Since inflation was predicted to fall below 3.3 per cent by mid-1986, Britain appeared to have made the same counter-inflationary fiscal adjustment as the ERM states had. Nonetheless, membership was likely to constrain any future plans for inflationary fiscal expansion.

The biggest potential macro-economic cost of ERM entry was in terms of the level of the exchange rate itself. During the third and fourth quarters of 1985, sterling averaged DM3.90 and DM3.71 respectively.[85] Even many of those who advocated membership believed that entry at DM3.70 would pose problems of competitiveness.[86] In 1985 Britain's manufacturing trade deficit with the EC was £9.1 billion, two-thirds of which was with Germany, and, at least in the short term, membership would have ruled out a depreciation in sterling to combat the situation.[87] Since growth was already disproportionately taking place in the oil sector, with manufacturing investment and output still below the levels of the late 1970s, membership was, therefore, likely to act as a constraint on export-led growth.

In terms of ministers' capital accumulation priorities, there was a more substantial case for ERM entry than had hitherto existed. By 1985 ministers appeared *to be actively seeking* to encourage particular sites of investment. Central to their strategy was the aim to recreate London as the prime European centre of finance. This process began in July 1983 when Cecil Parkinson, the Trade and Industry Secretary, agreed to stop the Office of Fair Trading's case against the Stock Exchange on the condition that the latter reformed itself. From late 1983 there was a flurry of activity in which both British and foreign big banks took over stock exchange firms. Meanwhile, combining with City firms, ministers used their statutory power to start deregulating and modernizing City practices. In the process the City became an unparalleled site for international capital operations with Japanese banks lending more from the City than British banks.[88]

The internationalization of this part of the economy was mirrored in the unprecedented encouragement given by the government to internal investment, especially from Japan. By 1986 one in seven of the British workforce was employed in foreign multinational companies.[89] Whilst other EC states had national strategies for capital restructuring in the manufacturing sector, the Thatcher government had effectively substituted an internal investment policy for industrial intervention. The net result was that Britain was left with few significant sectors of manu-facturing capital with secure markets, and its role in the world manu-facturing economy was increasingly becoming that of branch part-assembler of Japanese, American and German goods.[90]

At the same time the government was giving new support to the service sector. In 1984, for example, the Treasury made services eligible for regional development grants for the first time, despite the general move towards selective rather than automatic assistance in regional aid. Moreover, the commitment to privatization, deregulation and liberal-ization also disproportionately benefited the service sector, and minis-ters were making concerted efforts to liberalize trade in services both in the EC and GATT. In this climate, the service sector's share of GDP increased by 6.8 per cent between 1984 and 1989, having risen just 2.1 per cent between 1979 and 1984.[91]

These new capital accumulation priorities added an extra, if yet limited, dimension to the ERM policy debate. Although in terms of the service sector the issue was largely redundant since many firms do not export, there were clear benefits to membership for the most inter-nationalized parts of the economy. The City wanted the security of reduced exchange rate volatility and a counter-inflationary discipline. Multinational companies operating in Britain who tended to rely on importing components from abroad stood to benefit from ERM entry since it would fix sterling at a relatively high rate and provide some insurance against future depreciation. Nonetheless, it could not be said that either sector saw membership as imperative to their interests.

Although the review of ERM policy in 1985 had been precipitated by economic policy considerations, as in 1979 and 1980 membership was likely to yield benefits in terms of ministers' European agenda. As the negotiations on what was to become the Single European Act (SEA) were reaching a climax, Thatcher and Howe clearly did not want to be left behind in a second tier of states as a core group moved towards greater integration. In March 1985 Spain had decided to remain outside the ERM when it joined the EC the following year. This raised the possibility that the ERM itself might come to demarcate the tiers of EC integration. Meanwhile the major EC states and the Commission, who sought to promote closer integration, again wanted Britain to become part of the ERM. Believing that it was necessary for the development of a genuine single market and to further the ERM's credibility and competence, the Commission called for British entry throughout 1985.[92] Such calls were matched in the public comments of the German Finance Minister, Gerhard Stoltenberg, and the Bundesbank chief, Karl Otto-Pöhl. Of all the ERM states, Germany was perhaps the most keen on British membership and, indeed, made it their condition for any future development of the EMS. As well as wanting sterling to relieve the burden on the Deutschmark as the unilateral reserve currency, the Germans calculated that Britain would be a free-market ally within the system, particularly in regard to issues of capital movement.[93] In this context a decision to join the ERM potentially offered considerable benefits. If ministers were worried about a two-speed Europe, then participation in the system would thwart the threat of the ERM becoming the catalyst of that development. Meanwhile, since the other member states led by Germany had a significant interest in a change in British policy, then Thatcher and Howe could give themselves a significant bargaining card in the last stages of the SEA negotiations.

'On the contrary: I disagree'

In preparation for the Prime Ministerial seminar on 30 September Lawson instructed his officials to develop the Treasury paper in close collaboration with the Bank, explaining both the case for entry and the best way to present membership in public. In the words of one Treasury official, 'it was a prerequisite that the Bank should be on side', since for Thatcher its opposition would have been 'a cast-iron argument' against joining.[94] At the same time Lawson was particularly concerned to pre-empt any use by Thatcher of the so-called 'Walters' scenario' argument. Walters claimed that inside the ERM a poor Conservative showing in an opinion poll during a general election campaign would put sterling under pressure, forcing the government to raise interest rates and handing the election to the Labour Party. Lawson dismissed the argument himself, but he asked Geoffrey Littler to conjure a way around the alleged problem. Littler suggested the *'congé* plan. *In extremis*, the government could formally declare that sterling would be allowed to float until polling day and that on re-election the government would immediately restore sterling to the system at the previous parity.[95]

The 30 September seminar was attended by Lawson, Ian Stewart (the Financial Secretary), officials from the Treasury, Leigh-Pemberton and other Bank representatives, Howe and Brian Griffiths (the Head of the Policy Unit). Backed by Leigh-Pemberton, Lawson argued that entry was absolutely necessary to reinforce the government's anti-inflationary strategy, given the difficulty of interpreting the monetary indicators. For his part, Howe left European policy aside and argued that membership would strengthen the MTFS. Once again Thatcher concluded that she remained unconvinced and that further ministerial discussion was necessary before a decision could be taken. She would decide, she declared, which ministers to invite to take the decision and would circulate a list of questions that needed to be answered before the meeting.[96]

Shortly afterwards, Lawson asked the Treasury to prepare a further paper to be circulated in advance to all those who were to attend the second meeting. He set up a joint Treasury-Bank team both to write the paper and to respond to the questions from Number 10. When the Prime Minister's questionnaire arrived, Lawson reports, it read much as 'a rag-bag' of every conceivable objection to the ERM.[97]

Lawson's own paper, sent as a memo to Thatcher on 11 November, again stressed the benefits of membership as a counter-inflationary monetary framework, in view of the problems with the policy based on monetary targets:

After grappling with these problems as Chancellor for over two years now, I have come to the conclusion that joining the ERM of the EMS would deal with both the issue of substance and the issue of presentation, and is the only practicable means of doing so. The exchange rate is more readily comprehensible than monetary targets and we are already relying on it to a major extent as an indicator. To join the EMS would reinforce the discipline and commitment inherent to the MTFS, and be seen to do so. The interested public seem ready for it. Industry certainly is.[98]

Between September and November Lawson and the Treasury became more optimistic about the chances of success in convincing Thatcher. Recalling his over-sanguine expectations, one Treasury official commented:

I think I got personally to the point of believing that there might be a slightly better than evens chance. Because we had done our homework well; the seminar had gone not too badly ... One of the things that actually persuaded me that there might be a chance was the Hong Kong issue ... The idea that the Hong Kong dollar could be linked to the American dollar was not one that we thought was a natural subject of enthusiasm for Mrs Thatcher on any count, or indeed for Alan Walters. The odd thing was that it happened to be a former pupil of his who in Hong Kong had begun to raise the whole issue and got Alan's ear, and Alan persuaded the Prime Minister of this ... After she gave the green light, I could not help thinking: 'Her antipathy to any sort of fixed exchange rate is not total.'[99]

The second meeting took place on 13 November. With ministers and officials both in attendance, it was essentially an *ad hoc* meeting organized at the Prime Minister's discretion. The officials present were Middleton and Burns from the Treasury and Leigh-Pemberton and

Eddie George from the Bank of England. As for ministers, Thatcher asked Lawson and Howe, plus Willie Whitelaw (Deputy Prime Minister), Norman Tebbit (Conservative Party Chairman), Leon Brittan (Trade and Industry), John Biffen (Leader of the House) and John Wakeham (Chief Whip). Brian Griffiths and one of Thatcher's private secretaries were also present. In Lawson's view, Thatcher had asked Whitelaw and Brittan because she could not exclude them, and the other three ministers were invited on the grounds that she supposed they were opponents of membership. At any rate Lawson himself saw all the ministers, except Biffen, prior to the meeting to go over his paper.[100]

At the meeting Lawson, Howe and Leigh-Pemberton made the same case for membership that they had presented in September. They were supported by Brittan, who said that having previously been an opponent of membership he now believed in the need for a credible alternative to monetary aggregates and that the petro-currency factor no longer applied.[101] Brittan's position also reflected the view of DTI officials, who were keen supporters of membership, although never asked to contribute to the debate.[102] Of the ministers invited by Thatcher as likely opponents of membership, only Biffen, as a committed free floater, argued against entry. Not only did Tebbit and Wakeham speak in favour, but they instructed that membership would be a positive benefit in the government's relations with the party and its back benches.[103] Thatcher responded that, to the contrary, it would divide the party, leave the government with no control of interest rates, and that the *congé* plan would not work.[104] According to one Thatcher confidant:

> Lawson said: 'How can you stand up against it, when your
> Chancellor and Foreign Secretary are both agreed, that it is most
> urgent that we enter the ERM?' She replied that it was her
> constitutional responsibility to choose policy.[105]

Characteristically waiting until the end of the discussion, Whitelaw declared his support for membership.[106] For himself Whitelaw believed that having some means of regulating currencies in the EC which included sterling must make sense. At the same time he judged that when the Chancellor, Foreign Secretary and the Governor of the Bank of England were united on entry, then it was extremely hard to understand why the government should do otherwise.[107] In Lawson's description of the end of the meeting after Whitehall's declaration, Thatcher immediately replied, 'On the contrary: I disagree. If you join the EMS, you will have to do so without me.'[108]

Clearly not intending to resign, Thatcher had slammed the door on the ERM again.

Any plausible explanation of Thatcher's position must first recognize her rejection of the most fundamental benefits which membership would have brought, namely lower interest rates for a given rate of inflation. Certainly, it cannot be argued that Thatcher did not understand this attraction. A pro-ERM official recalled: 'I remember her saying at some moment when it seemed to me to be completely inappropriate that the great thing about ERM is that it would allow you to have lower interest rates than you would have otherwise.,[109] While all Prime Ministers and governments have an interest in low interest rates, if Lawson is to be believed, then Thatcher had a passionate desire to cut rates whenever possible. It is a point which Lawson returns to repeatedly in his memoirs. For example:

> Low interest rates had an unfailing appeal for Margaret. Despite her reputation as a diehard opponent of inflation, and her dislike of it was undoubtedly genuine, she was almost always in practice anxious to reduce interest rates, and thus, the mortgage rates.

> It was hard enough to persuade Margaret of the need to raise interest rates when I had the Bank with me.

> She was positively soft on interest rates.[110]

Thatcher herself admits:

> Nigel apparently now thinks that I was 'soft' on interest rates. Anyone who recalls our decisions from 1979 to 1981 will find that implausible ... Nevertheless, Nigel and I did have rather different starting points when it came to these matters. I was always more sensitive to the political implications of interest rate rises—particularly their timing—than was Nigel. Prime Ministers have to be. I was also acutely conscious of what interest rate changes meant for those with mortgages.[111]

Whatever benefit Thatcher saw in ERM membership had to be strong enough to override her clear preference for lower interest rates.

By contrast, Thatcher did not accept that ERM membership would bring any real benefits in EC policy. Uncomfortable with the European Council as a decision-making forum, Thatcher still did not want to trade one EC issue against another, and found it easier to play the nationalist card. In the words of one former Cabinet minister:

> She hated all those Council meetings. She would come back absolutely fuming ... they were all waffle, waffle, waffle, and I can just imagine that she had to sit there crossing her legs and uncrossing her legs, and wondering how long she had to go on

listening to all the bloody people from Greece and Portugal and all the rest.[112]

At the same time she believed that Britain was generally in a weak position with little or no bargaining power. An exasperated Foreign Office official recalled:

> I used to argue with her. She would say, 'Those crafty French, they'll win again, they always win.' I remember saying to her, 'Why are you so defeatist? It's an extraordinary attitude ... You know we've got a very good case here. We've got a lot of support, why do you think the French line will win?'[113]

Thatcher's own explanations of her opposition to membership centred on economic policy and were somewhat contradictory. In her memoirs, she writes about the 13 November meeting:

> By now I was more convinced than ever of the disadvantages of the ERM. I could see no particular reason to allow British monetary policy to be determined largely by the Bundesbank rather than by the British Treasury, unless we had no confidence in our ability to control inflation. I was extremely sceptical about whether the industrial lobby which was pressing us so hard to join the ERM would maintain its enthusiasm once they came to see that it was making their goods uncompetitive. I doubted whether the public would welcome what might turn out to be the huge cost of defending sterling within the ERM– which, indeed, might well prove to be impossible in the run-up to a general election and so be compounded by a forced devaluation.[114]

On two different occasions she declared that membership would be too deflationary and too inflationary, respectively. Then, in June 1986, Thatcher argued that Britain needed to retain the option of letting the exchange rate, rather than monetary policy or 'precious reserves', take the strain when there was speculation against sterling. Later in the year she told the *Financial Times*: 'I want to be absolutely certain that there can be no repetition of what happened before, when we came out of the snake [in 1972]. When we go in, we will go in strong and stay in.'[115]

Neither is it plausible to explain Thatcher's opposition mainly in terms of the influence of Alan Walters. In his memoirs Lawson reflects that in the questionnaire Thatcher sent before the 13 November meeting, 'curiously, about the only objection that was not included in the list of questions was that dubbed (by Alan Walters) the 'Walters' critique'.[116] In the same vein one Treasury official expressed his scepticism about Walters' influence:

The question of Alan Walters, I was inclined to dismiss and I still do. She never actually did what Alan told her or followed Alan's advice, but she found him absolutely a marvellous man to brief her with arguments to combat others with, but she was never a slave to his views.[117]

Those who talked with Thatcher on the issue understood her opposition in various terms. In the view of one Foreign Office official: 'Her main argument against the ERM was one of practicality. She was always telling one how Ted Heath had had to come out of the snake.'[118] At least one Bank of England official perceived that it was the problem of managing monetary policy in the pre-election period which troubled Thatcher: 'In the run-up to an election, if there was a sterling crisis, the government would have to raise interest rates and she did not want to be dictated to by the Bundesbank.'[119] Be that as it may, such an argument for non-membership would have only made sense if Thatcher was prepared to adopt an attitude of benign neglect towards sterling, which she manifestly was not. In November 1986 Thatcher made it clear that Lawson and herself would not countenance a devaluation in the run-up to the general election. As Sam Brittan argued in dismissing the argument, in the circumstances a much smaller rise in rates might be necessary once in the ERM than when doubts existed about the government's exchange rate objectives.[120]

Many people have understood Thatcher's opposition to membership as ultimately about a conception of sovereignty in relation to economic policy:

She thought that it was giving too much away in terms of sovereignty.[121]

She just did not like the idea of the Europeans getting involved in sterling ... I think she always feared too much European meddling in British affairs. She thought that the Bank and the pound and all the rest were things they should not be allowed to meddle in.[122]

It was the sense of sovereignty that she had, surrendering your political power to some outside body.[123]

She stood out on grounds of sovereignty, a concept she had read about somewhere but could never tell you where.[124]

[She saw it] as losing control over the economy. The government should not sacrifice that degree of ability to run the economy.[125]

Yet for a more analytical explanation, the question has to be asked how Thatcher's particular conception of sovereignty related to her understanding of the government's political interests. What particular freedom of manoeuvre outside the ERM did Thatcher believe was of sufficient benefit to outweigh the advantage of lower interest rates for a given rate of inflation? Certainly, joining the system would not have been simply the 'shift in emphasis' which Lawson, the Treasury and the Bank of England took it to be. As a fundamentally different way of operating economic policy, ERM membership would ultimately have reduced the government's freedom of manoeuvre beyond the area of monetary policy. The most likely political cost in the short to medium term was the potential conflict between the fiscal constraint inherent in the ERM and the desire to reduce income tax. Whilst Lawson and those ministers who supported membership in November 1985 clearly did not trade off interest rate cuts against income tax cuts in making their judgement, it is less clear whether Thatcher herself made the calculation. At any rate, there is no evidence that Thatcher ever articulated a detailed understanding of the relation between the constraints of ERM membership and her economic objectives. Nevertheless, as Chapters 4 and 5 will indicate, it is plausible to suggest that Thatcher had an instinctive grasp of a difference which she wished to hold on to between her government's economic policy and those of the Continental states in areas beyond monetary policy.

For Lawson the outcome of the meeting demanded a decision on his future. Three courses of action were open to him: he could have resigned, carried on fighting on the issue or simply accepted Thatcher's decision. Clearly depressed, Lawson did indeed appear to consider resignation, but claims that he was talked out of it by Whitelaw, Howe and Tebbit.[126] However, what Lawson does not explain in his memoirs is on what basis he saw himself staying in office: did he accept Thatcher's decision as final or not?

As one Cabinet opponent of membership has admitted, Lawson, together with Howe, would have been within their rights to demand a Cabinet meeting on the issue.[127] They would have been backed in their demand by Whitelaw, who was prepared to act on their behalf if they so wished.[128] Two ministers in Cabinet at the time commented that there was a reasonably good chance that Lawson and Howe would have been backed by the majority of the Cabinet.[129] Indeed, Thatcher herself remarks that 'I knew that I was in a very small minority within the Cabinet on this matter, though most of my colleagues were probably not overinterested in it anyway.[130]

There appear to be three possible reasons for Lawson's and Howe's lack of action. First, they were simply not prepared to act together. Lawson's demobilization of Howe and the Foreign Office in the summer suggested a general unwillingness to make common allies with him and his officials. In fact, for Lawson and the Treasury to have combined with

Howe and the Foreign Office would have flown in the face of the Treasury's understanding of its *raison d'être*. As one Foreign Office official remarked:

> I dare say there was a bit of reluctance of Treasury officials to plot with Foreign Office officials. The Treasury's view usually is that what is required is for the Prime Minister and the Chancellor of the day to be absolutely at one ... and [not] of allowing the Chancellor to plot with the Foreign Secretary.[131]

Second, Lawson and Howe may have considered that the Cabinet was irrelevant, either because it was harder to persuade Thatcher in this forum than in small gatherings or because economic policy was not a matter for Cabinet.[132] If so, there was no choice but to let the matter rest. As one former Cabinet Minister reflected on the situation:

> The nature of British government invests enormous authority in the Prime Minister and if the Prime Minister is a bad loser – and I promise you the previous Prime Minister was a very bad loser – then I think she could have probably survived.[133]

Third, Lawson and Howe may have reckoned that Thatcher's position as Prime Minister was vulnerable, and hence were confident that her veto was only a temporary problem. There is indeed some evidence that Lawson and Howe did not view the 13 November meeting as the end of the matter. In his memoirs, Lawson relates how in December he gave the green light to a secret mission of officials to Germany, which he had planned in the hope of a favourable outcome to the ERM discussions. On 7 December Middleton, Littler and Anthony Loehnis, a Bank of England official, went on a highly confidential mission to Bonn to discuss contingency planning in the event of Britain deciding to enter the ERM. They talked to both Finance Ministry and Bundesbank officials, and Loehnis examined the possibility of the Bundesbank providing a substantial line of short-term credit to support initial British membership. Interestingly enough, Lawson offers no explanation of the purpose of this mission in view of Thatcher's veto nor how he reconciled this with his belief expressed on the next page that 'I could not see Margaret changing her mind so soon after the drama of 13 November'.[134] At least one Thatcher confidant considered that Lawson and Howe reconciled themselves to the decision by supposing that Thatcher's own tenure in office was limited:

> Within the highest reaches of the Conservative Party and Cabinet, they were always anxious to get rid of her. They thought they would sit it out and that they would be in a powerful position when she was ruined by something or other. Westland was only just around the corner.[135]

Certainly, Lawson has made it clear publicly that he was contemplating that the Westland affair could finish Thatcher's premiership.[136]

Aftermath

After debating ERM membership on 13 November exclusively in terms of economic policy, ministers were quickly forced to face the consequences of Thatcher's intransigence in terms of their EC policy. In the final negotiations towards the SEA three issues stood out: the completion of the Single Market; the use of majority voting in the Council of Ministers; and the Community's future monetary development. On the monetary issue, what was in dispute was whether to write the EMS into the Treaty of Rome and the objective of monetary union into the SEA. To inscribe the EMS into the treaty would mean that any future development of monetary policy affecting EC institutions would be subject to the full reform process of Inter-Governmental Conferences (IGCs) and ratification by national parliaments. On 14 November Lawson minuted Thatcher on the matter, warning against accepting any reference to monetary union in the Treaty, or any amendment to the original EEC treaty concerning exchange rates.[137]

Four days later the British and German governments combined to oppose writing the EMS into the Treaty of Rome on the grounds that it would restrict the autonomy of their central banks to control monetary policy.[138] By December, with a summit looming in Luxembourg, monetary union appeared to be the main unresolved monetary issue. Opinion within the British government was clearly split as to the gravity of what was at stake. Lawson feared that any formal commitment to monetary union would be taken very seriously both by the major member states and the Commission.[139] Meanwhile Howe and the Foreign Office reassured Thatcher that any commitment in the treaty would be rhetorical rather than substantive.[140] In part, this may have reflected a belief that it was necessary to underplay this dimension of the treaty if Thatcher were to accept it rather than an objective assessment of the situation. One former minister commented on the Foreign Office's attitude: 'they felt that you know, Christ, if she knew what we were up to, it would be like getting our money back all over again.'[141] Nonetheless, there is no evidence that at this time other member states, rather than the Commission, had any real agenda on monetary union. Notwithstanding Lawson's concerns and the benefit of hindsight, it was only when certain ERM states became dissatisfied with the operation of the ERM that monetary union genuinely emerged on the Community agenda.

After a bilateral meeting in London with Chancellor Kohl, Thatcher went to Luxembourg convinced that she had continuing German support to oppose writing the EMS into the Treaty of Rome.[142] But once at the summit Kohl attacked Thatcher on Britain's refusal to join the ERM, and backtracked on the EMS. He then proceeded to broker a compromise deal in which the EMS was given legal status and the SEA contained a limited commitment to the 'progressive realization of economic and monetary union'. Thatcher, isolated, was left to resentfully sign the deal.[143]

In the short term, the government's defeat on this issue was of little significance. Writing the EMS into the treaty changed nothing in practical terms, and there were precedents reaching back to the early 1970s of commitments to monetary union from which nothing ever materialized. Neither was there any evidence that monetary union was on the foreseeable agenda of either France or Germany. Nevertheless, in the medium to long term, the potential costs of the defeat were considerably greater. If any member states were to start advocating monetary union on economic grounds, then the SEA provided a basis for arguing that this was a fundamental part of the Community's development. At the same time the SEA raised new questions about the viability of non-membership in the future. First, if the ultimate objective of the Single Market was to improve the efficiency of resource allocation in the EC, then was not sterling's non-participation in the ERM the cause of inefficient exchange rate volatility? Moreover, was it logical to have a Single Market without a common currency? Second, the prospect of a single financial market opened up the possibility of banks and other institutions conducting business in one EC state, whilst being subject to central bank regulation in other states. In these circumstances there would be an increased onus on co-operation among central banks to ensure effective national monetary policies, whilst Britain would remain apart from the Community's main monetary institution.[144]

The intense debate about ERM membership which raged inside the British government in 1985 was first and foremost about economic policy. Whilst there was a substantial case for ERM entry in terms of ministers' capital accumulation priorities, it was not a pressing one, and it was not until the Luxembourg summit that the government paid a clear European policy price for non-membership. Unsurprisingly, the economic policy debate which took place emerged within the parameters of the 1981–82 deliberations, despite the implications of the development of the ERM into a fixed exchange rate system. The sterling crisis blew the second Thatcher government off course because the conflict which had emerged in the first administration about how to effectively run a counter-inflationary monetary policy remained unresolved. Between June 1983 and December 1984 Thatcher and Lawson had dealt erratically with the question, at times vainly trying to resuscitate the monetary targets, and on other occasions denying its relevance. After January 1985 the economic calculations imposed on the government by the foreign exchange markets demanded that, at least in the short term, more coherent choices were made.

By the end of 1985, there was an effective resolution to the monetary dilemma in terms of policy, but it was a compromise to which there was no guarantee that Thatcher or Lawson would adhere as circumstances changed. Moreover, whatever the disadvantages of ERM entry would have been, Thatcher's veto of membership and estrangement from Lawson on the issue meant that sterling was left vulnerable to the kind of crisis which had precipitated the soul-searching of 1985. Thatcher could keep saying 'no', but she would ultimately not be able to end the clamour from within her own government for ERM entry, nor control the economic conditions which would add monetary logic to her ministers' arguments.

NOTES

1 *Economist*, 27 July 1985, p. 12.

2 H. Ungerer, O. Evans and P. Nyberg, (1989) *The EMS: Developments and Perspectives*, Washington: IMF, p. 2; *Economist*, 19 September 1987, p. 86; *Guardian*, 5 April 1991.

3 For a discussion of the substance of the 1983 French crisis, see P. Hall, (1986) *Governing the Economy: The Politics of State Intervention in Britain and France*, Cambridge: Polity Press. For a discussion of the internal struggle within the French administration, see R. Elgie, (1993) *The Role of the Prime Minister in France 1981–1991*, London: Macmillan.

4 For a discussion of the new ERM, see Ungerer *et al.*, *The EMS* and F. Giavazzi and A. Giovanni, (1989) *Limiting Exchange Rate Flexibility: The European Monetary System*, Cambridge: MIT Press.

5 N. Lawson, (1992) *The View from No. 11: Memoirs of a Tory Radical*, London: Bantam, pp. 450–51.

6 Ibid., p. 453.

7 D. Smith, (1987) *The Rise and Fall of Monetarism: The Theory and Politics of an Economic Experiment*, Harmondsworth: Penguin, pp. 119–20; W. Keegan, (1989) *Mr Lawson's Gamble*, London: Hodder and Stoughton, pp. 122, 135.

8 Lawson, *Memoirs*, p. 464.

9 *Ibid.*, pp. 464–65.

10 *Hansard*, 12 November 1984, p. 418.

11 *Times*, 6 August 1984.

12 *Financial Times*, 26 November 1984.

13 *Ibid*, 30 November, 1984; *Economist*, 24 December, 1983, p. 50.

14 Smith, *Monetarism*, p. 51; *Times*, 27 October 1984.

15 *Financial Times*, 24 October, 1984.

16 Lawson, *Memoirs*, p. 485.

17 *Ibid.*, pp. 484–85.

18 Non-attributable interview with Treasury official.

19 Lawson, *Memoirs*, p. 485.

20 For a full discussion of this episode, see R. Harris, (1990) *The Good and Faithful Servant: The Unauthorised Biography of Bernard Ingham*, London: Faber & Faber.

21 *Financial Times*, 14 January, 1985.

22 *Ibid.*, 25 January 1995.

23 *Ibid.*, 25 January 1985; 29 January 1985; *Economist*, 2 February 1985, pp. 15, 19.

24 Harris, *Bernard Ingham*, p. 125.

25 *Economist*, 2 February 1985, p. 15; *Financial Times*, 30 January 1985.

26 *Financial Times*, 2 February, 1985.

27 *Economist*, 9 February 1985, p. 90; 23 February, 1985, p. 104.

28 Lawson, *Memoirs*, p. 485.

29 Non-attributable interview with Treasury official.

30 Lawson, *Memoirs*, p. 486.

31 *Ibid.*, p. 487; M. Thatcher (1993), *The Downing Street Years*, London: Harper Collins, p. 695.

32 *Times* 31 January, 1985.

33 Keegan, *Lawson's Gamble*, p. 156; Lawson, *Memoirs*, p. 488.

34 *Financial Times*, 16 January 1985; *Financial Times*, 19 February 1985; *Times*, 8 February 1985; *Times*, 19 February, 1985. On 18 February 24 back-bench Conservative MPs led by Geoffrey Rippon signed a motion in the House of Commons calling on the government to enter the ERM.

35 Lawson, *Memoirs*, pp. 488–99; Thatcher, *Downing Street Years*, pp. 694–95.

36 Lawson, *Memoirs*, pp. 489–90; non-attributable interview with Treasury official.

37 Non-attributable interview with Treasury official.

38 Non-attributable interview with Treasury official.

39 Lawson, *Memoirs*, p. 486.

40 Non-attributable interview with Treasury official.

41 Non-attributable interview with Treasury official.

42 Non-attributable interview with Treasury official.

43 Non-attributable interview with Treasury official.

44 Non-attributable interview with Treasury official.

45 Lawson, *Memoirs*, p. 478.

46 Non-attributable interview with Treasury official.

47 Non-attributable interview with Treasury official.

48 Lawson, *Memoirs*, p. 486; Keegan, *Lawson's Gamble*, p. 156; non-attributable interviews with Bank of England official.

49 Smith, *Monetarism*, p. 52.

50 Non-attributable interview with Bank of England official.

51 Non-attributable interview with Bank of England official.
52 Lawson, *Memoirs*, pp. 489–91; *Times*, 17 September 1985.
53 Non-attributable interview with Treasury official.
54 Non-attributable interview with Treasury official.
55 Non-attributable interview with Treasury official.
56 Non-attributable interview with Treasury official.
57 Lawson, *Memoirs*, p. 888.
58 *Ibid.*, p. 491.
59 *Ibid.*, pp. 491–93.
60 *Ibid.*, p. 496.
61 Non-attributable interview with Treasury officials.
62 Non-attributable interview with Treasury official.
63 *Financial Times*, 21 February 1985; non-attributable interview with CBI official.
64 Non-attributable interview with CBI official.
65 House of Commons, (1985) *Select Committee on the Treasury and the Civil Service, 13 Report: Minutes of Evidence*, London: HMSO p. 16; non-attributable interview with CBI official.
66 Non-attributable interview with CBI official.
67 House of Commons, *13th Report: Minutes of Evidence*, pp. 3, 8, 11.
68 *Financial Times*, 21 February 1985.
69 House of Commons, *13th Report: Minutes of Evidence*, p. 13.
70 *Financial Times*, 21 February 1985.
71 Non-attributable interview with CBI official.
72 *Financial Times*, 22 March 1985.
73 *Ibid.*, 13 April 1985; *Times*, 24 June 1985; *Economist*, 23 November 1985, p. 35.
74 Non-attributable interview with City official.
75 *Financial Times*, 22 August 1985.
76 *Ibid.*, 21 October 1985.
77 *Times*, 4 November 1985.
78 *Financial Times*, 14 November 1985.
79 Non-attributable interview with IoD official.
80 *Financial Times*, 4 September 1985; *Times*, 4 September 1985; non-attributable interview with IoD official.
81 *Financial Times*, 4 September 1985; *Times*, 4 September 1985.
82 For a discussion of the Plaza agreement, see Ŷ. Funabashi, (1988) *Managing the Dollar: From the Plaza to the Louvre*, Washington: Institute for International Economics.
83 D. Lomax, (1987) 'The UK Case', in P. van den Bempt, (ed.) *The European Monetary System Towards More Convergence and Closer Integration*, Louven: Acco, p. 198; House of Commons, *13th Report: Minutes of Evidence*, p. 62.
84 C. Johnson, (1991) *The Economy Under Mrs Thatcher, 1979–1990*, Harmondsworth: Penguin, p. 281.
85 Keegan, *Lawson's Gamble*, pp. 171, 182.
86 See, for example, David Howell's evidence to the Treasury and Civil Service Committee: House of Commons, *13th Report: Minutes of Evidence*, p. 61.

87 House of Commons, (1985) *Select Committee on the Treasury and the Civil Service Thirteenth Report*, London: HMSO, p. xix.
88 For further discussion, see B. Jessop *et al.*, (1988) *Thatcherism*, Cambridge: Polity Press; B. Jessop, (1986) 'Thatcherism's Mid-Life Crisis', *New Socialist*, 36, 1986; B. Jessop, (1990) *Conservative Regimes and the Transition to Post-Fordism: The Case of Great Britain and West Germany*, Essex: Working Paper; K. Middlemas, (1991) *Power, Competition and the State*, Vol. 3, *The End of the Postwar Era: Britain Since 1974*, London: Macmillan; M. Reid, (1988) *All Change in the City*, London: Macmillan; M. Moran, (1991) *The Politics of the Financial Services Revolution*, London: Macmillan.
89 Jessop, 'Mid-Life Crisis', p. 15.
90 See Jessop, 'Mid-Life Crisis' and Jessop *et al.*, *Thatcherism*.
91 Johnson, *Economy Under Thatcher*, p. 268.
92 House of Commons, *13th Report: Minutes of Evidence*, pp. 98–99; *Times*, 16 January 1985; *Financial Times*, 16 January 1985.
93 *Financial Times*, 28 March 1985; *Financial Times*, 12 September 1985; *Financial Times*, 8 November 1985; *Times*, 30 November 1985.
94 Non-attributable interview with Treasury official.
95 Lawson, *Memoirs*, pp. 491–92.
96 *Ibid.*, pp. 494–96; Thatcher, *Downing Street Years*, p. 697.
97 Lawson, *Memoirs*, pp. 496–97.
98 *Ibid.*, p. 1056.
99 Non-attributable interview with Treasury official.
100 Lawson, *Memoirs*, pp. 497–98.
101 *Ibid.*, p. 498.
102 Non-attributable interview.
103 There is considerable evidence that the majority of the parliamentary party was now in favour of ERM entry. See Lawson, *Memoirs*, p. 499; *Financial Times*, 13 June 1985; *Times*, 23 March 1985; 24 May 1985.
104 Lawson, *Memoirs*, pp. 498–99. Lawson's account of this meeting has been fully backed by other participants in the interviews I have conducted.
105 Non-attributable interview.
106 Lawson, *Memoirs*, p. 499.
107 Non-attributable interview.
108 Lawson, *Memoirs*, p. 499.
109 Non-attributable interview.
110 Lawson, *Memoirs*, pp. 478, 666, 686.
111 Thatcher, *Downing Street Years*, p. 698.
112 Non-attributable interview with Cabinet Minister.
113 Non-attributable interview with Foreign Office official.
114 Thatcher, *Downing Street Years*, p. 696.
115 S. Brittan, (1989) 'The Thatcher Government's Economic Policy', in D. Kavanagh and A. Seldon, (eds.) *The Thatcher Effect*, Oxford: Oxford University Press, p. 33; *Financial Times*, 11 June 1986; 19 November 1986.
116 Lawson, *Memoirs*, pp. 496–97.
117 Non-attributable interview with Treasury official.
118 Non-attributable interview with Foreign Office official.
119 Non-attributable interview with Bank of England official.

120 *Financial Times*, 14 November 1985.
121 Non-attributable interview with Treasury official.
122 Non-attributable interview.
123 Non-attributable interview with Treasury official.
124 Non-attributable interview.
125 Non-attributable interview.
126 Lawson, *Memoirs*, p. 500.
127 Non-attributable interview.
128 Non-attributable interview.
129 Non-attributable interviews.
130 Thatcher, *Downing Street Years*, p. 698.
131 Non-attributable interview with Foreign Office official.
132 Lawson, *Memoirs*, p. 129.
133 Non-attributable interview with Cabinet Minister.
134 Lawson, *Memoirs*, p. 501.
135 Non-attributable interview.
136 Lawson, *Memoirs*, p. 679.
137 *Ibid.*, p. 893.
138 *Times*, 19 November 1985.
139 Lawson, *Memoirs*, p. 893.
140 Non-attributable interviews with officials.
141 Non-attributable interview with Cabinet Minister.
142 *Financial Times*, 28 November 1985; Thatcher, *Downing Street Years*, pp. 554–55.
143 *Financial Times*, 2 December 1985; 3 December 1985; *Times*, 3 December 1985; *Economist*, 7 December 1985, p. 58.
144 F. McDonald, and G. Zis, (1989) 'The EMS: Towards 1992 and Beyond', *Journal of Common Market Studies*, 27 (3), p. 192; *Financial Times*, 16 June 1988.

3

Whose Sterling Problem?: 1986–1987

'Inconsistencies', answered Imlac, 'cannot both be right, but imputed to man they may both be true.' – Samuel Johnson, *The History of Rasselas*

THE ERM: COMPETITIVE DISINFLATION AND THE *FRANC FORT*

During 1986 and the first half of 1987 the ERM continued to operate as a relatively fixed exchange rate system around the Deutschmark and with a counter-inflationary bias in both fiscal and monetary terms. Member states were determined to retain the existing currency parities save in exceptional circumstances. When the Chirac government came to power in France in March 1986, it worried that the political fallout of *cohabitation* with Mitterrand would put the franc under pressure. So, pre-empting the foreign exchange markets, on 6 April the ERM states agreed to a general realignment of currencies in which the German, Dutch, Belgian and Luxembourg currencies were all revalued, and the franc was devalued. Revealingly, however, the Italian government refused to devalue, despite some pressure on the lira and Italy's below-average inflation performance. Four months later Ireland, another traditionally weak currency state, was forced into a devaluation. But once again the motive was not to compensate for rising inflation; the Irish government reluctantly asked to devalue to deal with the problems caused by a significant appreciation in the punt against sterling.

Such general resolve to maintain exchange rate stability was given added significance by a dramatic fall in the price of oil between the first and second quarters of 1986. This offered governments the opportunity to offset other inflationary pressure in their economies. But, led by Germany, the ERM states maintained tight monetary and fiscal policies, allowing the full benefit of the fall to feed through into a lower inflation rate. As Figure 3.1 shows, France, Germany and Italy all achieved a substantial fall in inflation in 1986, and Italy secured a further fall in 1987.

The stance of the ERM states in 1986 marked a significant watershed, most notably for France. After the devaluation in April 1986, the French government endeavoured systematically to reduce wage costs, and by January 1987, they were indeed rising more slowly in France than in Germany. Yet French counter-inflationary zeal notwithstanding, the franc came under renewed pressure against the Deutschmark. Citing the positive comparative fundamentals in the real economy, the French refused to devalue, and insisted that the situation was a problem for the Deutschmark. The French central bank allowed its currency to fall through its ERM floor, so obliging the Bundesbank to intervene to support the franc. The Bundesbank ended up selling DM5 billion on the foreign exchange markets, its hitherto largest sum of intervention within the ERM, at considerable cost to the German money supply. The experience was enough to convince both the Bundesbank and the German government that a revaluation of the

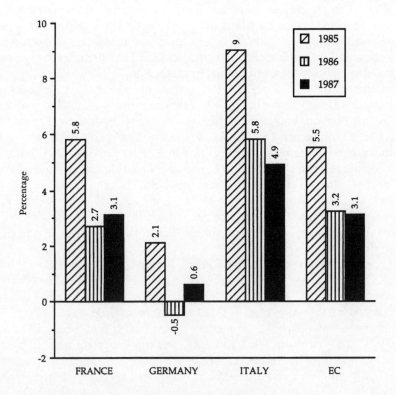

Figure 3.1: Inflation in the ERM States 1985-1987
(Source: Economic Outlook)

73

Deutschmark, not a devaluation of the franc, was now in order. On 11 January Germany, Holland, Belgium and Luxembourg all revalued their currencies with no concurrent devaluations. Henceforth, the French government was utterly determined to avoid any depreciation of the franc against the Deutschmark, whether by revaluation or devaluation, and permanently to emulate Germany's counter-inflationary performance. The guiding force of French economic policy was to be 'competitive disinflation', and the primary means to achieve it would be the *franc fort*.

DEVALUING FOR GROWTH: JANUARY–AUGUST 1986

Whilst the ERM states were seeking to strengthen their counter-inflationary credentials through an explicitly articulated commitment to exchange rate stability, the problem for the British government at the start of 1986 was how to run an exchange rate-based monetary policy without a public face. Thatcher had vetoed ERM membership without offering an alternative monetary framework to the one which Lawson had operated from mid-January 1985, and which Lawson himself believed could only work effectively inside the ERM. Left to work with a non-credible and unused M0 target and a *de facto* aim of exchange rate stability, those responsible for implementing policy were close to exasperation: 'In a sense, anything that one might have done as an alternative, we were already by definition doing ... The problem became how can you present this stuff better without the advantage of ERM.'[1] During the first weeks of January 1986, and with oil prices starting to fall dramatically, sterling came under pressure. On 9 January Thatcher reluctantly agreed to Lawson's proposal for a 1 per cent rise in interest rates to protect the currency. But in the following weeks sterling continued to fall. On 24 January Thatcher once more acquiesced to another 1 per cent rate rise, which in the event was rescinded before it was announced, when Leigh-Pemberton informed Lawson that sterling was recovering.

Having sought to stabilize sterling for these weeks in line with the 1985 policy, Lawson and Thatcher then quickly reversed course. Taking advantage of the halving of the price of oil between the first and second quarters of the year, they decided *to substantially devalue* sterling and offset the inflationary consequences against lower fuel prices. Between the fourth quarters of 1985 and 1986 sterling's effective rate fell by 16 per cent and its Deutschmark rate by 25 per cent. In the fourth quarter of 1986 sterling averaged DM2.86 compared to DM3.71 a year previously.[2] In his memoirs, Lawson rejects any suggestions that he either sought or welcomed the devaluation. Instead, he claims that whilst accepting that a 'halving of the price of oil made some exchange rate depreciation inevitable and necessary', he 'disliked intensely sterling's depreciation'.[3] His problem, though, was that 'there was a limit to what I could do, outside the ERM, particularly given Margaret's profound hostility to raising interest rates or maintaining any kind of exchange rate target'.[4] Thatcher herself, under a heading, 'Interest Rates and Inflation: 1986', does not actually accord a single word to the decisions about interest rates, the exchange rate, and their implications for inflation during the year.[5]

However, despite Lawson's protests, the evidence is very strong that he and Thatcher actively sought the devaluation, in direct contrast both to the 1985 policy and to what would have been possible inside the ERM. In the words of one Bank of England official:

> We found ourselves, more consciously that at any other time
> that I can remember, saying this is an event [the oil price fall]
> that actually does require us, justifies and requires us, *to seek* to
> depress our real exchange rate because we have to shift resources
> into the balance of payments from other sectors of the economy
> to substitute for the adverse movements in the terms of the
> trade in the oil sector. That was a judgement we would not have
> been able to attempt had we gone into the ERM.[6]

The Chancellor's actual actions as sterling fell during 1986 are simply impossible to reconcile with his later description of them. From February to September 1986 the Bank of England did not intervene to defend sterling, and Lawson cut interest rates in March, twice in April and in May. As sterling's decline accelerated during the second half of 1986, Lawson, on his own admission, made no attempt to convince Thatcher that an interest rate rise was necessary. Just as revealingly, he offers no explanation of why Thatcher's perennial dislike of interest rate increases should act as a 'limit on what [he] could do' in 1986 and not at other times when sterling was under pressure. Quite evidently, the Prime Minister and Chancellor allowed sterling to fall so as to boost the competitiveness of exports, and so stimulate a previously sluggish economy. As Keegan comments:

> The beauty of the 1986 devaluation from Lawson's point of view
> was that it was an essential prelude to the burst of growth in the
> real economy which led up to the 1987 general election, but
> there was no great political drama attached to it in the way that
> affects Labour governments on such occasions.[7]

With Lawson making a 1 per cent cut in the basic rate of income tax in the 1986 budget, his obvious and overriding aim that year was to push for growth. As reward for his efforts, the British economy grew faster than any other G7 economy during 1986, and unemployment finally began to fall in the second part of the year. But in using the oil price fall as a vehicle for growth, Lawson was pursuing a course very different from those of the ERM states whom he had been so keen to join just months previously. As Figure 3.2 shows, from 1985 to 1986 the effective exchange rate of all the ERM currencies rose, whilst that of sterling fell. Unsurprisingly, this meant that British inflation did not fall as fast as French, German or Italian, but British growth was over 1 per cent higher (see Figure 3.3).

Yet despite the discongruence between Lawson's economic policy course and what ERM membership would have required, during these months the Chancellor, in company with Geoffrey Howe, broke public

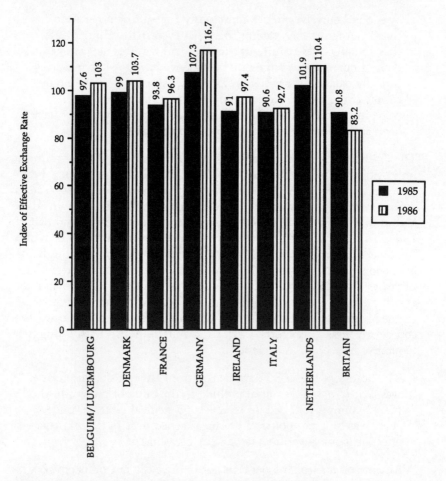

Figure 3.2: Comparative Effective Exchange Rates 1985-1986
(Source: Economic Outlook)

rank with Thatcher on the issue for the first time. On 16 April Lawson and Howe both made speeches advocating joining the ERM. Although Lawson claims that the timing of the speeches was coincidental, this rather defies belief. In his speech to the Lombard Association, Lawson noted that membership of a fixed exchange rate system was 'a pretty robust way' of managing monetary policy, and that the only way for Britain to benefit from such a discipline was inside the ERM. He then added that 'the government does not believe that the time is yet right for us to join.'[8]

For his part, Howe contended that Britain could not indefinitely postpone a decision on membership, and suggested that the final say should be left to the Treasury.[9] On 6 June Howe went further, and cast doubt on the validity of some of the reasons which had hitherto been

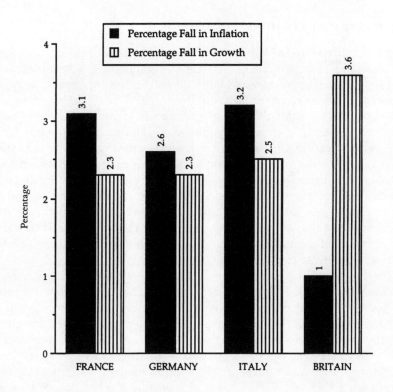

Figure 3.3: Comparative Falls in Inflation 1985-1986 and Growth 1986 (Source: Economic Outlook)

used to justify remaining outside the ERM such as sterling's petro-currency status:

> There are still some reasons which remain, and these perhaps are based as much on the habit of not belonging as anything else ... the position is not whether we are going to join. But that is an answer we cannot go on giving indefinitely.[10]

According to Lawson, these utterances did not result in any confrontation with Thatcher, because he, unlike Howe, foresaw that any further discussions would be futile.[11] But at least as plausible an explanation of Lawson's inaction is that he knew full well that the government was currently benefiting from a policy which was incompatible with entry to the ERM. The real significance of Lawson's and Howe's public words was that they demonstrated that the two of them would put membership back on the agenda if and when Lawson's decided he wanted to defend sterling again.

STILL 'NO': SEPTEMBER–DECEMBER 1986

The circumstances in which the ERM resurfaced as an issue between Lawson and Thatcher were not long in coming. During early September sterling started to fall towards DM3.00 for the first time ever. Judging that with the price of oil now stabilizing any further depreciation in sterling would translate into an increase in inflation, Thatcher and Lawson agreed to reverse policy. In effect, the devaluation policy was being sacrificed to the inflationary pressure growing elsewhere in the economy. Average earnings' growth had remained at 7.5 per cent since 1984, real disposable incomes rose by 4.2 per cent in 1986 and consumer demand was rising as a result of the cut in income tax and a credit boom was taking place induced by financial deregulation.[12] As September began, the Chancellor ordered the Bank of England to start to defend sterling, and on 3 September he made a record $4 billion FRN issue to boost the reserves.[13]

Notwithstanding the Bank of England's intervention, sterling continued to fall. On 23 September the currency came under intense pressure after the publication of a record monthly current account deficit of £886 million for August. But neither Lawson nor Thatcher wanted to raise interest rates before the Conservative Party conference, and instead turned to the Bundesbank for help. On 28 September Lawson and Leigh-Pemberton met with Stoltenberg and Pöhl during the annual IMF and World Bank meetings in Washington. Pöhl was initially reluctant to offer any assistance, but then agreed to consider a proposal from Lawson for a standby swap arrangement of the kind the Bundesbank had with the ERM states, and under which it effectively lent Deutschmarks for a specified time period. Furious at being kept waiting for an answer, Thatcher told Lawson that 'if the Germans would not play ball', she 'would pull the British Army out of the Rhine'.[14]

The next day Stoltenberg and Pöhl agreed to the swap deal, and that the Bundesbank would act as an agent of the British government in the foreign exchange markets. It was the first time since the days of Bretton Woods that the Bundesbank had undertaken such a commitment. Immediately it became apparent on 30 September that the Bundesbank was defending sterling, the currency stabilized, only to fall below DM2.90 within days. On 14 October, after the Conservative Party conference was over, Lawson raised interest rates to 11 per cent and re-coupled monetary policy to the exchange rate.

Once again Thatcher's and Lawson's apparent monetary and ex-change rate objectives were compatible with ERM membership. Indeed, even more than in 1985, membership offered clear monetary benefits. As Figure 3.4 indicates, after the interest rate hike in October, Britain, along with Spain as another non-member of ERM, continued to suffer from higher nominal interest rates than most of the ERM states. Britain was having to raise rates at a time when rates were falling elsewhere. In terms of real rates, Britain, unlike Spain, remained in an even poorer position with rates over 2 per cent higher than those in France, Germany, Holland and Italy. On long-term government bonds, Figure 3.5 shows that Britain and Spain both had substantially higher rates than the ERM states.

Financial commentators were very alert to the differential between British interest rates and those of the ERM states, and were quick to argue that the markets were demanding a British interest rate premium because of the lack of clarity in monetary policy. *The Economist*, for example, remonstrated thus:

> Higher than average interest rates means that Britain loses all the advantages that the anti-inflationary zeal of Mrs Thatcher and her ministers should have won for it. Just a few years ago, nobody would have believed that Italy with a budget deficit equal to 14 per cent of GDP, and a happy go-lucky record on inflation, would in 1986 be able to have lower interest rates in its long term government bonds than Thatcherite Britain. The moral is unmistakable: those countries with currencies inside the EMS gain twice over by having fairly steady exchange rates and also relatively low interest rates.[15]

Moreover, the interest rate premium was something of a gift for the opposition parties, and, unsurprisingly, they were now looking to make some political capital out of the issue. On 15 October David Owen, the leader of the SDP, called for swift ERM entry given sterling's depreciation.[16] On the same day the Shadow Chancellor, Roy Hattersley, announced that Labour would support entry to achieve greater exchange rate stability on certain conditions: a commitment to expansion and fuller employment inside the ERM; further convergence in the financial and economic approaches of member states; and increased mutual currency support and co-ordination of trade policies to protect countries which wished to expand.[17] Clearly achievement of such conditions would have transformed the ERM out of all recognition. But Labour's move was not without significance. Whatever the intellectual incoherence of Labour's position, it provided an additional means for rhetorically blaming the Conservatives for high and rising interest rates.

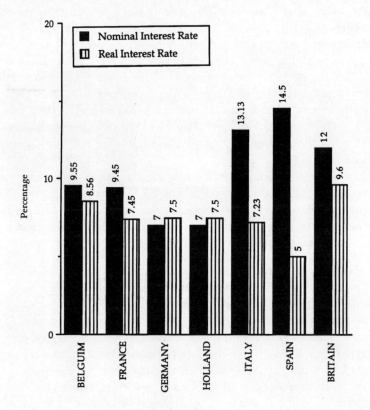

Figure 3.4: Comparative Nominal and Real Interest Rates October 1986
(Source: Economist Economic and Financial Indicators, October 25, 1986)

As a year previously, ERM membership offered Thatcher and Lawson lower interest rates for a given rate of inflation at a time when they were anxious to boost the economy. In October 1986 the Conservatives had only just caught up with Labour in the opinion polls, despite rising growth and falling unemployment.[18] After November 1985 devaluation had proved an alternative stimulus to the economy, but clearly this option no longer existed. Only ERM membership could provide lower interest rates to boost growth without an inflationary risk. However, probably for the first time, there was likely to have been a price in fiscal policy to ERM entry. In his 1986 autumn statement, Lawson announced a planned average increase in the volume of public expenditure of 1.75 per cent per year over the following four years, and promised further tax cuts. With the balance of payments moving into deficit because of rising imports, credit booming and wages rising, such fiscal

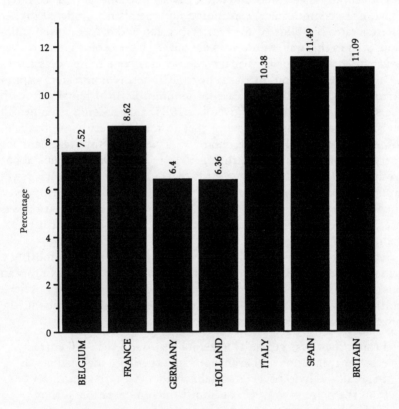

Figure 3.5: Comparative Long Term Government Bonds November 1986
(Source: Economist Economic and Financial Indicators, November 1, 1986)

expansion was likely to add fuel to an already smouldering inflationary fire. Given the commitment of the ERM states to counter-inflationary fiscal restraint, it is therefore difficult to see how sterling could have participated in the ERM without the policy being adjusted. As a result of sterling's depreciation during the year, membership would have imposed fewer costs in terms of competitiveness than was the case in 1985. Nevertheless, despite the effective devaluation, Britain's general manufacturing trade performance was continuing to deteriorate. If membership would no longer have been the obvious constraint on export-led growth that it would have been in 1985, it would have ruled out any further depreciation to deal with the large external deficit which was in prospect for the second half of 1987 and 1988.

Viewed as a whole, ministers now faced an apparent trade-off between short-term macro-economic objectives: ERM membership would mean lower interest rates, fiscal restraint and a counter-inflationary commitment, continuing non-membership offered higher interest rates but allowed for fiscal expansion and consequential inflation. Seen in this way, ministers were now facing a choice as to whether lower interest rates or further income tax cuts were more necessary to secure their re-election. At the same time, in terms of ministers' capital accumulation priorities, the case for joining the ERM remained much the same as it had been in November 1985. City opinion remained in favour of membership, believing that it would inject some financial discipline into the British economy, but were pressing less hard for entry than many in manufacturing industry who were anxious about sterling's volatility during the year.[19] Although there were clearly fewer costs for exporters in membership than there had hitherto been, given the increase in competitiveness from 1985, sterling's depreciation was not an added incentive for membership for the City or multinational companies operating in Britain.

The complexities of economic options apart, there was probably a stronger case for ERM entry in terms of the government's European policy agenda than had existed at any time since 1980. The official British view was that the ERM states were ambivalent about the prospect of sterling as a partner currency:

> I think there was generally a feeling that our recent and current economic, inflation and exchange rate experience meant that we were not likely to be a comfortable bedfellow in the ERM. So from the point of view of continued smooth operation of the ERM, they were not terribly anxious to welcome us in the near future. But there's always among the member states a feeling of common purpose and the need to develop that common purpose in an institutional way. And there was a feeling I think, even at

that time, that it was going to be difficult to move beyond the then present degree of integration to something at that time not specified without UK membership of ERM.[20]

Yet the evidence is that by this time the Commission and the other member states were more impatient on several grounds than ever before with British intransigence. Others were increasingly concluding that having sterling outside the ERM was problematic for their own monetary management. Throughout 1986 Pöhl vociferously insisted that there would be no Ecu-denominated accounts in Germany until Britain had joined the ERM.[21] For Ireland the problem was far more acute, since more than 30 per cent of its exports went to Britain. After Ireland was forced to devalue in August, the frustrated Irish Finance Minister, John Bruton, reflected that the Irish pound would continue to be vulnerable to devaluation when sterling was weak so long as the British currency was outside the ERM.[22] This growing tiredness with the British position in monetary circles was well summed up in the words of the President of the Dutch central bank, Wim Dulsenberg: 'My feeling is that the time is becoming riper every day.'[23]

Aside from monetary problems, sterling's position outside the ERM was now also an issue in the operation of the CAP and agricultural trade. France protested that as a result of sterling's depreciation against the ERM currencies in 1986, British lamb farmers were unfairly undercutting their French counterparts.[24] Meanwhile agricultural ministers had to sort out a messy dispute between Britain and Ireland over beef trade after the devaluation of the Irish green pound. In the eyes of the rest of the EC, these were examples of unnecessary problems which would not arise if Britain would only join the ERM.[25] Whilst the government could easily endure this kind of discontent, in October 1986 Britain was again holding the EC presidency. Wishing to speed up work on the Single Market, to liberalize transport and develop employment policy, Thatcher and her ministers were in practice making little headway. In this context, there might well have been a significant pay-off in finally deciding to place sterling inside the ERM.

Lawson Thwarted Again

Worried that sterling would remain unstable even after the interest rate rise, Lawson was anxious for Thatcher to reconsider her position on the issue.[26] Sceptical of his own ability to persuade Thatcher, Lawson turned to Pöhl, whom he knew Thatcher held in high regard.[27] With Pöhl due to come to London on 20 October, Lawson asked him to talk to Thatcher on the issue. Speculation in the media then mounted that ERM entry was now imminent.[28] But at their meeting Thatcher quickly told Pöhl that she would not discuss the issue. Immediately afterwards Bernard Ingham told the lobby that the government had no intention of entering the ERM before the next general election, and that in no way could sterling's current weakness be attributed to non-membership of the system.[29]

Thwarted again, Lawson tried another direct approach to Thatcher in their bilateral meeting on 21 October, but she bluntly instructed him that the issue was off the agenda until after the election.[30] Lawson contends that this left him with no option but to admit defeat: 'I was feeling increasingly frustrated. I was also becoming somewhat isolated, since my senior officials had come to the view that the Prime Minister had vetoed entry, and that was that—at least for the foreseeable future.'[31] But there were certainly potentially more effective allies than the Treasury whom Lawson simply renounced, namely Howe and other senior Cabinet Ministers, and he could have made further use of the heavy groundswell of opinion within the Conservative Party as a whole for ERM entry. Between September and December Lawson chaired the economic policy manifesto group. Of twelve members, all, save John Redwood, supported membership as a manifesto commitment, dividing only between those who favoured entry before and after the election.[32] Yet once more, Lawson was unwilling to forge an alliance with Howe to force a Cabinet meeting. At least one official close to both men, and a firm supporter of membership, was exasperated by their lack of action at this time:

> I tried to 'hot' Nigel Lawson and Geoffrey Howe up to demand a Cabinet session on the subject. Because I thought it would be very difficult for her to refuse a firm demand for a Cabinet discussion on the basis of a firm paper from the Chancellor and the Foreign Secretary. And that she would find herself with not too many supporters. I don't know why the hell they didn't do that. They never did.[33]

Indeed, despite their likely support for his position, Lawson evidently colluded with Thatcher in excluding other interested parties from the decision-making process. For example, Michael Jopling, the Agricultural Minister, and MAFF calculated that staying outside the ERM cost Britain 500 million Ecus a year in the CAP, and were hence strong supporters of membership. But they had no voice at all in the decision-making process. As one MAFF official reflected:

> When the British Minister of Agriculture wanted to have a bigger devaluation in order to get higher prices to UK farmers to compensate for UK inflation, the Commission would always propose a smaller devaluation. And Andriesson who was then the Commissioner for Agriculture would trot out the argument

that if Britain were in the ERM then it would be much easier. In that sense it made life harder for MAFF. But we wouldn't go back [to Number 10 or the Treasury]. It would not have carried any weight, since the Treasury did not want to give more money to farmers anyway.[34]

For the time being at least, it was if Lawson was more concerned that economic policy remain an exclusive domain of decision-making only for those directly and professionally concerned with it – whether at home or abroad – than he was for sterling to join the ERM.

Thatcher's veto of ERM membership in autumn 1986 now left a significant hole in monetary policy. For the Treasury, the problem was that Thatcher was rejecting one option without offering an alternative: 'She really, as far as I know, did not address the question of an alternative because the obvious alternative was a money supply target, but she knew we were in great difficulties with that. We were left in a kind of vacuum.'[35] Unsurprisingly, those close to Thatcher saw things differently, perceiving that any Prime Minister was too weak to run economic policy positively:

They [Prime Ministers] can give the Chancellor guidelines. But you've got open market operations, debt issues, I mean a whole host of issues which impinge on this, and the Prime Minister is just not set up to control what the Treasury is doing. The thing is that the way to control it is to fire the Chancellor.[36]

With no resolution to the problem in sight, the main protagonists took to a public war of words. On 12 November Leigh-Pemberton told a conference of Bundesbank officials and German business people that the reasons for Britain's non-membership of the ERM were 'entirely political'.[37] One week later the *Financial Times* published an interview with Thatcher in which she admitted that the issue would be reconsidered after the election, but gave full rein to her instinctive dislike of the system:

In an hour long interview . . . she said the economy was not 'quite strong enough yet' for EMS. 'We are getting stronger and one day we will go in.' She said repeatedly that entry would not be an easy or a soft option . . . Mrs Thatcher also argued that other EC countries should reconsider the rules, particularly the retention of exchange control in most cases. She also expressed concern about 'hitching our wagon to a Deutschmark standard and all the problems we used to have with devaluation if it comes.' She thought the pound would be tested and that would mean 'swinging up interest rates very sharply' since 'there is no way you can intervene to that great an extent'.[38]

As revealingly, she went on to take aim at the whole idea of assigning monetary policy to the exchange rate:

> Mrs Thatcher thought the pound had gone low enough against the Deutschmark. She underlined her dislike of increasing interest rates and market intervention. 'We may believe it [the pound] has gone enough but it is what the market believes and you know what the market is: 95 per cent of the movement is speculation and the other 5 per cent is trade.'[39]

Lawson responded the next day by telling the Treasury and Civil Service Select Committee that 'I think there is clearly a case for being part of an explicit regional fixed exchange rate system'.[40] On 26 November Howe reiterated his position to the CBI council:

> The phrase 'when the time is right' should be seen as a declaration of intent rather than the reverse . . . It is a legitimate expectation of the business community that politicians should try to increase domestic price stability. The EMS does represent a framework in which it would be possible to produce at least a measure of stability.[41]

Such public bickering was just what the Treasury was always desperate to avoid, especially as the war of words was starting to put pressure on sterling: 'It is absolutely essential that there should be agreement between the Prime Minister and the Chancellor on really important things. If and when they don't agree, you carry on until they do.'[42]

Although sterling strengthened in December, it was still unclear exactly what the rationale of monetary policy was now to be. According to Lawson, he believed that monetary conditions measured by M0 still warranted an increase in interest rates. On 10 December Lawson and Thatcher met to discuss his proposal for a 1 per cent rate rise. Lawson states that Thatcher was dismissive of the proposal and conceded only 'with the utmost reluctance' that interest rates could rise if there was 'a clear trigger'.[43] Presumably, a 'clear trigger' meant a further fall in sterling. So if Lawson's version of events is to be accepted, 1986 ended in deep contradiction: Lawson supported ERM membership, but otherwise wanted to assign monetary policy to a monetary aggregate; meanwhile, Thatcher rejected both ERM membership and assigning monetary policy to a monetary aggregate, leaving only an *ad hoc* option.

SHADOWING THE DEUTSCHMARK: JANUARY–JUNE 1987

If the problem at the end of 1986 was how to protect sterling from depreciation in this monetary vacuum, at the start of 1987 the opposite dilemma arose, as sterling started to strengthen in the wake of an improving short-term outlook for the economy. Thatcher and Lawson could now use monetary policy and intervention to place a cap on sterling, and pursue exchange rate stability outside the ERM; or they could allow sterling to appreciate, and wipe out the gain in competitiveness achieved in 1986. Precisely how they did choose to resolve this dilemma was to become a political dispute in itself.

What is indisputable is that at the G7 meeting of 21–22 February in Paris the British government signed the Louvre Accord on exchange rate management. This was an agreement to try to stabilize the dollar against the yen and the Deutschmark, and by implication against the ERM currencies. The G7 central banks were to take co-ordinated action if and when currencies diverged from the prevailing rates. More significantly, the states gave a commitment to increase fiscal policy co-ordination to try to combat the widening external imbalances between them. Germany and Japan agreed, nominally at least, to stimulate their economies, and the USA to a more restrictive policy. In terms of British policy, the Louvre Accord was ambiguous. Whilst the aim of Louvre was to stabilize the dollar–which included its rate against sterling–the means for achieving this goal was defined in terms of the Deutschmark to which sterling had no formal links.[44]

In practice, the outcome of Louvre was that the government used both monetary policy and reserve intervention to shadow the Deutschmark between a range of about DM2.90 to DM3.00. Between 22 February and the budget on 17 March sterling rose to over DM2.90. Lawson responded by cutting interest rates on 10 March to 10.5 per cent, whilst the Bank of England sold sterling and took massive sums into the foreign exchange reserves. As the upward pressure continued in the run-up to the general election, which the Conservatives looked certain to win, Lawson cut interest rates again to 10 per cent on 19 March, 9.5 per cent on 29 April and 9 per cent on 11 May.

But, despite the public nature of the Louvre commitment, the new exchange rate target went unannounced. Indeed the public presentation of monetary policy remained mired in contradiction. In his 1987 budget speech, Lawson declared that Money GDP was the operational guide to monetary policy. He set a target for M0 as a means to control Money GDP, whilst noting that other indicators would be monitored, of which the most important was the exchange rate.[45] He then told the Treasury Select Committee that keeping sterling in line with the Deutschmark was likely to be over the medium term 'a pretty good anti-inflation discipline'.[46] Meanwhile Thatcher told the *Financial Times* that 'there is no specific range–we are always free'.[47] In April, at the NEDC, Lawson said that sterling rates of about $1.60 and DM2.90 were 'about right', and that industry could base its plans on these rates. But the next day he felt compelled to tell a conference that these figures were in no way targets, and he had been simply stating the exchange rates prevailing at the time.[48]

For Thatcher and some of her acolytes this doublespeak was the result of Lawson's duplicity in deciding on the shadowing policy in the first place. They have alleged that Lawson usurped the economic policy decision-making process and had decided to shadow the Deutschmark without Thatcher's knowledge or consent. According to Thatcher:

> Extraordinarily enough, I only learned that Nigel had been shadowing the Deutschmark when I was interviewed by journalists from the *Financial Times* on Friday 20 November 1987. They asked me why we were shadowing the Deutschmark at 3 to the pound. I vigorously denied it. But there was no getting away from the fact that the chart they brought with them bore out what they said.[49]

Nicholas Ridley, in his memoirs, went further and claimed that Lawson, with the Bank of England as a keen accomplice, deceived Thatcher over the Louvre Accord itself.[50] In their books on Conservative economic policy, William Keegan and David Smith both wholeheartedly accept this version of events. Keegan contends that Lawson 'hoped to prove to Thatcher, with a dry run, that she need have no fears about sterling's chances of stability within the EMS'.[51] Meanwhile Smith suggests that Lawson could deceive Thatcher because she was reliant on Bernard Ingham for a summary of the day's press, and his 'blind spot' for economic and financial policy meant that her attention was never drawn to the speculation of the financial pages on the rationale of monetary policy.[52]

Lawson has always argued that Thatcher and he agreed a set of objectives for Louvre. After the summit, he and Thatcher concurred to roughly stabilizing sterling against the Deutschmark in line with the Accord, but without a specific target.[53] For Lawson this was an 'interim measure' which he hoped to replace with ERM membership after the election.[54] Before long, however, the markets began to assume that the policy was to defend a target of DM3.00. Then, in Lawson's words:

> At the markets meeting I held on 18 March ... I told the senior Treasury and Bank officials present that this market view was useful, and that we should validate it, by being ready to intervene as and when necessary ... Thus it was that the policy of shadowing the Deutschmark, as DM3 to the pound, was born.[55]

But, Lawson emphatically protests, the fact that the precise DM3.00 target was agreed on at a meeting at which Thatcher was not present did not mean that she was kept in the dark, and on 'a number of occasions' they discussed the policy openly.[56] Indeed, according to Lawson, Thatcher was positively enthusiastic about the policy in its initial stages because it added to the foreign exchange reserves. In a television interview, he recalled:

> Whenever she saw the Governor of the Bank of England she said 'Tell me, Mr Governor, how much have we taken in today?' That's to say taking in of the foreign exchange, the reserves. So she liked that policy.[57]

Lawson's account of the decision to shadow is far and away more plausible than those who have accused him of unilateralism. Certainly, it is true that the Prime Minister is not involved in the day-to-day operation of reserve intervention policy. The Bank of England possesses a general authority through the 1979 Banking Act, as it relates to the Exchange Equalization Account, to intervene in the foreign exchange markets on behalf of the government, and does not need approval for any specific intervention on any one day. However, the Prime Minister does not have to ask to see the reserve figures, and each night the Prime Minister's economic private secretary receives the Treasury's daily market report.[58] As one Treasury official remarked:

> Whether she would actually see them depends on the private secretary. But I am pretty sure that given the size of the movements that were in there, the private secretary would say, here you better have a look at this.[59]

Lawson's account of the relationship between the Louvre Accord and the DM3.00 target is additionally backed up by the evidence of Treasury officials. In a television interview, Geoffrey Littler, the then Second Permanent Secretary, defended the Chancellor:

> To the best of my recollection, we never thought of 3 Deutschmarks as being a ceiling until the combination of the market sensing that it might be, and the press of course choosing that as an obvious target with sex appeal in journalists' terms, more or less forced our hand. We found ourselves then in a band of sort of 2.80 or so up to 3 Deutschmarks willy-nilly. And if we'd failed to stay within that band, then the headline would have been, 'Policy Collapses.'[60]

Most crucially in Lawson's favour is the fact that Thatcher departed from her usual indictment of him in June 1991 when she admitted to *The Times* that she had known about shadowing, but said that allowing it was her 'great mistake.'[61]

It was not the Prime Minister but the Bank of England which was left out of the formulation and subsequent discussion of shadowing, despite its responsibility for implementing part of the policy. Whilst Lawson fails to discuss the issue, according to Bank officials, he would never even privately admit to them that the policy existed. Anthony Loehnis, a director of the Bank of England from 1981–89, recalled bitterly in a television interview:

> My recollection is that there was never any official admission of it [shadowing]. I mean clearly there was no public admission that that was what we were doing, but as I've already said, I don't think that there was any reference to it, you know in private between Bank and Treasury officials. You were just sort of intuitive that it was in terms of the responses that one got to tactical options that there might actually be.[62]

The Bank's own view was that shadowing was a 'total disaster'.[63] In the words of one former official:

> Shadowing was the worst of both worlds because the markets don't really believe it ... You have to defend the target without credibility. You have to put more effort into defending it because they [the markets] can't really believe you should be defending it.[64]

Although the Bank believed that Thatcher did reluctantly acquiesce to the decision, it laid the blame for not being consulted on Lawson's inability to positively convince Thatcher of the policy's merits:

> He [Lawson] could not give it the proper airing and debate in the decision-making process that should normally attend these things because he was actually wanting to do something which he knew his neighbour next door would not actually agree to ... It was a private-enterprise attempt to be a proxy member of the ERM.[65]

Seen in full perspective, shadowing was born out of the monetary vacuum produced by Thatcher's veto of ERM membership, and in itself created yet more internal divisions over exchange rate management. Thatcher, Lawson and the Treasury formulated a policy which they were not prepared to discuss with the Bank of England. Whilst the Governor and majority opinion in the Bank remained committed ERM supporters, they were now asked to implement a particular exchange rate policy which they found unpalatable both in origin and substance. Most crucially, Thatcher and Lawson clearly decided to shadow the Deutschmark for different reasons. Lawson wanted a stable exchange rate policy to prove that sterling was ready for ERM membership. Meanwhile Thatcher was prepared to accept the policy so long as it was not broadcast in public. Rather than being a prelude to membership, Thatcher evidently saw shadowing as an alternative to it – a means of accruing some of the benefits of exchange rate stability without conceding defeat to Lawson.

Yet whatever the macro-economic benefits which the two protagonists saw in the policy, it offered very little in other dimensions. Whilst industry welcomed the reduction in exchange rate volatility, the City's predilection for an explicit financial discipline remained as firm as ever.[66] Moreover, in terms of European policy, shadowing was at best redundant. Lawson and the Treasury did want to claim some kudos from the ERM states for stabilizing sterling against their currencies:

> The policy evolved from our concern that the exchange rate was falling too far and too fast in 1986, and this evolution ran through to the time when we locked into the Deutschmark. Once we had got to a situation where sterling was stable, we were concerned to demonstrate to the EC that, even if we were not in the ERM, at least give us credit for achieving stability outside the system.[67]

However, as the Foreign Office perceived, this was a rather forlorn hope; as one official commented, shadowing 'proved very unsatisfactory – it brought all the inconveniences of membership with none of the advantages'.[68] Indeed, shadowing did nothing to abate the pressure for ERM entry from elsewhere in the Community, especially from the Bundesbank. On 29 May 1987 Pöhl declared: 'Britain's membership would certainly give the EMS more weight and a new quality. We shall change the previous stance of rejection.'[69] At home and abroad the issue was not going to lie in rest for long, whatever the hopes that lay behind the shadowing experiment.

SHADOWING AND ERM MEMBERSHIP

If Lawson and the Treasury believed that shadowing was a 'dry run' for ERM membership, it is interesting to assess the relationship between the two options. Certainly, shadowing involved some practical and technical problems which could have been avoided inside the ERM. Shadowing did not give Britain access to the short-term borrowing facilities of the ERM, or guarantee European central bank intervention to support sterling. The essentially informal arrangement of co-ordinated intervention under Louvre was not the same as the obligatory support provided by the European system. At the same time shadowing created a different relationship between the speculators and sterling than with the ERM currencies. It is very likely that sterling would have come under far less upwards pressure inside the ERM than it did under shadowing. Without a formal cap on sterling's upper limit backed by collective intervention, speculators were given a likelier option on the upward movement of sterling from which they were looking to profit.[70]

In terms of monetary policy itself, shadowing was at best a quasi form of membership. It committed the government to exchange rate stability against the ERM anchor currency, and used both monetary policy and reserve intervention to achieve that end. However, this did not mean that the relationship between sterling and monetary policy worked as it would have done inside the ERM. If relatively high interest rates were the premium demanded in autumn 1986 for non-membership, shadowing did not abolish that premium. Although it provided an exchange rate target and an effective floor for sterling, this position was not explicitly communicated to the foreign exchange markets. The absence of a formal target, combined with the public divisions between Thatcher and Lawson, continued to cause uncertainty, and did not provide the security necessary to reduce interest rates. The rationale for the interest rate cuts in the first half of 1987 lay in the markets' new found faith in the strength of the British economy and the likelihood of the government's re-election, not in shadowing itself. In this respect, if and when sterling came under pressure again, shadowing could not reduce the interest rate premium over the ERM states necessary to defend the currency.[71]

Yet these inevitable differences apart, the shadowing experiment revealed a fundamental incongruity between how Lawson and the Treasury saw ERM membership and the reality of the system itself. What shadowing left unanswered was how Lawson, and the Treasury, believed that Britain could match the counter-inflationary performance of the ERM states in view of their attitude towards fiscal policy, credit controls and wage restraint. Shortly after shadowing began, Lawson used the 1987 budget to cut the basic rate of income tax to 27 per cent.[72] As Figure 3.6 indicates, in both 1986 and 1987 the British government gave a fiscal stimulus to the economy at a time when France, Germany and Italy were pursuing deflationary fiscal policies to control demand. Such fiscal expansion was all the more distinctive because it occurred at the same time as monetary policy was being loosened. Inside the ERM there would have been an obligation to tighten fiscal policy to offset the lower interest rates produced by sterling's appreciation. Rather than using monetary and fiscal policy in tandem as the ERM states did, shadowing was an exchange rate policy exclusively defined in monetary terms.

So if shadowing was a 'dry run' for ERM entry, how did Lawson believe he could reconcile his fiscal approach with the demands that participating in the system would have imposed. Certainly, there is no evidence that Lawson envisaged using fiscal policy differently once inside the ERM. Fiscal expansion, via income tax cuts, was not incidental to the 1987 budget, but central to the Conservatives' electoral strategy. Indicative of the political advantage that ministers believed they held over Labour on the issue were Lawson's words in a radio interview in January 1987: 'There is a fundamental difference of philosophy between the Labour Party and the Conservative Party. The Conservative government believes in bringing tax down and the Labour Party quite clearly believes in putting income tax up.'[73] The 1987 *Conservative Campaign Guide* raised the rhetorical stakes even higher:

There are compelling economic arguments for lower taxation.
But there are also fundamental considerations of political
principle. If the government does not trust a family to spend its
own money, what will it trust the family to do? It is no accident
that the Conservative Party, the only political party committed

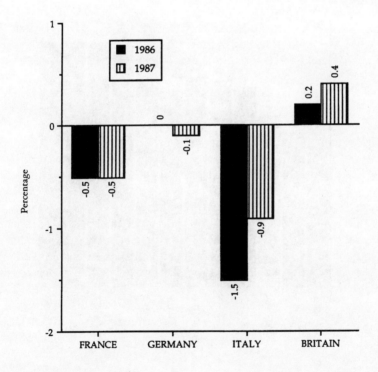

Figure 3.6: Comparative Fiscal Stimulus as a Percentage of GNP 1986-1987
(Source: Economic Outlook)

to the family and opposed to the encroachment of the state, is also the only political party committed to bringing taxes down.[74]

At the same time a low income tax regime was an important plank of ministers' efforts to make Britain the centre of inward investment in the EC. As Figure 3.7 shows, by June 1987 Britain possessed easily the lowest marginal tax rates on average wages among the richest EC states. In the whole Community only Greece and Portugal levied less marginal tax. Although ERM membership would not have categorically ruled out further income tax cuts, it would have placed taxation policy in the context of exchange rate management. Inside the ERM cuts would have to be related to the state of monetary policy, and, just as significantly, possible increases countenanced.

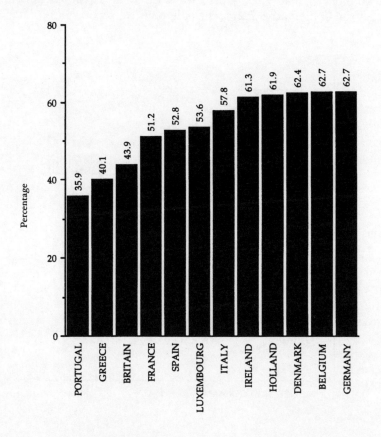

Figure 3.7: Comparative Marginal Tax Rates on Average Wages June 1987 (Source: Economic Outlook)

Neither can it be said that fiscal policy was decided by Thatcher at Lawson's expense. Lawson himself publicly rejected fiscal demand management in a speech in July 1988: 'Inflation is pre-eminently a monetary phenomenon. Interest rates are the essential instrument of monetary policy . . . The notion that fiscal policy should be used to fine-tune demand is to hark back to the failures of the 1960s and 1970s.'[75] Lawson similarly rejected the idea that changes in taxation levels could be part of a counter-inflationary fiscal policy, telling the Treasury Select Committee in 1988 that '[tax changes as part of fiscal policy] are extremely inflexible . . . very slow acting and the reversal of them is extremely complicated'.[76] Indeed, if Lawson is to be believed, he was the architect of the government's fiscal strategy not Thatcher. In October 1986 Thatcher was worried that fiscal policy was too lax in view of the size of the PSBR, but Lawson was unperturbed.[77] Whereas he planned the 1987 income tax cuts in this period, she was prepared to raise taxes.[78] Somewhat absurdly, it appears, Lawson supported ERM entry and a fiscal approach incompatible with it, whilst Thatcher rejected membership but accepted the main constraint it would have placed on economic management.

For its part, the Treasury was less enthusiastic about the 1987 cut in income tax, and initially argued for a cautious budget.[79] But there is no evidence in the comments of officials that this was because they conceived ERM membership in a more realistic way to Lawson. According to Lawson himself, the Treasury typically disapprove of tax cuts, judging that they are undeserved and will invariably be wasted by the public.[80]

The origins of this discrepancy in objectives can be traced back to the way in which the benefits of joining the ERM were conceived in 1985. As seen earlier, after the sterling crisis, for Lawson and his officials, membership represented an alternative counter-inflationary monetary means to achieve the ends of the MTFS. Retaining the assumption of the MTFS that inflation is essentially a monetary phenomenon, they did not believe, in contrast to the ERM states, that it was necessary to manage aggregate demand in order to control inflation. Indeed, Lawson did not even appear to believe that fiscal policy was expansive in 1986–87, and denied that increasing demand without a parallel increase in supply was inflationary. Rather, he measured the effect of fiscal policy by the size of the PSBR, which was in this case diminishing through privatization revenues.[81] In so doing, he clung to the vestiges of the proposition of the original MTFS that the impact of fiscal policy on inflation occurred through the relationship between the PSBR and £M3. Its proven intellectual dubiousness aside, such an attitude could hardly have made sterling a comfortable bedfellow with the ERM currencies.

Credit Controls

This divergence of fiscal approaches was compounded by Lawson's perspective on controlling credit. From 1985 to 1987 there was an inflationary explosion of credit in the British economy. In the early 1980s the Thatcher government had removed a variety of restrictions on lending, but, after a surge in 1981, sterling bank lending to the private sector remained relatively steady. Then between 1985 and 1986 bank lending doubled to reach a level about 25 per cent higher in real terms than the previous peak in 1972.[82] The expansion in credit during 1985–87 was further reflected in the growth of the broad monetary aggregate £M3, which includes sterling current accounts of the private sector with banks, deposit accounts and public sector accounts. As Figure 3.8 shows, the annual percentage increase in £M3 shot up from 9.5 per cent in 1983–84 to 18.7 per cent in 1986–87. With large mortgages easily available, rising house prices became a significant

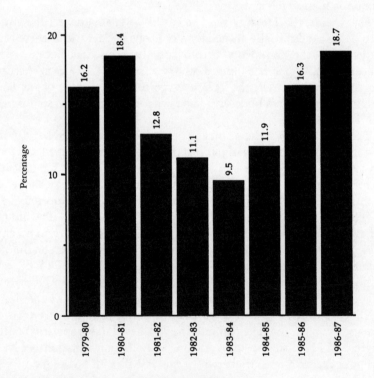

Figure 3.8: Sterling M3 Growth 1980-1987
(Source: C. Johnson, The Economy Under Mrs Thatcher, p. 274)

source of inflationary pressure. In the six quarters from January 1986 to June 1987 indexed house prices rose 34 percentage points compared to 17 in the previous eighteen months. But despite its inflationary consequences, Thatcher and Lawson made no effort to check the credit boom. Indeed, in the 1987 budget Lawson did not even set any kind of broad money target as a yardstick to measure credit expansion.[83] His view, shared by the Treasury, was that in a deregulated financial world it was impossible to directly manage credit without exchange controls.[84]

Privately, Lawson and others tended to the view that the credit expansion itself was not dangerous. Describing the prevailing attitude, one Treasury official remarked:

> You had gone in for deregulation. You had got a much more efficient financial system out of it. There was a stock adjustment going on while people adjusted their debt – asset ratios to the new deregulated environment. And as soon as that stock adjustment was over, everything would sort of come back and you'd be on a rather golden path with the stock of credit higher but the growth of credit from then on no higher. The problem was that we had absolutely no idea how long that stock adjustment was going to take.[85]

During the Conservatives' second term of office only a consumer credit tax briefly emerged as a possible method of control. Such a tax was first proposed by Lawson in 1985, but he dropped the idea after Thatcher refused to countenance applying it to mortgages.[86] In January 1987, in preparation for the budget, Lawson and the Treasury agreed to a 5 per cent tax on all consumer credit payments except mortgages. However, after the Bank told Lawson that a tax announced in March 1987 could not be introduced until July 1988, Lawson 'dropped the whole idea without even bothering to put it to Margaret'.[87]

By contrast, all the ERM states, to a lesser or greater extent, controlled credit, and did not incur the same kind of credit boom in this period. From 1985 to 1987 Britain had easily the highest broad money growth among the G7 European states, as Figure 3.9 indicates. Yet Lawson and the Treasury, or indeed the Bank of England, did not believe that there was any contradiction between their attitude towards credit expansion and their support for ERM membership. In their view, Germany did not use credit controls, and since Germany was the ERM benchmark, there was no need for Britain to control credit if it were to join:

> 'We didn't think that Germany practised credit controls. They had a different way of running their monetary system . . . They

ran a form of monetary base control. I don't think we regarded it as equivalent to control of credit.'[88]

Lawson was particularly dismissive of any suggestion that the Bundesbank operated effective monetary reserve requirements (a system in which banks are required to lodge a fixed percentage of their deposits as cash with the central bank):

> The only substantive difference between Britain and Germany was that in Germany there were mandatory, and much larger reserve requirements– . . . [This] merely encouraged the Frankfurt banks to escape the impost by channelling business through offshore centres.[89]

However, this position was based on two fallacies. First, whilst it is true that the Bundesbank ceased to attach much operational significance to its monetary reserve requirements in the 1980s, this did not

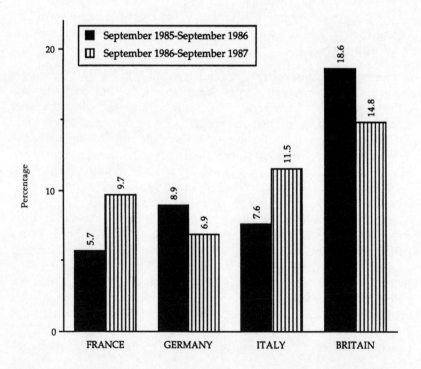

Figure 3.9: Comparative Broad Money Growth 1985-1987 (Measured by M3 except for Italy by M2)
(Source: Economic Outlook)

mean that Germany shared Lawson's and Thatcher's *laissez-faire* attitude towards credit. As the utility of its monetary reserve requirements declined, the Bundesbank turned to open-market policy instruments, using short-term purchases and sales of government bonds and other securities to regulate liquidity in the banking system.[90] At the same time Germany maintained a broad money target to measure credit after British ministers decided that such targets were not reliable.[91] When the outcome of German and British policy towards credit expansion is compared, it is very difficult to sustain Lawson's argument that the German system was little different than that which operated in Britain. As Figure 3.10 shows, whilst the German ratio of household debt to income remained relatively stable between 1983 and 1987, the British ratio increased dramatically.

Second, whatever Lawson's assessment of German credit policy, in terms of ERM membership it would have been more appropriate to use

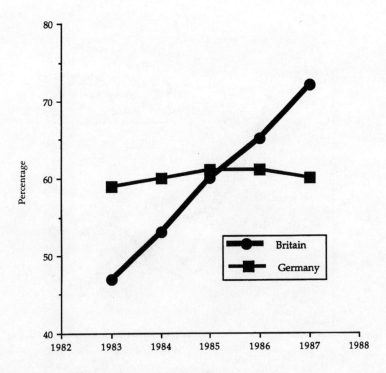

Figure 3.10: Household Debt to Disposable Income Ratio in Germany and Britain 1983-1987
(Source: The Guardian, October 9, 1992)

the other ERM states as his yardstick. To sustain their currencies these states needed to reduce inflation to as near German levels as possible by whatever means they could. Consequently, all the other ERM states did control credit, practising both monetary reserve requirements and continuing to set a broad money target throughout the decade.[92] Since credit expansion was an inflationary problem for Britain, it was rather irrelevant as to how low-inflation Germany did or did not control credit. Inside the ERM the onus would be to reduce inflation whatever its cause.

Wage Control

A similar story of misunderstanding and incongruity existed in relation to Lawson's attitude towards wage increases. Throughout 1986 and 1987 wage rises were a significant source of inflationary pressure in the British economy, which the Prime Minister and Chancellor did nothing to control. As Figure 3.11 shows, in these years the differential between

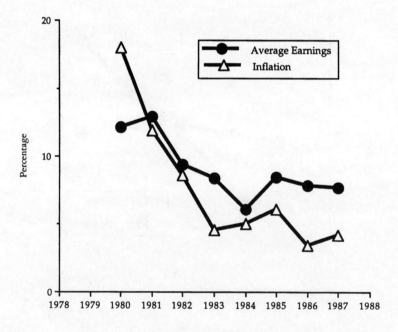

Figure 3.11: Increase in Average Earnings Compared to Inflation 1980-1987 (Source: Annual Abstract, Monthly Digest of Statistics)

increase in average earnings and inflation in Britain was significantly higher than between 1981 and 1984. More crucially, Britain achieved neither the steady low-level percentage increase in wage costs of Germany nor the reductions secured by other states, most notably France. Figure 3.12 demonstrates that while the annual increase in unit labour costs fell from 1985 to 1987 by 3.15 per cent in France and 5.05 per cent in Italy, they fell only 0.5 per cent in Britain.

Unlike the ERM states, the Thatcher government did not have a policy to control wage increases, having renounced any form of incomes policy on its entry into office in 1979. With the Heath government's statutory incomes policy blamed for its defeat in 1974, formal wage restraint was an unthinkable option for Thatcher and Lawson:

> Wage restraint was certainly not on the agenda ... The whole history of the 1970s led to the view that incomes policies had been singularly ineffective for two reasons. Firstly, they just led

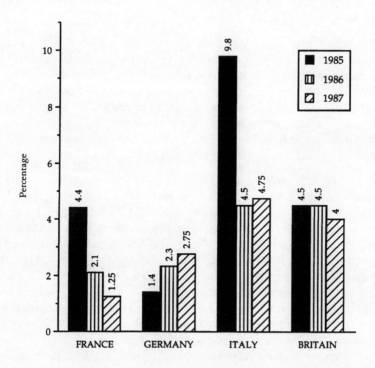

Figure 3.12: Comparative Percentage Annual Increase in Unit Labour Costs (Source: Economic Outlook)

to a wage explosion as soon as they ended. And secondly, that a wage policy would lead to inflexibilities in the economy ... The only time I ever heard incomes policy seriously mentioned was in the Cabinet in 1981.[93]

Meanwhile the Treasury was just as opposed to formal wage restraint as ministers. It too regarded the 1970s experience as an unmitigated failure.[94] Indicative of its attitude was the resigned defeatism of one Treasury official:

We tried it [an incomes policy] and it does not seem to have succeeded. If it works, you don't need it and if you need it, it doesn't work ... It is a tragedy of the British economy that it appears to require quite deep recession to check, even to 'check' (whatever that means) wage inflation.[95]

To the extent that Lawson and the Treasury did recognize that the level of wage increases in 1986 and 1987 would translate into inflation, they believed that the ERM itself would be the most effective policy instrument to combat the problem:

We seem to be stuck with earnings increase of 7 per cent plus ... It [the wage problem] led back to the need to have a more competitive labour market, and I think it led back to the ERM too. We were impressed by the wage experience of France and Germany, and we felt that membership of the ERM had had an impact on wage negotiations. In the sense that wage negotiations were helped when there was not a devaluation option to override an inflationary wage settlement.[96]

However, this attitude stood in contrast to the actual experience of France and Germany which had institutional structures designed to restrain wage increases independent of ERM membership. In effect, Germany practised, as Johnson describes, 'a covert form of voluntary incomes policy'.[97] The Bundesbank and the Council of Economic Experts (CEE) set implicit parameters for wage bargaining. The CEE was specifically charged with the means of maintaining price stability, and made wage restraint the central objective of its policy recommendations. Meanwhile, at the end of each year, the Bundesbank announced a rate at which the money supply would be allowed to expand over the subsequent twelve months, and specified what this entailed for wage settlements. Through a network of informal and collaborative business-labour forums, the exhortations of the CEE and the Bundesbank were generally accepted by wage bargainers on both sides.[98] Given the discrepancy between the German approach and the British attitude, one senior CBI official remarked:

I don't think they properly understood just what convergence involved. I think they thought that by being in it [ERM] that itself would impose the [wage] discipline. Because clearly if our costs went up quicker than the exchange rate in a fixed parity would allow us to go up, then those companies would lose their profitability, they would be in decline and jobs would be lost ... I think they were putting in the end result with the hope of controlling one of the inputs.[99]

Viewed together, fiscal policy, credit controls and wage restraint all raised fundamental questions about how Lawson and the Treasury believed they would be able to match the counter-inflationary perform-ance of the ERM states in the medium to long term, whilst renouncing the means those countries used to achieve it. Indeed, in the face of rising inflation the only option Thatcher and Lawson had left themselves was to allow sterling to appreciate to reduce import prices – which was the one counter-inflationary policy ruled out *per se* by ERM membership. Whilst revaluation remained possible within the ERM, it is difficult to see how a relatively inflationary currency would have come under enough appreciatory pressure to warrant an upwards realignment. The reality is that Lawson wanted to enter a counter-inflationary fixed exchange rate system with a bare counter-inflationary cupboard.

These discrepancies in Lawson's approach raise an interesting ques-tion as to the nature of Thatcher's opposition to ERM entry: was Thatcher aware of the counter-inflationary difficulties which would have arisen inside the ERM in 1986–87?; did such a judgement form any part of her opposition to ERM membership?; and did Thatcher's conception of sovereignty on ERM membership involve the wish to hold on to a peculiarly British approach towards inflation? Such an explanation of Thatcher's position would be dependent on her possess-ing a better understanding of the ERM's operation than Lawson, the Treasury or the Bank of England did. In the case of fiscal policy, this argument is hard to sustain, at least if Lawson is to be believed that Thatcher was less committed to fiscal expansion than himself. If Thatcher preferred a more restrained fiscal policy than Lawson, it can hardly stand as a reason for her rejecting Lawson's case to enter the ERM with its emphasis on fiscal restraint.

Only in the case of credit controls is there evidence that Thatcher saw a contradiction between ERM membership and her's and the Chan-cellor's approach. Asked about whether Thatcher was aware that ERM membership might be a backhand path to credit controls, a close adviser replied: 'Yes, very much so; nannying she called it. I don't think it was a major part of her objection to it. I think she took the view that if we went in we wouldn't have credit controls; they would have to change to our way.'[100] Alan Walters, in an article in the *Evening Standard* in April 1991, said that he had been expecting Lawson to raise credit controls ever since 1985–87, since all the other ERM states practised them.[101] Clearly, Thatcher's views on credit controls are not sufficient to explain her view of the ERM. However, it is perhaps not difficult to conceive that Thatcher's view on credit controls fitted into a general belief that there was 'our way' and a 'Continental way' of running the economy. In her *Financial Times* interview in November 1986, for example, she fumed about the exchange controls still practised by the ERM states.[102] Nor is it difficult to perceive how Thatcher could see electoral benefit in presenting the Conservative Party as preserving 'our way' of economic management against outside forces.

In many ways the development of events from the start of 1986 through the first half of 1987 were testament to Thatcher's veto of ERM entry in November 1985. There was a significant case to be made for joining the ERM, in terms of both the government's agenda within the EC and its desire to support the growth of the City, but there was no huge cost in staying out on either account. Moreover, in macro-economic terms, Thatcher and Lawson had reaped crucial rewards from sterling's independence from the system. Through 1986 and 1987 the two ministers presided over an economic boom and rising levels of prosperity, which would in all likelihood have been impossible without the stimulus provided first by the depreciation of sterling, and then income tax cuts and credit expansion. Lawson was to receive many accolades for winning the Conservatives the 1987 general election, but, ironically, if he had triumphed over Thatcher in November 1985 that election success might have been put in very serious jeopardy. Whether Lawson, or even Thatcher, understood it or not, in June 1987 they both owed much to the Prime Minister's obduracy 20 months previously.

Nonetheless, as she celebrated the election victory, in no way could Thatcher hope that the ERM issue had been banished. Just because Lawson would not accept what benefits had been gained from staying outside the ERM did not mean that he would not pressurize her to replace shadowing with membership now that the election was won. Moreover, so long as Thatcher accepted exchange rate stability as the rationale of monetary policy, Lawson would have monetary logic on his side for reasons which dated right back to the sterling crisis of 1985. What Thatcher could not know was that during her third term in office a new European dimension was going to add fuel to Lawson's fire, and ensure that her problems with errant ministers and the ERM were only just beginning.

NOTES

1 Non-attributable interview with Treasury official.
2 W. Keegan, (1989) *Mr Lawson's Gamble*, London: Hodder and Stoughton, pp. 182, 187.
3 N. Lawson, (1992) *The View from No. 11: Memoirs of a Tory Radical*, London: Bantam, pp. 650–51.
4 *Ibid.*, p. 651.
5 M. Thatcher, (1993) *The Downing Street Years*, London: Harper Collins, pp. 698–99.
6 Non-attributable interview with Bank of England official.
7 Keegan, *Lawson's Gamble*, p. 186.
8 *Financial Times*, 17 April 1986.
9 *Financial Times*, 27 April 1986.
10 *Financial Times*, 17 April 1986; 21 April 1986; 7 June 1986; *Times*, 7 June 1986.
11 Lawson, *Memoirs*, p. 653.
12 *Economic Outlook*, December 1986, p. 92; D. Smith, (1992) *From Boom to Bust: Trial and Error in British Economic Policy*, Harmondsworth: Penguin, pp. 78, 127.
13 Lawson, *Memoirs*, p. 654; Smith, *Boom to Bust*, pp. 72–73; *Times*, 4 September 1986.
14 Lawson, *Memoirs*, p. 656.
15 *Economist*, 18 October 1986, p. 15.
16 *Financial Times*, 16 October 1986.
17 *Ibid.*
18 D. McKie, (ed.) (1992) *The Election: A Voters' Guide*, London: Fourth Estate, p. 287.
19 *Financial Times*, 27 February 1986; *Times*, 8 March 1986; 14 April 1986.
20 Non-attributable interview with Bank of England official.
21 *Financial Times*, 18 April 1986; 21 October 1986; 13 November 1986; *Times*, 21 October 1986.
22 *Financial Times*, 5 August 1986.
23 *Ibid.*, 19 September 1986.
24 *Ibid.*, 19 November 1986.
25 *Ibid.*
26 Lawson, *Memoirs*, pp. 661–62.
27 *Ibid.*, p. 663.
28 *Times*, 20 October 1986.
29 Lawson, *Memoirs*, p. 663; *Financial Times*, 21 October 1986; *Times*, 21 October 1986.
30 Lawson, *Memoirs*, p. 663.
31 *Ibid.*, p. 663.
32 *Ibid.*, pp. 663–64.
33 Non-attributable interview.
34 Non-attributable interview with MAFF official.

35 Non-attributable interview with Treasury official.
36 Non-attributable interview.
37 *Financial Times*, 13 November, 1986.
38 *Ibid.*, 19 November, 1986.
39 *Ibid.*
40 Lawson, *Memoirs*, p. 665.
41 *Financial Times*, 27 November, 1986; *Times*, 27 November, 1986.
42 Non-attributable interview with Treasury official.
43 Lawson, *Memoirs*, p. 667.
44 For a discussion of the Louvre Accord, see Y. Funabashi, (1988) *Managing the Dollar: From the Plaza to the Louvre*, Washington: Institute for International Economics.
45 *Hansard*, 17 March, 1987, pp. 169–70; *Economic Outlook*, June 1987, p. 93.
46 C. Johnson, (1991) *The Economy Under Mrs Thatcher, 1979–1990*, Harmondsworth: Penguin, p. 59.
47 Keegan, *Lawson's Gamble*, p. 217.
48 *Ibid.*, p. 195.
49 Thatcher, *Downing Street Years*, p. 701.
50 N. Ridley, (1991) *My Style of Government: The Thatcher Years*, London: Hutchinson, pp. 201–02.
51 Keegan, *Lawson's Gamble*, pp. 193–95.
52 Smith, *Boom to Bust*, p. 104.
53 Lawson, *Memoirs*, pp. 682, 783.
54 *Ibid.*, p. 683.
55 *Ibid.*, p. 683.
56 *Ibid.*, p. 789.
57 Channel Four, (1993) *A Brief Economic History of Our Time*, 14 February
58 Lawson, *Memoirs*, pp. 39, 784; non-attributable interview with Treasury official.
59 Non-attributable interview with Treasury official.
60 *A Brief Economic History of Our Time.*
61 *Times*, 29 June, 1991.
62 *A Brief Economic History of Our Time.*
63 Non-attributable interview with Bank of England official.
64 Non-attributable interview with Bank of England official.
65 Non-attributable interview with Bank of England official.
66 Non-attributable interview with CBI official; *Times*, 13 March, 1987; 12, May 1987.
67 Smith, *Boom to Bust*, pp. 102–03.
68 Non-attributable interview with Foreign Office official.
69 *Financial Times*, 30 May, 1987.
70 W. Hutton, (1989) 'Put Simply, Money Matters', *New Statesman*, 23 June, p. 14.
71 Keegan, *Lawson's Gamble*, p. 198.
72 *Ibid.* p. 195.
73 Conservative Party, (1987) *The Conservative Campaign Guide 1987*, London: Conservative and Unionist Central Office, p. 46.
74 *Ibid.* p. 27.

75 *Financial Times*, 8 July, 1988.
76 Johnson, *Economy Under Thatcher*, p. 64.
77 Lawson, *Memoirs*, p. 661.
78 *Ibid.*, pp. 664, 667, 685.
79 Smith, *Boom to Bust*, pp. 80–81.
80 Lawson, *Memoirs*, p. 686.
81 *Ibid.*, p. 661.
82 T. Congdon, (1992) *Reflections on Monetarism: Britain's Vain Search for a Successful Economic Strategy*, Aldershot: Edward Elgar, p. 138.
83 Johnson, *Economy Under Thatcher*, Table 9.
84 Lawson, *Memoirs*, p. 853.
85 Non-attributable interview with Treasury official.
86 Lawson, *Memoirs*, p. 366.
87 *Ibid.*, p. 367.
88 Non-attributable interview with Treasury official.
89 Lawson, *Memoirs*, pp. 853–54.
90 D. Marsh, (1992) *The Bundesbank: The Bank that Rules Europe*, London: Mandarin, p. 62; Bundesbank, (1989) *The Deutsche Bundesbank: Its Monetary Policy Instruments and Functions*, Frankfurt: Bundesbank, p. 63.
91 *Guardian*, 9 October, 1992.
92 G. Holtham, and N. MacKinnon, (1990) *Controlling Inflation: Two Views*, London: Fabian Society, p. 34; *Guardian*, 11 November, 1991; 22 July, 1992.
93 Non-attributable interview with Treasury official.
94 Non-attributable interview with Treasury official.
95 Non-attributable interview with Treasury official.
96 Non-attributable interview with Treasury official.
97 Johnson, *Economy Under Thatcher*, p. 218.
98 C. Roberts, (1979) 'Economic Theory and Policy-Making in West Germany: The Role of the Council of Economic Experts', *Cambridge Journal of Economics*, 3, pp. 83–89.
99 Non-attributable interview with CBI official.
100 Non-attributable interview.
101 W. Ellis, (1991) *John Major*, London: MacDonald, p. 262.
102 *Financial Times*, 19 November, 1986.

4

Strife at Home and Abroad: 1987–1989

The choosing of ministers is a matter of no little importance for a prince; and their worth depends on the sagacity of the prince himself. The first opinion that is formed of a ruler's intelligence is based on the quality of the men he has around him. When they are competent and loyal he can always be considered wise, because he has been able to recognize their competence and to keep them loyal. But when they are otherwise, the prince is always open to adverse criticism; because his first mistake has been in the choice of his ministers.

Machiavelli, *The Prince*

The Corinthians to the Spartans, 432 BC
'It is also, perhaps, responsible for a kind of ignorance which you show when you are dealing with foreign affairs ... To our minds, you are quite unaware of this difference [between you and the Athenians]; you have never yet tried to imagine what sort of people these Athenians are against whom you will have to fight – how much, indeed how completely different from you. An Athenian is always an innovator, quick to form a resolution and quick at carrying it out. You, on the other hand, are good at keeping things as they are; you never originate an idea, and your action tends to stop short of its aim ... Think of this, too: while you are hanging back, they never hesitate; while you stay at home, they are always abroad; for they think that the farther they go the more they will get, while you think that any movement may endanger what you have already.' – *Thucydides*, 1: 68, 70

FROM ERM TO MONETARY UNION

Between June 1987 and June 1989 the ERM enjoyed a period of unprecedented stability and no adjustments were made to any of the system's parities. In circumstances which had previously produced realignments, the member states demonstrated a resolve to maintain the value of their currencies. During a bout of dollar weakness in October 1988, which boosted the Deutschmark, the franc fell to the bottom of its band. But the French government remained faithful to the *franc fort*, and raised interest rates even though French growth was already sluggish. With unit labour costs relative to Germany moving in

France's favour, the French government was simply not willing to forego the long-term credibility rewards it had built up in the foreign exchange markets by its commitment to competitive disinflation.

Nonetheless, even in the second half of 1987, most of the ERM states, and most significantly the French government, were keenly aware of the economic costs of their participation in the system. For those states with higher inflation than Germany, maintaining a roughly stable nominal exchange rate against the Deutschmark meant accepting an appreciation of their currency in real terms. Unsurprisingly, in the circumstances, the majority of ERM states were now confronting a deteriorating external account, and the German trade surplus with the rest of the EC increased from DM30 billion in 1986 to DM46 billion in 1988. Most significantly, the French manufacturing trade deficit with Germany increased by over one billion Deutschmarks from 1986 to 1987. Although the French external account had started deteriorating as early as 1985, the fall in the dollar from its mid-1980s peak now reduced the opportunity to balance the deficit with Germany with surpluses with the USA. At the same time as inflation converged among the ERM states towards German levels, unemployment continued to rise. Despite the monetary advantage that ERM membership yielded in the form of lower interest rates for a given rate of inflation and the stimulus this gave to the ERM economies, economic growth was not translating into rising levels of employment. As Figure 4.1 shows, unemployment in France and Italy had risen to the highest levels within the G6.

From June 1987 the French and Italian governments began to suggest that these costs were unnecessarily imposed by the nature of German hegemony inside the ERM. So long as the Bundesbank persisted in keeping Germany monetary policy relatively tight in the face of low inflation, there was no prospect of sufficient growth to reduce unemployment. Moreover, whilst German fiscal policy remained re-strictive, the other ERM states would risk a further deterioration in their current accounts if they were to unilaterally expand their econo-mies to try to reduce unemployment. Nor as the ERM was presently constructed, was there any provision for co-ordinated fiscal action to achieve successful collective expansion.

Increasingly frustrated, in the second half of 1987 the French government made a series of public calls for a new power-sharing arrangement within the ERM. These precipitated several rounds of high-levels negotiations to find a means to share the burden of inter-vention more equitably between different states, and so save the reserves of weak currency states. These negotiations culminated in the Basle-Nybourg reforms, which were finally agreed in September 1987, and licensed the financing of non-obligatory intra-marginal intervention through recourse to a Very Short-Term Financing Fund. The fund allowed weak currency states to borrow reserves from other member states, subject to certain conditions, including quantitative limits. In practice this created a presumption that the Bundesbank would lend Deutschmarks to weak currency states before their currencies reached their fluctuation margins rather than when they were breached, as had hitherto been case.[1]

Yet, even as the agreement was signed, the tensions between Germany and the weak currency states proved difficult to contain. De Larosière, head of the Bank of France, described the agreement as 'presumably automatic'; and, in a similar vein, the Belgian Finance Minister, Mark Eyskens, observed that creditor central banks would bear 'the burden of proof' should they at any time refuse the necessary

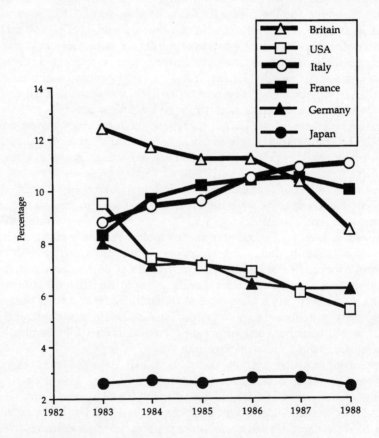

Figure 4.1: Comparative Annual Unemployment Rates 1983-1988 (Standardised OECD figures)
(Source: Economic Outlook)

credits.[2] Meanwhile Pöhl anxiously stressed the limits of the agreement by asserting the right of the creditor central bank to assess the prevailing monetary conditions, including its own domestic environment, before giving any funds.[3]

Unsurprisingly, therefore, although monetary co-operation did increase after Basle-Nybourg – unprecedentedly in November 1987 Germany and France jointly announced interest rate changes in opposite directions – French dissatisfaction remained unallayed. Concluding that growth would be restricted so long as the Bundesbank counterinflationary agenda dominated European monetary affairs, France now tried to divide the German government from its central bank. During November 1987 the French and German governments negotiated a draft treaty to create a Franco-German council, which would act as an economic policy co-ordinating mechanism between the two states. The council, which was expected to meet four times a year, placed both states' central banks on an equal footing and bound each to co-ordinated objectives to be determined by the council. Attaining such terms was a huge French victory because the council itself would be determining the yardstick for policy co-ordination, rather than simply accepting the primacy of the Bundesbank goal of price stability. In the event, though, French hopes of liberation from the German central bank were short-lived. When the Bundesbank discovered the terms of the treaty, the negotiation of which it had been excluded from, it pressurized the Kohl government into amending the treaty so as *to explicitly protect* its autonomy and commitment to maintain price stability. To all intents and purposes, the Franco-German council was redundant.[4]

Rebuffed in its bilateral efforts, the French government now looked for a new Community solution to its economic problems. For Mitterrand and his Prime Minister, Jacques Chirac, if there were no way either to ignore or change the behaviour of the Bundesbank within the ERM, the answer was to create a European central bank to manage a single Community currency, in which German monetary representatives occupied simply one more seat around a European table. By this means, France hoped, it would retain the counter-inflationary credibility of the *franc fort*, without its excessive monetary and fiscal costs in terms of growth. In this context starting in January 1988, French ministers made a series of calls for the Community to begin discussing the possibility of monetary union.[5] They were quickly supported by the Italian government, which was similarly frustrated by relatively low growth and rising unemployment. Of course, the German government, and the Bundesbank in particular, could be expected to have given the idea a cold reception since its whole *raison d'être* was to weaken their economic influence. Nevertheless, despite its disquiet, the Kohl government, which was holding the Community presidency, indicated its willingness to begin at least preliminary discussions on the subject for the Hanover summit in June 1988.[6]

France's aspirations for a monetary union did not represent an entirely new departure within the Community. The issue had first been discussed in the late 1960s as the foundations of Bretton Woods fractured. In 1970 the EC states agreed to the Werner plan to achieve monetary union by 1980. But the commitment quickly withered amidst the currency instability induced by the collapse of Bretton Woods, and was formally abandoned in 1974.[7] Three years later the Commission President, Roy Jenkins, tried to rekindle the idea, but his counsel for a common currency and a European central bank fell on deaf ears, serving only as presentational fodder for Schmidt's and Giscard's proposal to create the ERM. Yet the historical antecedent notwithstanding, the French initiative in 1988 on monetary union was always unlikely to prove just another false dawn in the Community's development; it was the response of a government which, through bitter experience, had become acutely aware of the costs of exchange rate management in the contemporary monetary environment, and saw a single currency as, perhaps, the last possible way out of the morass. Against the odds, France had avoided a premature German veto of the whole idea, and whilst the ERM may have been the source of French dissatisfaction, it also provided, for the first time, an institutional base on which a single currency could be created.

ECONOMIC AND EUROPEAN TROUBLES: JUNE 1987 – JUNE 1988

If in June 1987 the French government was starting to chafe at the costs of ERM membership, Nigel Lawson was hoping that the Conservatives' third general election victory would lead to Thatcher finally deciding to join the system, given the apparent success of shadowing the Deutschmark. Four days after the election Lawson told EC finance ministers that the debate within the government was more open, and that the reforms to the system that were being discussed could be conducive to Britain entering the ERM in the autumn.[8] But again Thatcher was to disappoint her Chancellor. At a bilateral meeting on 27 July she refused his request for new discussions on the issue, and insisted that the earliest the matter could be reconsidered was January 1988, and, then, there would be no repetition of the kind of meetings held in 1985.[9]

Confronted with another Thatcher veto, Lawson was again left looking for alternative ways to pursue exchange rate stability. First, and foremost, this meant continuing to shadow the Deutschmark. But Lawson now also endeavoured to strengthen the broad international structures of exchange rate management. Assisted by Terence Burns, the Treasury economic adviser, during the summer of 1987 Lawson drew up a proposal to institutionalize the Plaza and Louvre Accords into a permanent worldwide regime of 'managed floating'. He then presented the idea, to Thatcher's annoyance, to the annual IMF meeting in September 1987, where it received a less than enthusiastic reception.

However, this setback was marginal compared to the problems which were now to erupt between Thatcher and himself over shadowing. In July 1987, after the announcement of a significant current account deficit for May, the pre-election upward pressure on sterling abated. With inflation having risen slightly to 4.4 per cent in July, on 7 August Lawson took advantage of sterling's position to raise interest rates from 9 to 10 per cent. But the respite in the appreciatory pressure proved to be temporary, and over the next few months the Bank of England had to substantively intervene to stabilize sterling. By September Thatcher, having been counselled by Alan Walters, was becoming anxious about the level of intervention necessary to sustain shadowing, and told Lawson that she feared that the extra liquidity would lead to renewed inflation.[10] Yet it was also clear that intervention alone could not stem the tide into sterling, and after the stock market crash of 20 October Lawson cut interest rates on 26 October, 5 November and 4 December, leaving them at 8.5 per cent.

When the DM3.00 ceiling still appeared in danger, the final interest rate cut notwithstanding, Lawson sensed that it would be more effective for the Bank to intervene in Deutschmarks than dollars as it had hitherto. But, after the Bundesbank reacted angrily to the suggestion – since it contravened the EMS agreement on purchases of other member states currencies – Leigh-Pemberton refused Lawson's request.[11] On 8 December Thatcher again made clear to Lawson her apprehension about the whole intervention issue, but agreed that he should order the Bank to intervene in Deutschmarks irrespective of the EMS agreement.[12] Three days later the Banks' efforts seemed in vain with sterling trading at DM2.997. Yet just as it seemed to Lawson that the DM3.00 ceiling would have to be abandoned, the end to which Thatcher's feelings were increasingly pointing, sterling started to fall.[13] Indeed by February Lawson felt sterling safe enough to raise interest rates to 9 per cent.

But the interest rate rise proved merely to be the lull before the full storm, and at the start of March sterling came under renewed upward pressure, hovering just slightly below DM3.00, despite massive intervention. The foreign exchange markets, convinced of the DM3.00 ceiling, now believed that they possessed a one-way bet on its appreciation. Lawson was forced to reduce his horizons, hoping that the ceiling could survive until the budget on 15 March.[14] But on Friday 4 March Thatcher demanded that he abandon the sterling target and end intervention when the markets reopened the following Monday. Whilst

Lawson accepted Thatcher's principal demand, she conceded that some limited intervention to smooth the markets could continue on the condition that she was given half-hourly reports on developments.[15] On Monday 7 March sterling surged, and within days stood at DM3.10.

If shadowing had begun as a messy compromise between a Prime Minister and Chancellor who could not agree on the ERM issue, then it ended in the same kind of muddle. Whilst Lawson, as he knew, could not resign in view of the impending budget, Thatcher feared sacking him because of his popularity among Conservative MPs.[16] In policy terms, Lawson hoped that sterling could be restabilized at around DM3.08 with further intervention and interest rate cuts if necessary; meanwhile Thatcher, although unrelenting on the former, was prepared to accept the latter to limit the currency's appreciation.[17] On 17 March Lawson did indeed cut interest rates from 9 to 8.5 per cent, leaving the government with half an exchange rate policy. But any harmony of words was far harder to achieve, particularly since Lawson's commitment to the DM3.00 target was widely reported in the media. On 8 March Thatcher told the House of Commons that 'there is no way in which one can buck the market', and so hammered home a very public wedge between herself and her Chancellor.[18] Two days later, with sterling at DM3.06, Lawson warned against any further rise.[19] He then told the Treasury Select Committee: 'Any further significant rise in the exchange rate, certainly against the Deutschmark would, in my opinion, be unlikely to be sustainable.'[20] As Smith comments: 'The markets were therefore faced with the bizarre situation of a Chancellor trying to talk the currency down, while the Prime Minister appeared to be relishing its rise.'[21] The public war of words only intensified on 24 March, when Howe firmly backed Lawson's case for exchange rate stability, and praised 'the increasingly valuable experience of stability in the ERM'.[22]

Yet if the internal clashes of March 1988 are analysed in terms of the ERM question, the fact remains that, as in the latter years of the Conservatives' second term of office, there was a serious contradiction between Lawson's support for membership and his general approach to economic management. Once more Lawson could certainly have pursued his monetary aims more successfully inside the ERM, since the existing ambivalence in policy only made stabilizing sterling more difficult. But, with sterling strong and nominal and real interest rates low in comparison to previous years, membership no longer offered the clear monetary benefits that it had in November 1985 or autumn 1986. As Figure 4.2 shows, British nominal rates were now lower than those in Italy, and real rates were lower than those in Belgium, France and Holland as well. Only on long-term government bonds was Britain in a relatively poor position.

More crucially, Lawson's fiscal policy was now more incompatible with ERM entry than ever before. Although the 1987 autumn statement had planned for a fall in public expenditure, fiscal policy in 1987–88 continued to be expansive. Lawson's budget in 1988 provided a big boost to demand, introducing income tax cuts totalling £6 billion per annum, by reducing the basic rate from 27 to 25 per cent and the top rate from 60 to 40 per cent. At the same time, by limiting mortgage tax relief to one allowance per household from August 1988, the budget inadvertently gave a further huge stimulus to the housing market, as people rushed to take advantage of the old regulations. Such expansion was possible because revenue was flooding into the Treasury through increased tax payments, a reduced social security budget and, most significantly, privatization. This meant that there was a budget surplus of £3.2 billion for 1987–88, and a projected surplus of £14.4 billion for 1988–89. Lawson used what he dubbed the Public Sector Debt Repayment to deny that the budget was fiscally expansive, but he was in

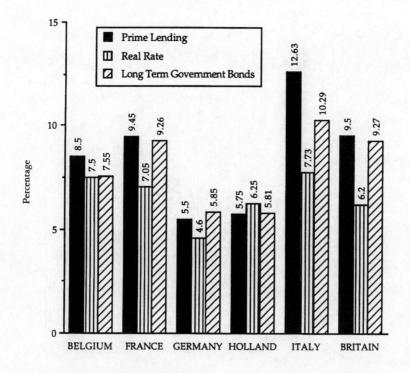

Figure 4.2: Comparative Interest Rates March 1988
(Source: Economist Economic and Financial Indicators, March 26, 1988)

reality denying the most elementary relationship between taxation and demand.[23] Indeed, the net effect of an expansive fiscal and monetary policy was that Britain was taking significant inflationary risks in comparison with the ERM states whom Lawson was so anxious to join.

At the same time, by March 1988, it was clear that it would now be much harder than in earlier years to sustain sterling at a fixed rate in the medium term since a large balance of payments deficit was looming. In July 1987 the Treasury had announced a £500 million deficit for May, and by the end of 1987 the deficit stood at £4.182 billion. With the economy growing as it was, the imbalance in the external account could only widen, particularly since imports were now increasing at twice the rate of exports, and Britain's manufacturing base was nowhere near strong enough to provide for rising domestic demand. As Figure 4.3 shows, the manufacturing trade deficit expanded from £3 345 million in 1985 to £11 223 million in 1987 and £20 808 million in 1988. In these circumstances, it could only be expected that if sterling were

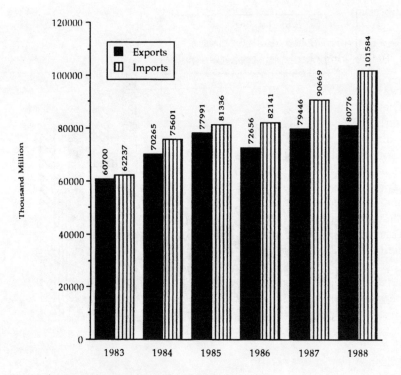

Figure 4.3: Exports and Imports 1983-1988
(Source: Economic Outlook)

indeed to join the ERM, before too long any parity would come under sustained downward pressure, as the foreign exchange markets assessed the risk of a future devaluation.

After Thatcher called a meeting with Lawson and Leigh-Pemberton for 25 March to try to restore order within the government, Lawson and the Treasury produced a paper laying out options for the future conduct of policy. Three options were presented: first, that sterling be a factor among others in monetary policy; second, to announce an explicit commitment to exchange rate stability but within an unpublished band; and, third, to enter the ERM. Although Lawson, despite the prevailing economic conditions, still saw ERM membership as the best alternative, he saw the value of restating it as an option at this time purely in terms of persuading Thatcher to accept the second possibility.[24] However, the compromise which was finally reached on the 25 March between Thatcher and Lawson was considerably less than the Chancellor's objectives. The two ministers agreed only that exchange rate stability was desirable, and that intervention had a role to play in achieving this, but there would be no exchange rate target of any kind as the objective of policy. The net result was a cap on sterling's appreciation with future interest rates cuts if necessary, much to the consternation of Leigh-Pemberton who was firmly against any further loosening of monetary policy, whatever sterling's position.[25]

Before long, however, even this compromise was supplanted, and Lawson's, let alone Thatcher's economic objectives, moved even further away from what ERM membership would have demanded. On 11 April Thatcher and Lawson agreed to cut interest rates to 8.5 per cent, after sterling rose above DM3.12.[26] But a month later the war of words began again when, on 12 May, Thatcher, responding to a question from Neil Kinnock, pointedly failed to back Lawson's view that any further appreciation in sterling would damage industry.[27] The next day Howe departed from his press-released text to say that the government could not 'go on for ever' discussing ERM, adding the qualification of 'when the time is right' to the underlying commitment to join.[28] Once more Thatcher and Lawson met to discuss their differences, with Thatcher deliberately excluding Howe from the exchange.[29]

What transpired at their meeting is a matter of fierce dispute between the two protagonists. According to Lawson, they agreed an answer for her to give at Prime Minister's question time if pressed again on sterling. Then, he relates, Thatcher suggested a half per cent interest rate cut to strengthen the appearance that they were both committed to an exchange rate policy and 'to my eternal regret, I accepted this poisoned chalice.'[30]

By contrast, Thatcher claims that the interest rate cut was Lawson's initiative:

I had been told by the Treasury in advance of the meeting that Nigel wanted a further interest rate cut ... I had got part of what I wanted ... in that sterling had been allowed to rise to DM3.18. So I was not unhappy to have the suggested interest rate cut I knew he wanted ... Above all, however, this reduction of the interest rate on Tuesday 17 May by half a point to 7.5 per cent was the price of tolerable relations with my Chancellor, who believed that his whole standing was at stake if the pound appreciated outside any 'band' to which he might have semi-publicly consigned it.[31]

In her next appearance in the House of Commons, Thatcher agreed that there was 'utter unanimity' between herself and Lawson over economic policy.[32] Unsurprisingly, though, within Downing Street the battle lines were intensifying, particularly when Thatcher's former economic adviser, Alan Walters, began to give interviews criticizing Lawson's monetary management, and arguing for an increase in interest rates. Somewhat characteristically, as events were now developing, Thatcher responded to this criticism of her Chancellor by asking Walters to return to his old job from May 1989 in a part-time capacity.

Nevertheless, June saw the start of a temporary respite to the feuding, when Thatcher and Lawson were finally forced to confront the inflationary nemesis for the mix of policies they had been pursuing since 1986. Having stood at 3.3 per cent in January 1988, inflation had risen to 4.6 per cent in June. Meanwhile house price inflation was running at 30 per cent, and the growth of narrow and broad money was accelerating. Demand was growing much faster than domestic supply, and wages were rising far above prices. Unsurprisingly, given this activity, the balance of payments was plunging further into deficit, registering £12 billion for the first half of the year. In this context, in the space of a few days at the end of May and the beginning of June, sterling fell from DM3.19 to DM3.09. Thatcher and Lawson united again to raise interest rates to 8 per cent on 3 June, 8.5 per cent on 6 June, 9 per cent on 22 June, and 9.5 per cent on 29 June.

Their apparent aim was not simply to stabilize sterling but to encourage its appreciation as a counter-inflationary weapon. Significantly, in so doing they rejected the alternatives of curbing the housing market, controlling credit, encouraging wage restraint or increasing taxes – all of which would have directly addressed the sources of inflation. Moreover, by choosing a tight monetary policy and an appreciating exchange rate as their sole counter-inflationary tool, Lawson and Thatcher were rejecting the whole approach of the ERM states to economic management, and leaving their monetary as well as fiscal policy incompatible with ERM membership. Indicatively, a year earlier

Italy had faced a similar problem of rising demand, a deteriorating current account and pressure on the lira. After raising interest rates, the Italian government had introduced a package of tax measures, which included a rise in VAT, and then imposed additional qualitative controls on bank lending.[33]

Such further divergence in policy from the ERM states raised not only the old question of how if Britain were to enter the ERM, as Lawson wished, inflation would be controlled but how a parity could be sustained in the face of such a large deficit in the external account. But Lawson, and the Treasury, were now as prepared to ignore the threat to successful ERM membership posed by the balance of payments deficit as the incompatibility of their counter-inflationary framework. In a speech to the IMF in 1988, Lawson pronounced that the balance of payments was no longer an important economic indicator, and that it was not necessary for it to be in equilibrium for policy to be successful, since any deficit could be financed by importing capital from overseas. Only if a balance of payments deficit reflected excessive government borrowing and spending, Lawson asserted, was corrective action necessary.[34] But what Lawson's doctrine ignored was how Britain could maintain a reasonable degree of confidence in sterling given the size of the deficit. Since international investors were being asked to use their savings to finance domestic consumption as much as investment, beyond the short-term lure of high interest rates, there was little incentive to export capital to Britain. At the same time investors could only believe that the British government would not allow sterling to depreciate to the extent to which they could also believe that the government would accept the consequent costs in interest rates, lost output and employment. Without that market confidence, any government would ultimately find it difficult to pursue exchange rate stability.

Hanover

Yet if Thatcher and Lawson were taking British economic policy off in an increasingly divergent direction to the ERM states, the onset of discussions about the possibility of monetary union in the EC was ultimately going to create a new incentive for ERM entry. After the success of the Single European Act, Britain's relations with its EC partners had deteriorated again in June 1987 when, at the European Council in Belgium, Thatcher alone had opposed the Delors plan for the reform of the budgetary process, CAP and regional and social policy. For the remainder of 1987 the Thatcher government refused to reach any deal on these issues other than on its own conditions, despite a general belief that the proposals accommodated more of Britain's demands than those of any other member state. Only in February 1988, and lacking allies, did Thatcher and Howe effectively concede defeat and agree to a budgetary reform plan, which included increasing regional and social expenditure.

During this protracted dispute monetary and financial affairs had moved to the forefront of the EC's agenda, first with the reform of the ERM, and then in regard to capital liberalization and monetary union. Once this occurred, it was never going to be long before Britain's non-membership of the ERM would resurface as a concern for the other EC states. As the final Basle-Nybourg agreements were drawn up in September 1987, EC finance ministers pressed Lawson on the issue, arguing that Britain was free-riding on the benefits of the ERM system without accepting the cost of membership.[35] Whilst on this occasion the Irish government alone publicly criticized Britain, the onset of the monetary union debate from January 1988, and the impending Hanover summit, ensured a new round of open attack on the British position.[36]

When the French Prime Minister, Jacques Chirac, first proposed a European central bank, he urged British entry to the ERM so that the Community could move forward monetarily.[37] In the following weeks, the Italian and German governments, the Dutch and German central banks and the Commission all expressed similar sentiments.[38] Indeed Italy went so far as to say that it would give up its unique wide 6 per cent ERM bands, if Britain were to join the system.[39] During March Stoltenberg made two unusually strong calls for Britain to reverse policy, arguing that its intransigence was delaying the general process of integration and the development of pooled reserves within the EMS in particular.[40]

By mid-1988 the pressure to enter the ERM had mounted further. In May Lord Cockfield, the senior British Commissioner, intervened in the matter, asserting that sterling's participation in the system was a necessary part of the Single Market and capital liberalization.[41] On 10 June Mitterrand vainly pressurized Thatcher in bilateral talks.[42] Two days later France and Germany issued a joint threat to block the capital liberalization directive, to which Britain was deeply committed, unless Britain reversed its position.[43] It was the first time that other EC states had sought to impose a direct cost on Britain for staying outside the ERM. But, with France already starting to remove some of its exchange controls, the threat lacked potency, and on 24 June the EC finance ministers reached a final agreement on the directive, with Lawson successfully striking down a draft declaration calling for 'equal participation by 1992 of all countries in the EMS'.[44]

Yet whatever the new salience of the issue in European terms, there appears to have been scant discussion about ERM membership in the run-up to the Hanover summit. Lawson claims that little debate took place, because Thatcher refused to consult him prior to Hanover due to their conflict over economic policy. Instead, she relied for advice almost entirely on Charles Powell, her Private Secretary on Foreign Affairs.[45] In this manner, Thatcher decided that Britain could not oppose the establishment of a committee on monetary union, as other states wished, even though no minister supported the idea of a single currency. In the perception of one Thatcher confidant:

> There was no option. The trouble was always with these things
> in the Community, you get carried along step by step. At each
> stage you try to minimize it, but there was always enough there
> to get to the next stage.[46]

Irritated by her lack of room for manoeuvre, Thatcher aimed to expunge any mention of a European central bank from the terms of reference, and ensure that the committee was comprised of central bank governors rather than economic experts.[47] The latter provision was allegedly based on an assurance from Chancellor Kohl that any group of central bankers would oppose monetary union: 'We were told – "Push these guys in there. They'll all hate it. They'll kill it stone dead." '[48]

At the Hanover summit on 27–28 June the EC states unanimously agreed to the objective of the 'progressive realization of monetary union', as set out in the SEA, and to establish the Delors committee – to be composed of EC central bank governors and co-opted experts and chaired by Delors – to outline 'concrete steps towards this union'.[49] On her return from Hanover Thatcher presented the omission of any explicit mention of a European central bank from the committee's terms of reference as a victory for Britain, telling the House of Commons:

> With regard to the European central bank, we have taken part
> in the SEA which went through the House and which said that
> we would make progressive steps to the realization of monetary
> union, and we have set up a group to consider that. Monetary
> union would be the first step, but progress towards it would not
> necessarily involve a single currency or a European central
> bank.[50]

For Lawson, it was 'extraordinary' that Thatcher had deceived herself that monetary union could be possible without a European central bank;[51] her naivety had precipitated a disastrous outcome at Hanover for which she alone bore responsibility because 'she simply failed to understand what she was about.[52]'

Certainly, Thatcher's post-summit statement starkly contrasted with Mitterrand's assertion that a European central bank followed from monetary union.[53] Evidently, Thatcher was confident she had agreed to something less for the Delors committee than the ERM states envisaged. As one former Foreign Office official remarked: 'I am completely amazed that Thatcher agreed to the terms of reference of the Delors committee.'[54] Similarly, a Commission official concluded that 'Thatcher did not realize what she signed up for at Hanover.'[55]

Nevertheless, some of Lawson's scorn towards Thatcher warrants serious scepticism. In 1989 Thatcher told one minister that the only reason that she agreed to a committee on monetary union was because the Foreign Office assured her that its conclusion would be of little consequence.[56] Moreover, a senior Treasury official, asked about Lawson's claim that he was ostracized on the issue, responded that Thatcher did take Treasury advice in the run-up to Hanover.[57] Indeed, the underlying cause of the British problem on the issue was that no one in the government, including Lawson and the Treasury, grasped that the other member states were actually serious about monetary union. One Treasury civil servant admitted: 'I don't think in mid-1988, we [the Treasury] were taking it [monetary union] very seriously. I don't think we began to take it very seriously until we actually got to the Delors Report.'[58] Another official defended the Treasury's tardiness by arguing that it was in a structurally weak position to assess the monetary union debate:

> One of the problems in the early stages was following
> discussions. Jacques Delors worked extremely hard to keep it
> out of financial circles. He did his utmost to mobilize the
> Foreign Affairs Council, so that we in the Treasury were actually
> finding it quite difficult to discern what was going on.[59]

Be that as it may, the Treasury apparently concluded that other finance ministries were no more interested in monetary union than themselves: '[Delors] knew that the monetary committee would not be enthusiastic.'[60] Seeing Britain at the heart of monetary affairs in the Community — because their technical expertize made them part of an inner sanctum on the monetary committee — Treasury officials considered neither that they saw monetary matters in any different respect to their counterparts nor that Britain's monetary influence was weakened by sterling's position outside the ERM:[61]

> We negotiated all the financial side of the directives leading up
> to 1993, and I always reckoned we got much more than our fair
> say. It isn't true that people said, 'you're not in ERM so we're
> not going to listen to you.'[62]

Yet the claims of Treasury officials apart, the reality was that the British government had simply misunderstood the origins of the Hanover agreement. Whilst, as seen earlier, the interest in monetary union was born out of the harsh economic experience of some Community states, British ministers and officials tended to believe that Delors and his Commission colleagues were forcing the debate as part of their own supposed compulsion for political integration. One Treasury official described monetary union as 'a Commission dream', and recounted that he could not recall any interest among the Community member states until April 1989.[63] Another senior official alleged that the initial push for monetary union came from Delors putting political pressure on Mitterrand as the 'big statesmanlike thing to do; I'm sure Delors put it to him on that basis'.[64] Rather than perceiving that there was any economic rationale to the French position in 1988, the Treasury saw only political motives: 'the French motive was basically to tie Germany into the EC; they detected that it might just move off to the East'.[65] Indeed, one official charged, France did not become dissatisfied with the ERM until 1990.[66] Significantly, this interpretation of events was shared by those who directly advised Thatcher:

> I think that Delors concluded that after the Single Market, this would be the next big step, not principally for economic but for political reasons. He saw this as the key to political union and a federal Europe. That's why he pursued it so vigorously ...
> Delors was absolutely central to the pressure for economic and monetary union. Now, we all know that the French developed their own reasons for favouring it, principally because they got fed up being dependent on the Deutschmark and the Bundesbank determining their economic policy, and wanted to grab a share of that themselves through Europe. But that I think was a rationalization, quite frankly – an exploitation of a policy stance that Delors originally took.[67]

It is difficult not to conclude that if the decision made at Hanover to establish the Delors committee turned into a disaster for the Conservative government, responsibility lay not just with the Prime Minister but went right through the government. Isolated outside the ERM, British policy-makers simply failed to grasp how the other Community states understood and conceptualized the problems of monetary management.[68]

At the same time the establishment of the Delors committee in June 1988 quickly added yet another dimension to the dilemmas which already confronted Thatcher and Lawson over ERM membership. One week after the Hanover summit, the Chairman of the Stock Exchange, Nicholas Goodison, told a group of MPs that outside the ERM Britain's interests in the monetary union debate would be ignored. As a result, he argued, London's position as the leading financial centre in Europe could be threatened.[69] Similarly, the *International Financial Outlook* of

Lloyds Bank warned that continuing to stay outside the ERM would run the risk of isolating the City. In such circumstances, Lloyds argued, Frankfurt would be the likely host of any European central bank, and so displace London as the operational centre of exchange and money markets in the EC.[70] Evidently, the City now feared that potential isolation within the Community was likely to strike at the heart of London's position as a financial centre. Compared to New York and Tokyo, London was without a large economic hinterland. It had succeeded in transcending that weakness through its liberal rules of operation, and its claim to the whole of the EC as its economic backyard. But capital liberalization within the Community was likely to reduce the singular attraction of the City in regulatory terms. Moreover, any move towards further EC monetary development without British participation made it less tenable to assert that the Community functioned as London's economic hinterland.

In this context, with the City now criticizing non-membership as a direct threat to its own interests, Thatcher and Lawson could only expect more vociferous pressure from this quarter on ERM entry in the future. At the same time City anxiety of this kind was always likely to translate into increased fervour on the issue from sections of the Conservative backbenches. In an article in the *Financial Times* in July 1988, Michael Heseltine warned:

> Technically, the ERM and our attitude to the Delors committee are not linked. Britain could leap a stage and without joining still play a positive role in the arrangements which will flow from Delors. But such clinical simplicity ignores the cause of the controversy over EMS ... Europe believes we have dug in. Psychologically and politically, 'they've heard it all before'. We will never play our full role if we stay outside the institutions of Europe and complain of their discrimination. It is almost surrealist to look at Europe's leading economies today with lower interest rates and lower inflation than ours and suggest that German rigidity underlying the ERM is incompatible with Britain's economic self-interest.[71]

Viewed as a whole, the mire facing Thatcher, Lawson and Howe on the ERM was deepening: internally divided among themselves, pursuing an economic policy which was taking them ever further away from the ERM states, plunged into a debate on monetary union they neither wanted nor understood, the question mark now raised over the future of the City had provided Heseltine with an issue on which to focus his latent leadership challenge.

THE DELORS COMMITTEE: JULY 1988 – MARCH 1989

This morass of conflicts and contradictions was to be fully exposed during the Delors committee's nine-month deliberations, and with the subsequent publication of the Delors Report. Domestically, Thatcher's and Lawson's monetary and fiscal policy remained incompatible with ERM membership. After the four interest rate rises in June 1988, Lawson raised interest rates to 10 per cent on 5 July, to 10.5 per cent on 19 July, to 11 per cent on 8 August and to 12 per cent on 26 August. Unsurprisingly, sterling steadily appreciated. Clearly, now, welcoming this rise in the currency, Lawson raised rates again to 13 per cent in November, when sterling came under downward pressure after an announcement of the worst monthly balance of payments deficit on record. Thereafter, sterling continued to appreciate, averaging DM3.23 in the first quarter of 1989, and reaching a peak of DM3.27 in February.

Evidently, if Lawson and Thatcher could not agree on the ERM, they were united in rejecting the kind of counter-inflationary policies which membership would have required. Although inflation continued to rise, reaching 7.9 per cent in March 1989, they chose to rely solely on a rising currency and accompanying high interest rates to deal with the problem. In September 1988 an IMF report warned that if the growth in demand did not slow down, the government needed to tighten fiscal policy and consider raising taxes, or otherwise face a further rise in inflation and deterioration in the current account.[72] Lawson dismissively responded that 'we must continue to resist those siren voices who want to use fiscal policy in a vain attempt at short term demand management'.[73] Indeed, rather than tightening fiscal policy, in the 1989 budget the Chancellor gave the economy a further stimulus with £2 billion worth of tax cuts through changes to National Insurance.

Yet, in now characteristic fashion, as Lawson was busy repudiating the tools of the ERM trade, Thatcher and he were continuing their feud over membership in their own private terms. Faced with Thatcher's repeated rejection of the ERM option, in September 1988 he secretly instructed his officials to devise an alternative proposal for an independent but accountable Bank of England with an explicit statutory obligation to maintain price stability.[74] On 25 November Lawson sent a memo to Thatcher outlining his proposal, and recommending a white paper publication on budget day 1989, with legislation in the following November. When Thatcher and he subsequently discussed the matter and Thatcher displayed little interest, Lawson concluded that their feud over the ERM counted against him in any monetary discussion before a word had even been spoken.[75]

Meanwhile the public war of words was unabated. In October 1988 Thatcher pronounced dismissively that with capital liberalization the ERM would break up.[76] Pending that doomsday, on 23 January 1989 Bernard Ingham informed the press that Thatcher was virtually ruling out ERM membership during the remainder of the government's term in office, and that she did not believe that re-election would change her mind.[77] Still refusing to admit defeat, the next day Lawson responded that obstacles to sterling's participation in the system were diminishing, and that the Single Market would make exchange rate stability increasingly important.[78]

Amidst these circumstances, with the Chancellor and Prime Minister feuding about joining an exchange rate system which their mutual economic policy effectively disqualified them from, pressure from within the EC for Britain to become an ERM member mounted. In part, this was the result of the progress being made towards capital liberalization within the Community. While Thatcher was declaiming that liberalization would destroy the ERM, practice was increasingly suggesting otherwise. In May 1987 Italy had been forced to abandon its first effort to remove some of its capital restrictions after the lira came under pressure, but through the second half of 1988, it successfully accomplished the task while maintaining the lira parity.[79] With such progress taking place towards a single financial market, Britain's critics were given added ammunition to argue that non-membership was an anomaly. In January 1989 Leon Brittan replaced Lord Cockfield as the British senior Commissioner. Almost immediately, he began to argue publicly that sterling needed to be in the ERM, both as a counter-inflationary discipline for the economy and so that Britain could put at least a temporary break on further institutional monetary development.[80] One month later the Spanish government sought to raise the stakes again by announcing that it might delay its own entry to the system until Britain had joined.[81]

Against this background the deliberations of the Delors committee took place. Robin Leigh-Pemberton, Britain's representative on the committee, was at best agnostic on the question of monetary union. In the words of one Bank official:

> I don't think the Bank of England was or is opposed to
> monetary union in principle. Many of us would feel that if that
> is a destination which we reach as a result of having had a really
> meaningful Single Market which over a period has brought our
> economies increasingly closer together, so that they are
> practically integrated ... then at a certain point in that process,
> you lose very little and potentially gain quite a bit more, by
> locking in to a monetary union. It's the notion that that process

is one that can be used as a driving engine for economic integration that I think some of us are pretty sceptical of.[82]

The Bank's position contrasted with those of Thatcher and Lawson, who were both adamantly opposed to the whole principle of a single currency, fearing that its inevitable, and appalling, consequence was a European superstate.[83]

Nevertheless, Leigh-Pemberton and his Bank colleagues were adamant that Britain needed to play a full role in the discussions on the matter:

> I think we thought it would be absolute folly not to take the
> debate seriously. I think that most of us felt in our bones that
> the terms in which the debate was being conducted were a little
> bit removed from reality. But nevertheless one had to go
> through the debate, and as necessary inject doses of reality when
> we thought it was lacking.[84]

Certainly, Thatcher and Lawson are quick to discount any suggestion that they themselves did not take the Delors committee's work seriously, and both have stressed that they sought to use Leigh-Pemberton to secure a report that they could accept. According to Lawson, Thatcher and he saw the papers from the start of the committee in September on a *sub rosa* basis, and quickly became worried that the likely report would make recommendations to which they were firmly opposed. On 14 December 1988, therefore, Thatcher held the first of a series of meetings with Leigh-Pemberton, Lawson, Howe, Charles Powell and Brian Griffiths. The ministers agreed that the Governor should seek to assemble the widest possible opposition within the committee both to the recommendation of any particular course of action, and to any early EC treaty amendment. To this end, they considered, Leigh-Pemberton's best hope was to build an alliance with Pöhl.[85] If this approach was unsuccessful, it was, Lawson alleges, because Pöhl, after promising Leigh-Pemberton his support, refused to engage himself seriously in the committee's negotiations.[86] Consequently, when a draft of the Delors committee's report was circulated in February 1989, Thatcher and Lawson were confronted with something which they found totally unacceptable. They were left to vainly try to persuade Leigh-Pemberton to submit a minority report, stressing that it was beyond the committee's competence to pronounce upon the shift in political sovereignty that monetary union would entail. Refusing to bow, Leigh-Pemberton concentrated on removing some of the prescriptive language from the report.[87]

However, Lawson's and Thatcher's accounts are contradicted on several counts, all of which suggest that neither took the work of the Delors committee particularly seriously, notwithstanding Lawson's announcement in August 1988 that the government would create a unique market in short-term Treasury bills denominated in Ecus.[88] Whilst Lawson states that the committee started meeting in September, and the formal meetings did indeed commence on 13 September, informal discussions appear to have begun on 12 July.[89] As one Treasury official acknowledged: 'The way the committee started was a bit confusing, and it was difficult to get hold of what was actually going to be discussed.'[90] On this basis, therefore, there was no consultation between Leigh-Pemberton and Lawson and Thatcher until some five months after the committee began its effective work. Indeed, one Treasury insider admitted that the department had no discussions with Leigh-Pemberton about a strategy for negotiation until some months after the committee began; and another acknowledged that Leigh-Pemberton was very much left on his own in the committee.[91] According to a former Foreign Office official:

> Robin Leigh-Pemberton did not have any instructions of any kind in all that year of the Delors report ... He never saw Mrs Thatcher after he signed it to discuss it. I mean, she just went around saying that he was a bloody idiot to go along with it.[92]

Left unadvised in the formative stages of the committee, Leigh-Pemberton and the Bank simply informed Lawson and the Treasury about proceedings. In the words of one senior Bank official:

> The Treasury were kept in touch with what was happening, but more by way of letting them know what had happened at each meeting. And then Governor-Chancellor level to some extent, and to a much more detailed extent at a somewhat more junior level, we were sensitized to Chancellor-Treasury thinking.[93]

With Leigh-Pemberton personally concluding that a unanimous report would actually reflect some compromises with his scepticism, Thatcher's and Lawson's failure to persuade him to submit a minority report is unsurprising.[94]

Thatcher's and her ministers' apparent detachment from the Delors committee was not matched in other Community states. Although Pöhl remained, in the words of one Bank official, 'pretty autonomous' from the German government, this reflected the Bundesbank's independence rather than lack of government attention to the committee's work. More significantly, French ministers, who had a similar institutional relationship to the Bank of France as their British counterparts to the Bank of England, clearly looked to their representative, De Larosière to pursue their interests.[95] As one Bank of England official close to the negotiations recalled:

I don't know how much prior [French] consultation, preparation and instruction went on. I would suspect quite a lot, mitigated only to the extent that Larosière is a fairly powerful figure. Nevertheless, to my mind, it is *inconceivable* that he would have argued a line on any particular aspect of the [Delors] report that was not deemed by the Treasury [i.e. Finance Ministry] to be consistent with French government thinking.[96]

Having been outmanoeuvred, British ministers and the Treasury resorted to blaming Leigh-Pemberton's personal inadequacies for the situation.[97] Accusing the Governor of incompetence, one Treasury official retorted: 'He was a bit out of his depth in central banking circles ... He saw being Governor as a part-time job in his spare time from being Lord Lieutenant of Kent.'[98] Another recounted: 'I think Nigel Lawson was pretty fed up with the way that Robin Leigh-Pemberton allowed himself to be carried along ... He spoke scathingly of the inability of the Governor to stop it.'[99] Thatcher and Lawson, and indeed Lawson's officials, would not acknowledge that sterling's non-membership of the ERM had placed any limit on the Governor's potential influence in the committee. The Bank of England begged to differ:

He did not go into those discussions with the best hand. Our non-participation was a weakness in the hand, certainly ... If you want to be arguing that the Community should not be advancing as fast down the EMU road as some of the more ambitious institutional developers might be seeking, it is very difficult to argue that, footdragging a *non-communitaire* card as seen by those who want to rush ahead. [It's as] if not only are you not wanting to run the next race as far or as fast as the others but you haven't actually finished the race before ... We were not deemed to be a full-time professional player.[100]

As concluded the Foreign Office, who 'were very aware that the revival of the EMU objectives revived also the political as well as the economic disadvantages of non-membership of the ERM'.[101] There was simply little ground on which Leigh-Pemberton could forge alliances inside the committee, or others outside it:

I do not recall that we saw the Germans as particular allies on issues of monetary union. In some things they were helpful, for example in favouring economic convergence, but not in others. In some areas we had more scope for making deals with the French, who always hoped to have us on their side to exert concerted influence on the Bundesbank. But with either country our absence from the ERM was a deterrent to striking alliances.[102]

Apparently unwilling to grapple with the weakness that staying outside the ERM imposed on their position in the monetary union debate, Thatcher and Lawson remained unable to grasp the relationship between the operation of the ERM and the whole issue of a single currency in the first place. Throughout the period of the Delors committee they persisted in addressing the debate in exclusively political terms. Thatcher, in particular, took to painting monetary union as part of an alien plot for a federal Europe, deliberately conceived to abolish the sovereignty of the nation-state. On 18 September 1988 Thatcher protested that a central bank would mean that:

> Each country would have to give up control over the future of
> its own economy, over its own currency, so that neither
> Parliament nor government would have a say in what happened,
> in what steps had to be taken to uphold the value of the
> currency.[103]

Two days later, in her infamous Bruges speech, Thatcher became even more forthright: 'We have not successfully rolled back the frontiers of the state in Britain, only to see them reimposed at a European level with a European superstate exercising a new dominance from Brussels.'[104] For his part, on 25 January 1989 Lawson delivered a similarly withering attack:

> It is inevitable that there are those who tire of [completing the
> internal market] and flutter towards the flame of economic and
> monetary union, or other great ideas. And others who have
> never much liked hacking at regulation and bureaucracy anyway
> and are only too keen to escape with dreams of EMU instead.[105]

Cocooned in their incomprehension, Thatcher and Lawson may have at last found some common ground on European monetary matters, but they were soon to have to face the fact that this new debate could only take their dispute on the ERM to its somewhat inevitable finale.

THE ROAD TO MADRID: APRIL–JUNE 1989

To Thatcher and Lawson's consternation, the Delors Report was published on 17 April as the unanimous findings of its 17 members. It outlined three stages necessary to reach monetary union, and argued that a decision to enter upon the first stage should be a decision to embark on the entire process. Stage One was to begin in July 1990, and would entail closer co-ordination of monetary policy, the abolition of remaining exchange controls and the participation of all member states in the ERM. Stage Two would be a transition period, creating a European System of Central Banks (ESCB) with limited powers, composed of a central institution and individual national banks. Statutorily committed to price stability, the ESCB would be independent from member states and Community institutions. In Stage Three the ESCB would assume sole responsibility for monetary policy and exchange rate management *vis-à-vis* non-EC currencies. After the currencies of member states were irrevocably fixed against each other, a single currency would be issued.[106] In order to make monetary union successful, the report prescribed, economic convergence between member states was essential. To this end, it would be necessary to increase regional aid, improve macro-economic policy co-ordination and, most importantly, impose binding rules on the size of member states' budget deficits. Finally, the report recommended that preparations begin immediately for an IGC to negotiate any necessary changes to the Treaty of Rome.[107]

Outside Britain the report was generally received enthusiastically. Unsurprisingly, differences did exist between states, led by France, Italy and Spain, who wanted to move rapidly towards a single currency, and those, like Germany, who envisaged a long period of economic convergence and institutional consolidation before Stage Three was reached.[108] But, in vociferously condemning the report as it did, the British government stood alone within the Community. Even the Bundesbank, quite evidently the institution most threatened by monetary union, concluded that 'outright opposition to EMU would be sterile and counterproductive', and the best path was 'to seek to obstruct it by posing conditions which would simply not be acceptable to the other countries'.[109] Lawson's retort was that Britain could not accept the massive transfer of sovereignty into a political union that monetary union would entail. Britain could only accept Stage One, the Chancellor insisted, and would seek to block any proposal to proceed with an IGC.[110]

Nonetheless, quite obviously, the reaction of British business to the Delors Report was not the same as that of the government, and its position redefined again the choices which confronted Thatcher and Lawson over the ERM. Since manufacturing and financial sector companies and organizations generally supported the idea of monetary union, they now concluded that sterling's entry to the ERM was essential, not simply desirable, to minimize Britain's isolation in the Community. As one Treasury official reflected wryly:

> You could not meet an industrialist who didn't think that it
> was the answer to the world ... It [ERM membership] was just

there all the time, day after day after day, so the line of saying we'll join some time was becoming increasingly untenable.[111]

For its part, the CBI saw three main advantages to monetary union: it would reduce the costs of hedging on exchange rate volatility; it would reduce transaction costs; and it would demand of member states the inflation convergence which the CBI sought. Given these advantages, the CBI believed, British industry would be seriously damaged if it were forced to embrace costs that its competitors were avoiding.[112] Meanwhile most of the City welcomed the prospect of a single currency as a means of strengthening the position of European companies and a necessary component of a single financial market. Any decision not to participate in any union, the City apprehended, would represent a direct threat to its most fundamental interests as a financial centre. In the words of one City official:

> If the others went ahead with economic and monetary union, and it looked as though the UK were going to stay out, then a whole lot of companies, both EC and non-EC banks and insurance companies, would start thinking if they should still regard London as the financial centre of Europe and where the centre of gravity would move to. They would start hedging their bets by putting some of their operations in Paris or Frankfurt.[113]

Within this context staying outside the ERM assumed a new meaning for the City. In March 1989 a senior National Westminster Bank official wrote in *Banking World*:

> The uncertainty relating to future UK membership of ERM may limit the ability of London, in the future, to claim its rightful place as the premier financial centre of Europe. It would be easy to be complacent and point to the enormous strength of the City and the size of the markets, but the success of the EMS and the ERM in particular, is now being accepted by many observers. Increasingly, the UK looks out of line on this topic.[114]

Shortly afterwards Barclays Bank told the House of Lords Select Committee on the European Communities: 'The pace of change now facing the EC makes it vital that the UK plays its full part in the reshaping of Europe in the 1990s. This it can only do effectively as a full participant in the EMS.'[115]

Significantly, the publication of the Delors Report coincided with an increasing anxiety in the City about its future competitiveness. The competitiveness of any financial centre is primarily determined by the regulatory framework in which it operates.[116] During the 1980s London established itself as the financial centre of the EC through a process of deregulation which culminated in the Financial Services Act. But the advent of the Single Market and capital liberalization meant that the other ERM states were now moving towards British-style deregulation. By April 1989, many of the directives for the single financial market were already in place, and other states' centres were well advanced in their preparation for the completion of the venture. Increasing numbers in the City believed that the Financial Services Act now left the City over-regulated in comparison to its competitors, and facing two specific threats: first, that some European business, previously driven offshore to London could now be repatriated; and second, that harmonization could give the potential for each financial market to make use of other advantages to become an international centre.[117] In Robin Leigh-Pemberton's words:

> We can no longer class London as a cheap place to do business; and we must be sensitive to the cost of operating here. We start with great natural advantages, not least that we have achieved that 'critical mass' which enables a market to function effectively as a major international, as well as a domestic, financial centre. But it may be that only a small shift in the balance of advantage would be enough to start a process of attrition. And I am well aware that other centres – in Europe and elsewhere – are far from devoid of attraction or potential.[118]

Worried about the lack of collective City input into Britain's EC policy, as early as May 1988 the Bank of England had worked to create a City European Committee of British Invisibles to examine all Community issues affecting the City. Chaired by Michael Butler, a former Permanent Representative to the Community, the committee operated primarily as a policy consultation body, with members joining in a personal capacity from all main areas of the City's activity.[119] Although in 1988 the European Committee had rather lacked coherence, the monetary union issue had given it an opportunity to establish a collective identity and voice. After the Delors Report was published, Butler went to Thatcher with a mandate from the committee to pressurize her for a more constructive response to both the single currency and ERM questions. Whilst sceptical about the appropriateness of immediate entry in view of economic conditions, Butler counselled Thatcher that Britain could not expect to influence developments on monetary union unless it was regarded as making a serious effort to create the conditions necessary for sterling's participation in the ERM.[120]

If Thatcher wanted to protest that she had heard it all before, quite clearly there was a new component to the issue. Of its own volition, the government had bound part of its own political interests up with the future of the City. By 1989 the broad financial service sector was the engine of growth of the British economy, employing 2.6 million people. It represented 19.8 per cent of GDP in 1989 compared to 11.6 per cent in 1979. Between 1985 and 1989 the financial sector grew at an annual average of 8.9 per cent, compared to 4.1 per cent for manufacturing industry and 4.2 per cent for the non-financial service sector.[121] In this context when the City charged that being outside the ERM was a direct threat to its interests, Thatcher and Lawson faced a greater incentive to join the system in terms of their capital accumulation priorities than ever before.

Nonetheless, the most immediate problem for ministers was how to handle the Madrid summit in June, where a formal decision would be taken as to how to proceed with the Delors Report. Initially they appeared simply disoriented, as one Treasury official recalled: 'It was quite difficult after the Delors Report was actually published to discover what the government's attitude actually was, and as we were supposed to be working for the government, it was a period of some confusion.'[122] But, for their part, Lawson and Howe quickly concluded that any successful strategy to halt the momentum towards monetary union was dependent on ERM entry. Howe now considered that the person most likely to change Thatcher's mind was Ruud Lubbers, to whom she was personally and politically close. Despite Lawson's scepticism, Howe proceeded to arrange a mini-summit with the Dutch government for 29 April, under the auspices of discussions on NATO modernization.[123] But pre-empting her Foreign Secretary, Thatcher made clear to Lubbers her resistance to entry before the formal discussions even began. According to Lawson, she then berated Lubbers over NATO, after which Thatcher and himself rowed over shadowing, leaving the Dutch ministers as helpless spectators.[124]

When Lawson returned to the fray in a bilateral meeting with Thatcher on 3 May, she rebuked him that joining the ERM would not strengthen the government's hand against monetary union, and that as far as she was concerned the issue was dead.[125] Lawson was left to conclude that they were now engaged in a deadly power struggle:

It was evident to both of us that the discussion was getting nowhere; but the terms in which she brought it to a close were particularly revealing. 'I do not want you to raise the subject ever again,' she said; 'I must prevail.' It was those last three words that said it all. The economic and political arguments had become an irrelevance. Joining the ERM, as she saw it, had become a battle of wills between her and me; and it was to be her will that prevailed.[126]

Undeterred, Lawson returned to the issue on 20–21 May at an *Ecofin* meeting to discuss the Delors Report. There, the finance ministers agreed to a quick start to Stage One, and to take a future decision about whether to call the IGC necessary to proceed with Stages Two and Three. With British membership of the ERM a necessary part of Stage One, Lawson assured his fellow finance ministers that entry 'is not a question of whether, it is a question of when'.[127]

Yet for all Lawson's continuing predilection for membership, the reality was that entry now offered the government more limited economic benefits than at any time since 1985. Thatcher's and Lawson's dispute on the issue was making their efforts to use an appreciating exchange rate as a counter-inflationary weapon increasingly untenable. In May, heavy Bank of England intervention notwithstanding, sterling came under sustained downward pressure as the balance of payments deficit mounted and the dollar rose. On 17 May, with Lawson and Howe's support for the ERM well known, Thatcher pronounced in a radio interview that inflation not ERM membership was to remain the overriding priority, and sterling weakened further.[128] Two days later, in another radio interview, Thatcher publicly blamed Lawson's shadowing of the Deutschmark for rising inflation, and questioned whether the ERM could survive capital liberalization. Provocatively, she continued, 'I do not know any serious commentator who at the moment has suggested that we go in until we have tackled our inflation and got it down.'[129] Once more the foreign exchange markets sold sterling.[130] Furious with Thatcher, Lawson contemplated resigning, and the two only reached another accommodation when Thatcher apologized to Lawson, saying that her remarks had been taken out of context.[131] Although Thatcher's apology was widely reported, it could neither dispel the impression of a Prime Minister and Chancellor locked in intractable conflict nor stabilize sterling. Indeed, on 22 May Thatcher attacked the ERM again, assuring her listeners that Britain would not join the system until inflation was under control and 'maybe not even then'.[132] With sterling persistently vulnerable to this kind of uncertainty, Lawson was forced to raise interest rates to 14 per cent.

In this context the monetary calculations confronting Thatcher and Lawson about ERM membership shifted from what had hitherto been a fairly consistent position from 1985. As Figure 4.4 shows, although British nominal interest rates were significantly higher than the ERM states, real rates were now lower than those in Belgium, Holland and Italy. More crucially, though, with inflation rising as it was and sterling weak, the capacity to reduce interest rates was now of dubious benefit. Once sterling stopped rising, high interest rates became Thatcher's and Lawson's only counter-inflationary tool. Inside the ERM, given the premium of British rates over most other states, interest rates were likely to have to be reduced to keep sterling within its band. Yet, as Figure 4.5 shows, by May 1989 British inflation and annual wage increases were much higher than elsewhere within the Community. Without counter-inflationary policies other than high interest rates, particulary some means of controlling wage rises, Thatcher and Lawson would not be able to achieve the inflation convergence necessary to maintain a sterling ERM parity in the medium to long term, even leaving aside the matter of the external deficit.

Some sense of these macro-economic difficulties now led the Bank of England to reconsider its attitude towards the ERM. On the one hand, 'the whole question about London's position as a financial centre [was] preoccupying the Bank', which led to officials compiling a report on the

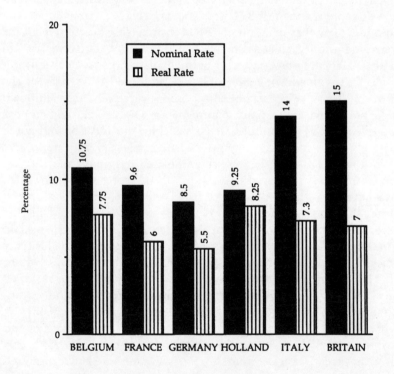

Figure 4.4: Comparative Interest Rates May 1989
(Source: Economist Economic and Financial Indicators, May 27, 1989)

position of the City in relation to monetary union.[133] As one official described the growing uneasiness:

London's position as a financial centre is a factor which clearly does weigh quite strongly with everybody in the Bank. We consider the City to be a major economic asset, and we're therefore concerned lest there be any development that undermine that, prejudice it, in anyway. And I think most people would agree that the financial community, particularly financial institutions from elsewhere, happening to locate their European institutions here, or considering whether to locate their European institutions here, would take into account the question of whether we were in a single currency union or outside it ... How important it would be, different people inevitably take slightly different judgements. Yes, in principle,

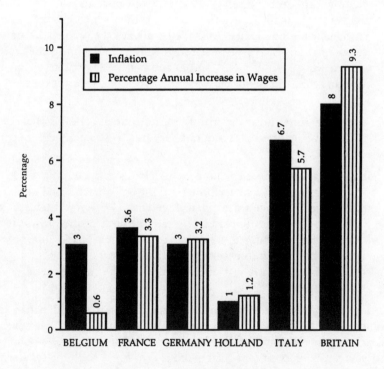

Figure 4.5: Comparative Rates of Inflation and Wage Increases May 1989
(Source: Economist Economic and Financial Indicators, May 27, 1989)

it would be prejudiced, but is it just a marginal consideration or is it a fundamental one? . . . I think probably most people feel, short term, either uncertainty as to whether we would join, or even knowledge that we weren't going to join wouldn't have much significant adverse effect. But that over time, particularly if associated with our not being part of the union, other policy decisions were taken at a Community level by members of the union, our influence over events is likely to be eroded. If financial institutions see that, or expect that to be the outcome, then that in turn will affect whether they locate themselves in the decision-making centre or in somewhere which is clearly outside the union.[134]

Outside the ERM, the Bank judged, British concerns would go unheeded, with other states retorting:

'If you want us to listen to your view of the way forward to further monetary integration, you at least have to come up to where we all are at present.' . . . It puts one at some disadvantage in all negotiations about things which change permanent arrangements. And there's always the potential that we will not be able to carry as much weight in deciding the outcome as we would wish, and as another member state with our economic and historical weight, if you like, would expect to achieve.[135]

At the same time, however, the Bank no longer believed that ERM entry could be justified on economic grounds.[136] In Leigh-Pemberton's words:

It would be a mistake to enter the mechanism in circumstances where our anti-inflationary policy might be compromised or undermined. This could happen if we wished to keep interest rates high for domestic reasons but . . . we were pushed towards lowering interest rates to keep sterling within its band. It would therefore be unwise to enter the mechanism with the UK economy significantly out of balance with other major member countries.[137]

Evidently, the Treasury-Bank axis on the matter, which had prevailed since 1985, had broken down. The Treasury was far less apprehensive than the Bank of England that the City would be penalized outside a monetary union. Asked about the threat to the City, a senior Treasury figure observed: 'it's not very obvious that it is true'.[138] Neither did the Treasury share the Bank's view that rising inflation made joining the ERM untenable. Indeed, the Treasury still saw membership as a useful counter-inflationary monetary framework, as well as deeming it necessary to halt the Delors Report.[139] Effectively, there was now 'no difference of view between the Treasury and the Foreign Office on these matters',[140] especially since the latter regarded '[ERM membership] as a litmus test of whether we were serious about Europe'.[141]

In this context, Lawson and Howe joined forces for the first, and only, time against the Prime Minister. At the start of June Howe proposed to Lawson sending a joint memo to Thatcher, outlining the case for entry in the context of the decisions to be taken on monetary union at Madrid. Sceptical about its utility, Lawson nonetheless agreed that their respective officials should draft a paper. Subsequently, a memo was drafted, arguing that it would be very damaging simply to oppose monetary union at Madrid, and the aim should be to avoid agreeing to any IGC. To this end, therefore, Britain should give a non-legally binding undertaking that sterling would enter the ERM by the end of 1992, on the conditions that inflation fell and all EC exchange controls were abolished. Britain could then seek the postponement of any decision on Stage Three until work was carried out on how it would operate.[142]

Whilst the memo was still being drafted, Lawson returned to the public offensive. On 11 June he denied that shadowing caused inflation, and accused Alan Walters of misjudging the ERM question.[143] The next day, giving evidence to the Treasury Select Committee, Lawson argued that if the other member states believed that sterling would enter ERM within a reasonable time period, then Britain could play a more influential role in the monetary union debate. Moreover, for the first time he specified a set of conditions for ERM entry, differing only from the draft memo in that the exchange control condition was restricted to the *major* EC states.[144] Since France and Italy were due to abolish controls by mid-1990, it was reasonable to infer that Lawson was saying that sterling would enter the system sometime in 1990. On 14 June Lawson agreed to sign the proposed memo, subject to a number of amendments and that it be sent on Foreign Office paper.[145] In the view of a Treasury official who worked on the memo, it was a step into new territory: 'What was extraordinarily unusual was something that comes out in the Lawson memoirs that he and Geoffrey, Howe signed a joint minute. That is very, very rare in Whitehall.'[146] Perceiving a potential ambush on receiving the missive, Thatcher reluctantly agreed to see her two ministers on 20 June.[147]

In the days prior to the meeting, events conspired to apparently strengthen Lawson's and Howe's hand. In the elections to the European Parliament on 15 June, the Conservatives slumped to their worst performance in a national election in the post-war period, receiving just 34.7 per cent of the vote and losing 13 seats to Labour. In part the poor performance reflected a growth in the government's general unpopularity: in the *Guardian* average monthly poll the Conservatives had fallen from a 6 per cent lead over Labour in January to an 8 per cent deficit in June.[148] But at the same time, the government had clearly paid a price for a public feeling that it was too negative in its approach to Europe. Already isolated on monetary issues, in May 1989 British ministers had unilaterally dismissed the Commission plan for a social charter to protect worker rights in the EC. In this respect, with the Community increasingly moving onto its obvious political territory, Labour could effectively present itself as the united and pro-European party working for British interests, and depict the Conservatives as petty isolationists, a strategy which was made even easier by the latter's crudely nationalist advertising.

Throughout the campaign the Conservatives' strategy left many in the party uneasy, and both the leader of the Conservative MEPs, Henry Plumb, and Edward Heath made scathing attacks on the style and substance of Thatcher's European leadership. If Michael Heseltine had already set his stall as a pro-European with the publication of a new book, *The Challenge of Europe: Can Britain Win?*, it was evident that the mood of back-benchers had swung in a pro-ERM direction. As one opponent of membership recalled, Conservative MPs now 'believed Britain's problems would be ameliorated by a German fixed-rate regime; there was a very powerful mood disposed to membership of the ERM'.[149] To add fuel to Lawson's and Howe's fire, on the day of the election, a Gallup poll revealed that 93 per cent of chief executives of large British companies and City institutions believed that sterling should be inside the ERM.[150]

Meanwhile direct pressure on the issue from within the Community mounted. On 16 June Spain announced that it would be joining the ERM three days later.[151] Since Spain similarly suffered from above-average inflation, the decision drew attention to precisely what the justification of the British position was. Spain also gave voice to the view growing elsewhere in the Community, including in Germany, that if Britain did not act quickly on ERM entry, monetary union could progress without it. Quite clearly, as a joint communiqué from France and Germany on 19 June made clear, other Community states wanted decisive progress on the Delors Report at the Madrid summit.[152]

On 20 June Thatcher, Lawson and Howe met to discuss the joint memo. Rejecting any idea of setting a timetable for membership as economically unwelcome and politically futile, Thatcher agreed only that the three of them would give the matter further consideration.[153] What happened next is a matter of dispute between the protagonists. According to Lawson, Howe received a memo from Charles Powell the next day, outlining an alternative set of conditions for joining the ERM to use at Madrid, apparently devised by Alan Walters. These conditions were a reduction in inflation, exchange control abolition, the creation and successful implementation of a level playing field in Europe on the monetary front and the final completion of the Single Market to Britain's satisfaction. Regarding the conditions as totally unacceptable, Lawson and Howe then sent another joint memo to Thatcher on 23 June, arguing that the open-ended nature of the 'Walters' conditions would be counterproductive at Madrid and requesting a further meeting. Most crucially, they also agreed that if Thatcher did not adopt these conditions they would both resign.[154] By contrast, Thatcher makes no mention of any memo from Powell, and implies that the second Lawson-Howe memo which she received came out of the blue.[155] But she reluctantly agreed to see her Chancellor and Foreign Secretary on Sunday 25 June, before she and Howe left for Madrid in the evening.[156] Unable to gain any concession from her, Howe and Lawson made their resignation threat, leaving Thatcher fuming and adamant that she would 'never allow this to happen again'.[157]

When Thatcher and Howe arrived in Madrid they were not even on speaking terms. But when the summit started Thatcher quickly deployed a conciliatory tone, and set out a series of conditions for sterling joining the ERM: the convergence of British inflation with other EC states; the abolition of all exchange controls; further progress towards the completion of the Single Market; free competition in financial services; and the strengthening of European competition policy. Later during the summit she agreed with the other states to accept the Delors Report as the means to achieve monetary union, starting Stage One by 1 July 1990, and followed by an IGC when adequate preparation was completed.

The media were quick to hail the summit as a major shift in Thatcher's position on the ERM. Yet with Thatcher claiming that the Madrid conditions were based on a paper Alan Walters had given her in May 1989, this was open to dispute.[158] For his part, Lawson rejected Walters's claim to the conditions, arguing that the last three conditions were 'as long as a piece of string' and 'could be interpreted as having been satisfied at any time,' whereas Walters and Powell had originally ruled out membership until well into 1993.[159]

But whilst conditions 'as long as a piece of string' could be interpreted 'as having been satisfied at any time', they could also be interpreted as never having been satisfied. Even more significantly, the Madrid conditions contained no deadline for membership as demanded by Lawson and Howe.

Officials who worked on the joint memo saw the Madrid conditions as a defeat for Lawson and Howe:

It was a slight movement. But at the time it seemed to those of us who had been working on it all as a grave disappointment ... I'd worked on the joint paper and the purpose of the paper was to persuade the Prime Minister that ERM membership at an early stage, not with the Single Market, but within a matter of months would be appropriate. It seemed to set up hurdles which meant we would not be able to join for quite a while. I think those of us who were closely involved regarded it as a setback.[160]

In the words of a former Cabinet Minister, 'she gave sufficient ground to make everyone believe she had given more ground than she had done'.[161] Or, as a Thatcher confidant observed:

I would argue that the conditions for our joining ERM were made more difficult by her statement in Madrid, not brought closer and that was a deliberate act of defiance of them [Lawson and Howe]. In effect, they had to climb down when she came home and pretend to be satisfied with what they'd done ... What we did was spell out the conditions which would have to be met if sterling were to join the ERM, and when you actually spelled out the conditions, it became quite clear that the hurdles were a good deal higher than the rather vague general formulation that we'll join when the time was right.[162]

Indeed Lawson also admits that ultimately Howe and himself were outmanoeuvred, since given the way the conditions were heralded 'a resignation ... would have been bizarre and incomprehensible'.[163] In the view of a Thatcher confidant: 'I think their bluff was called. I don't think they intended to resign or expected to have to.'[164] Effectively, having shelved four years of keeping their distance, Lawson and Howe were little closer to persuading Thatcher to accept ERM membership than they had been before.

If the debate between 1985 and 1988 about ERM membership had largely been about economic policy, and in particular perceptions about monetary policy, by the end of the Madrid summit, the question was quite clearly far more complicated. Yet confronted with new incentives to join the ERM, both as an act of European policy and to strengthen the City, Thatcher had successfully held her position. But the problem for Thatcher was that, whilst she had outmanoeuvred her two most senior ministers, the ground on which she was standing was becoming ever less solid. Lawson and Howe could be managed, but just how was her government going to stop, or indeed influence, an accelerating debate on monetary union and ultimately an IGC with important consequences for the City, on the sidelines of the Community?

In terms of economic policy, there were more grounds for hope. First, since Thatcher was commonly believed to have given ground at Madrid, the perception of uncertainty, which the foreign exchange markets had been punishing in the previous months, was likely to abate. Second, Spain's accession to the ERM in June 1989 revealed just how difficult sterling would have found life inside the ERM, given Lawson's and Thatcher's approach to economic management. When Spain decided to enter the system it abandoned its previous counter-inflationary policy based on a tight monetary regime and an appreciating exchange rate. In May 1989 Spain had faced rising demand and a deterioration in the balance of payments. In response the Spanish government had cut public expenditure and increased corporate withholding taxes. Then, shortly after the peseta entered the ERM, Spain reintroduced credit ceilings and increased withholding taxes on personal incomes.[165] Nevertheless, the fact remained that British interest rates were high and the foreign exchange markets have notoriously short memories. Lawson's advantage on the ERM issue had been that generally membership would be able to deliver lower interest rates for a given rate of inflation. With inflation still rising, and every further increase in interest rates threatening a hard landing for the economy, any prolonged weakness in sterling could only strengthen the short-term economic attraction of ERM entry.

NOTES

1 For a discussion of the Basle-Nybourg reforms, see H. Ungerer et al., (1989) *The EMS: Developments and Perspectives*, Washington: IMF.
2 E. Kennedy, (1991) *The Bundesbank: Germany's Central Bank in the International Monetary System*, London: Pinter, p. 94.
3 *Ibid.*, p. 94.
4 *Ibid.*, pp. 95–97; K. Dyson, (1994) *Elusive Union: The Process of Economic and Monetary Union in Europe*, Harlow: Longman, pp. 123–25.
5 *Financial Times*, 8 January 1988; 19 January 1988; 10 February 1988; 25 February 1988; 1 June 1988; 27 June 1988.
6 *Ibid.*, 25 February 1988; 18 March 1988; 27 June 1988. On the key role that Hans-Dietrich Genscher played in the German response, see Dyson, *Elusive Union*, Chapter 5.
7 For a discussion of the discussions about monetary union in the 1960s and 1970s see Dyson, *Elusive Union*, Chapter 3.
8 *Financial Times*, 16 June 1987.

9 N. Lawson, (1992) *The View from No. 11: Memoirs of a Tory Radical*, London: Bantam, p. 732; M. Thatcher, (1993) *The Downing Street Years*, London: HarperCollins, p. 700.

10 Lawson, *Memoirs*, p. 784.

11 *Ibid.*, p. 787.

12 *Ibid.*, pp. 788–89.

13 *Ibid.*, p. 792.

14 *Ibid.*, p. 794.

15 *Ibid.*, pp. 794–95; Thatcher, *Downing Street Years*, pp. 702–03.

16 Lawson, *Memoirs*, p. 795; Thatcher, *Downing Street Years*, p. 703.

17 Lawson, *Memoirs*, p. 795; D. Smith, (1992) *From Boom to Bust: Trial and Error in British Economic Policy*, Harmondsworth: Penguin, pp. 136–38.

18 Smith, *Boom to Bust*, p. 137.

19 *Ibid.*

20 *Ibid.*, p. 138.

21 *Ibid.*

22 *Financial Times*, 25 March 1988.

23 Lawson, *Memoirs*, p. 811.

24 *Ibid.*, pp. 830–32.

25 Smith, *Boom to Bust*, p. 138; Lawson, *Memoirs*, p. 832.

26 Lawson, *Memoirs*, p. 832.

27 *Financial Times*, 13 May 1994.

28 *Ibid.*, 14 May 1988.

29 Thatcher, *Downing Street Years*, p. 704.

30 Lawson, *Memoirs*, p. 836.

31 Thatcher, *Downing Street Years*, p. 705.

32 Lawson, *Memoirs*, p. 842.

33 *Economic Outlook*, December 1988, p. 111.

34 Lawson, *Memoirs*, pp. 854–59.

35 *Financial Times*, 9 September 1987; 12 September 1987; 14 September 1987.

36 *Ibid.*, 14 September 1987.

37 *Ibid.*, 8 January 1988.

38 *Financial Times*, 19 January, 1988; 28 January, 1988; 2 February, 1988; 25 February, 1988; 3 March, 1988; 18 March, 1988.

39 *Ibid.*, 19 January, 1988.

40 *Ibid.*, 28 March, 1988.

41 *Ibid.*, 10 May, 1988.

42 *Ibid.*, 11 June, 1988.

43 *Ibid.*, 14 June 1988; *Financial Times*, 15 June, 1988.

44 Ungerer *et al.*, *The EMS*, pp. 33–34; *Economist*, 9 July, 1988, p. 26.

45 Lawson, *Memoirs*, p. 902.

46 Non-attributable interview.

47 Lawson, *Memoirs*, pp. 902–03.

48 Non-attributable interview.

49 *Financial Times*, 27 June, 1988; 28 June, 1988.

50 Lawson, *Memoirs*, p. 904.

51 *Ibid.*, p. 902.

52 Lawson, *Memoirs*, p. 904.
53 *Ibid.*
54 Non-attributable interview with Foreign Office official.
55 Non-attributable interview with Commission official.
56 *Financial Times*, 26 June 1989.
57 Non-attributable interview with Treasury official.
58 Non attributable interview with Treasury official.
59 Non-attributable interview with Treasury official.
60 Non-attributable interview with Treasury official.
61 Non-attributable interviews with Treasury officials.
62 Non-attributable interview with Treasury official.
63 Non-attributable interview with Treasury official.
64 Non-attributable interview with Treasury official. Although Delors certainly played a role in persuading Mitterrand that a European solution was the only answer to France's economic problems, his active role in the debate was totally dependent on the French government's, in particular, support for monetary union.
65 Non-attributable interview with Treasury official.
66 Non-attributable interview with Treasury official.
67 Non-attributable interview.
68 Even Dyson who sees integration in a somewhat more deterministic fashion than understood in this book reflects, 'The victory of sound money ideas was not primarily attributable to the EC Commission and Jacques Delors.' Dyson, *Elusive Union*, p. 256.
69 *Financial Times*, 7 July 1988.
70 *Times*, 11 July 1988.
71 *Financial Times*, 20 July 1988.
72 D. McKie, (ed.) (1992) *The Election: A Voters' Guide*, London: Fourth Estate, p. 72; *Financial Times*, 26 September 1988.
73 *Financial Times*, 26 September 1988.
74 Lawson, *Memoirs*, pp. 868–69.
75 *Ibid.*, p. 871.
76 *Financial Times*, 10 October 1988.
77 *Ibid.*, 25 January 1989.
78 *Ibid.*, 26 January 1989.
79 Ungerer *et al.*, *The EMS*, p. 20; F. Giavazzi, (1989) *The Exchange Rate Question in Europe*, Brussels: The European Commission, p. 3.
80 *Financial Times*, 11 February 1989; *Financial Times*, 25 February 1989; *Times*, 11 February 1989; *Times*, 22 February 1989; *Times*, 25 February 1989.
81 *Times*, 7 February 1989.
82 Non-attributable interview with Bank of England official.
83 Lawson, *Memoirs*, p. 892.
84 Non-attributable interview with Bank of England official.
85 Lawson, *Memoirs*, pp. 906–08; Thatcher, *Downing Street Years*, pp. 708.
86 Lawson, *Memoirs*, p. 908.
87 *Ibid.*, pp. 908–09; Thatcher, *Downing Street Years*, p. 708.
88 *Financial Times*, 3 August 1988.

89 *Times*, 11 July 1988; non-attributable interview with Bank of England official.

90 Non-attributable interview with Treasury official.

91 Non-attributable interviews with Treasury officials.

92 Non-attributable interview with Foreign Office official.

93 Non-attributable interview with Bank of England official.

94 Non-attributable interview with Bank of England official.

95 Non-attributable interview with Bank of England official.

96 Non-attributable interview with Bank of England official.

97 Non-attributable interview with Foreign Office official.

98 Non-attributable interview with Treasury official.

99 Non-attributable interview.

100 Non-attributable interview with Bank of England official.

101 Non-attributable interview with Foreign Office official.

102 Non-attributable interview with Foreign Office official.

103 *Financial Times*, 19 September, 1988.

104 *Ibid.*, 21 September 1988.

105 *Ibid.*, 26 January 1989.

106 Committee for the Study of Economic and Monetary Union, (1989) *Report on Economic and Monetary Union in the European Community (The Delors Report)*, Luxembourg: Office of Publications of the European Communities.

107 *Ibid.*

108 *Financial Times*, 19 April 1989; 20 April 1989; 27 April 1989.

109 D. Marsh, (1992) *The Bundesbank: The Bank that Rules Europe*, London: Mandarin, p. 245.

110 *Financial Times*, 18 April 1989.

111 Non-attributable interview with Treasury official.

112 House of Lords, (1990) *Select Committee on the European Communities, 27th Report: Minutes of Evidence*, London: HMSO, pp. 119–22.

113 Non-attributable interview with City official.

114 J. Tugwell, (1989) 'Europe 1992: Clearing Banks Face the Challenge', *Banking World*, 7(3), p. 27.

115 House of Lords, *27th Report: Minutes of Evidence*, p. 252.

116 See M. Moran, (1991) *The Politics of the Financial Services Revolution*, London: Macmillan.

117 Moran, *Financial Services Revolution*, pp. 6, 56; A. Clark (1989), 'Europe 1992: Regulatory Implications', *Banking World*, 7(9), p. 35; A. Smith, (1989) 'Europe 1992: A Truly International Securities Market', *Banking World*, 7(5), p. 31; Tugwell, 'Europe 1992', p. 28; Bank of England (1989), 'The Single European Market Survey of the UK Financial Services Industry', *Bank of England Quarterly Bulletin*, 29(3), pp. 409–12.

118 R. Leigh-Pemberton, (1989) 'Europe 1992 and the City', *Bank of England Quarterly Bulletin*, 29(2),p. 225.

119 Non-attributable interviews with City officials.

120 Non-attributable interview with City official.

121 Moran, *Financial Services Revolution*, p. 5; C. Johnson, (1991) *The Economy Under Mrs Thatcher, 1979–1990*, Harmondsworth: Penguin, p. 268.

122 Non-attributable interview with Treasury official.

123 Lawson, *Memoirs*, pp. 913–14.

124 *Ibid.*, pp. 915–16.

125 *Ibid.*, p. 918; Thatcher, *Downing Street Years*, p. 709.

126 Lawson, *Memoirs*, p. 918.

127 *Ibid.*, p. 920; *Financial Times*, 22 May 1989.

128 *Financial Times*, 18 May 1989.

129 *Ibid.*, 20 May 1989.

130 *Ibid.*

131 Lawson, *Memoirs*, p. 921.

132 W. Keegan, (1989) *Mr Lawson's Gamble*, London: Hodder and Stoughton, p. 229.

133 Non-attributable interviews with Bank of England officials.

134 Non-attributable interview with Bank of England official.

135 Non-attributable interview with Bank of England official.

136 *Financial Times*, 12 May 1989.

137 R. Leigh-Pemberton (1989), 'The Future of Monetary Arrangements in Europe', *Bank of England Quarterly Bulletin*, 29(3), p. 374.

138 Non-attributable interview with Treasury official.

139 *Financial Times*, 27 April 1989.

140 Non-attributable interview with Foreign Office official.

141 Non-attributable interview with Treasury official.

142 Lawson, *Memoirs*, pp. 928–29.

143 *Financial Times*, 12 June 1989.

144 Lawson, *Memoirs*, pp. 923–24; *Financial Times*, 13 June 1989; 14 June 1989.

145 Lawson, *Memoirs*, p. 930.

146 Non-attributable interview with Treasury official.

147 Lawson, *Memoirs*, p. 931; Thatcher, *Downing Street Years*, pp. 710–11.

148 McKie, (ed.) *Voters' Guide*, pp. 277–78.

149 Non-attributable interview with Cabinet Minister.

150 *Financial Times*, 16 June, 1989.

151 *Ibid.*, 17 June, 1989.

152 *Financial Times* 8 June, 1989; *Financial Times*, 20 June, 1989; *Times*, 20 June, 1989.

153 Lawson, *Memoirs*, pp. 931–32; Thatcher, *Downing Street Years*, p. 711.

154 Lawson, *Memoirs*, pp. 930–31.

155 Thatcher, *Downing Street Years*, p. 712.

156 Lawson, *Memoirs*, pp. 930–32.

157 Thatcher, *Downing Street Years*, p. 712.

158 Lawson, *Memoirs*, p. 934; Thatcher, *Downing Street Years*, p. 712; Smith, *Boom to Bust*, p. 164.

159 Lawson, *Memoirs*, p. 934.

160 Non-attributable interview with Treasury official.

161 Non-attributable interview with a former Cabinet Minister.

162 Non-attributable interview.

163 Lawson, *Memoirs*, pp. 934–35.

164 Non-attributable interview.

165 *Economist*, 16 June, 1990, p. 111; *Financial Times*, 17 June, 1989.

5

There is no Alternative: 1989–1990

And certainly, the mistakes that we make, and female mortals make, when we have our own way, might fairly raise some wonder that we are so fond of it. George Eliot, *Middlemarch*

ERM, MONETARY UNION AND GERMAN REUNIFICATION

During the second half of 1989 and 1990 the ERM states were able to exploit the monetary union project to reap further benefits from their commitment to maintain exchange rate stability. Since the foreign exchange markets believed that currencies would eventually be irrevocably fixed, they required less premium to persuade them to hold currencies other than the Deutschmark. As a result, interest rates within the ERM started to converge towards the German level. As Figure 5.1 shows, from January 1988 to July 1990 the differential between Italian and German nominal rates fell by 4.5 per cent, and between French and German rates by 3.45 per cent. Similarly, as Figure 5.2 indicates, the differential between French and German long-term government bonds fell by 3.19 per cent over the same period. At the same time monetary union operated as an insurance policy for the major ERM states to fully liberalize capital movements. Without any pressure arising on their respective currencies, France and Italy removed all their remaining exchange controls between January and May 1990.[1]

Yet given that this manifest stability was concurrent with the external shock of the destruction of the Berlin Wall, it was effectively bought by storing up serious problems for the future. Once German reunification became a certainty, the question of how it was to be financed in a non-inflationary way raised fundamental questions for the future of the ERM. Since the Kohl government was unwilling to raise taxes, and indeed cut income tax in 1990, and West German workers were demanding higher wages to protect themselves from the thousands of East Germans crossing the border, the Bundesbank inevitably became anxious about the inflationary outlook. Having already raised its interest rates, from the end of 1989 the Bundesbank began seeking a realignment of ERM currencies in which the Deutschmark would be revalued to absorb the mounting inflationary pressure. Between the fall of the Wall and the start of 1990 the Deutschmark had gained nearly 11 per cent against the dollar and yen, due to rising German interest rates and the prospect that reunification would create a new economic superpower. Whilst all the ERM currencies, except the Dutch guilder, had come under sustained downward pressure against the Deutschmark in the fallout, the Bundesbank warned that without a further significant appreciation in the German currency, it would continue to tighten monetary policy. Despite the potentially serious deflationary consequences of the Bundesbank threat, the French government reacted irately to the idea of a realignment. Determined not to compromise the *franc fort*, French ministers appealed to their German counterparts to suppress discussion of

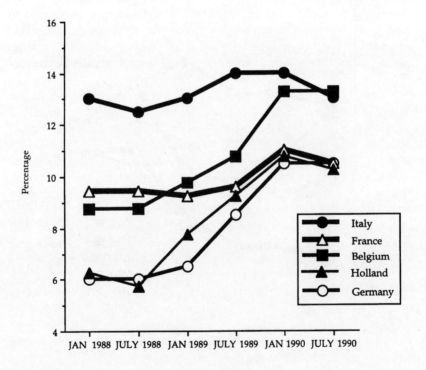

Figure 5.1: Comparative Nominal Prime Lending Rates 1988-1990
(Source: Economist Economic and Financial Indicators, 1988-1990)

the subject by the Bundesbank. In the face of this pressure, Kohl backed the French government and ruled out any realignment. Consequently, on 5 January only a marginal adjustment to currencies took place, with the lira moving into the 2.25 per cent ERM bands, whilst devaluing but 3.7 per cent against the Deutschmark. Indeed, within a few months Holland and Belgium were operating unofficial 0.5 per cent bands to further consolidate their existing currency parities.

In effect, the ERM states were choosing to ignore not only the likely consequences of the deflationary bell which the Bundesbank had started to toll but the fact that the convergence of economies which the post-1983 ERM had created was coming to an end. In the short term it was possible for the ERM states to act as if nothing had changed. Indeed, during 1990 the prospect of German reunification did provide some economic stimulus to other states. With the German economy growing

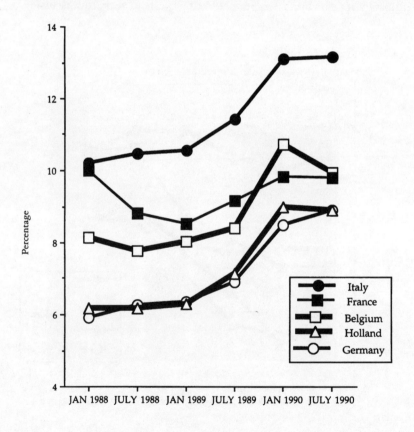

Figure 5.2: Comparative Long Term Government Bond Rates 1988-1990
(Source: Economist Economic and Financial Indicators, 1988-1990)

at a rate of 4.5 per cent – higher than at any other time during the ERM's existence – and demand surging after the Germany monetary union of 1 July, the ERM states made spectacular gains in export volumes to Germany (see Figure 5.3). By dramatically cutting their trade deficits with Germany, the ERM states were able to acquire Deutschmarks without deflationary action. Inside the ERM the Deutschmark temporarily weakened, and on the back of high Spanish interest rates the peseta rose to become the system's strongest currency.[2] But, whatever the short-term freedom of manoeuvre, the fact remained that the German economy was suffering inflationary pressure from a source absent elsewhere within the ERM states, and, given the Kohl government's choices, the Bundesbank was inevitably going to use monetary means to tackle the problem, whatever the ensuing consequences for the rest of Europe.

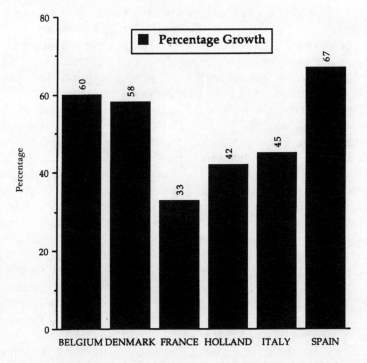

Figure 5.3: Comparative Percentage Growth of Imports into Germany Fourth Quarter 1989-Fourth Quarter 1990
(Source: The Guardian, April 15, 1991)

WHITHER THE MADRID CONDITIONS?: JULY – DECEMBER 1989

Meanwhile the potential benefits of the Madrid conditions to the Thatcher government's EC policy were lost within days of the summit. Whilst Thatcher was still in Madrid, she proclaimed that Britain rejected the Delors Report, and would be putting forward its own proposals for monetary union, even though she had just agreed that work on the report should begin and no alternative ideas existed. This revelation so took Lawson and his officials by surprise that when Peter Middleton first heard the news on his car radio, he nearly crashed into a tree.[3]

On her return to the House of Commons, Thatcher again speculated that the ERM might not survive the abolition of exchange controls in France and Italy.[4] If her rhetoric was not sufficient to convince observers of Thatcher's personal resolve on European monetary matters, on 24 July she sacked Geoffrey Howe as Foreign Secretary to try to strengthen her position within the Cabinet. In replacing Howe, Thatcher overrode the most obvious candidate, Douglas Hurd, and chose the less European-minded John Major. Since Major came to the Foreign Office without any apparent conviction on the issue, Thatcher clearly hoped that she would be free of the kind of pressure to fulfil the Madrid conditions that had led to their creation in the first place.

With his hand again weakened, Lawson was left by Thatcher to try to devise a credible alternative to the Delors Report. He decided upon a scheme of competing currencies, published by the Treasury on 2 November as 'An Evolutionary Approach to Europe'. Rather than proceeding to Stages Two and Three of the Delors Report, the paper suggested, the Community could make all its currencies fully legally interchangeable. Good currencies would gradually threaten to drive out the bad until eventually the EC might find itself with a single currency. Unsurprisingly, given that the plan did not offer the essential benefit which others wished to secure from monetary union, namely the end of Bundesbank hegemony, no support for Lawson's proposal was forthcoming. Other Community governments simply insisted that sterling's entry to the ERM was an effective precondition for Britain's voice to be heard on monetary union. In November Onno Ruding, the Dutch Finance Minister, warned that Holland would only be prepared to pay attention to British concerns on monetary union if sterling were inside the ERM.[5] Just as ominously, Pöhl cautioned that whatever its potential economic problems with membership, Britain could not expect to influence the monetary union debate outside the system.[6]

Clearly, the other Community states did not regard the Madrid conditions as sending any meaningful message on ERM entry. In the words of one official: 'The Madrid conditions were received with all the enthusiasm of Crystal Palace on a wet afternoon.'[7] Through the second half of 1989 the Commission, in a series of comments, criticized the whole rationale of the Madrid conditions that economic adjustment was necessary before sterling could join the system.[8] In its annual economic report published in October 1989, the Commission concluded that Britain would be better off inside the ERM and ending its 'excessive reliance' on high interest rates to curb inflation.[9]

Meanwhile, in terms of economic policy, Thatcher and Lawson were unable to use the Madrid conditions to create any degree of certainty in the foreign exchange markets about their attitude towards sterling. During July and August the press reported that Alan Walters was criticizing Lawson's monetary policy at City lunches. Although Walters vigorously denied this, and claimed that Lawson planted the stories himself, an indelible impression remained that the Prime Minister and Chancellor were bitterly divided.

At the start of October, after the announcement of a £2 billion trade deficit for August, sterling weakened again to hover just above the DM3.00 level for the first time since shadowing was abandoned. On 5 October the Bundesbank raised its interest rates by 1 per cent, and immediately Lawson and Thatcher agreed to a similar move in British rates to try to keep sterling above DM3.00. But any renewed confidence that the swift action could have brought was quickly undermined when, on the eve of the Conservative Party conference, the *Sunday Times* published a story that Walters had opposed the interest rate rise, and that Thatcher had only reluctantly sided with Lawson. Moreover, the newspaper alleged, Thatcher would not sanction any further increase in rates to defend sterling. If indeed Thatcher was prepared to accept Walters's advice to decouple monetary policy from the exchange rate again, with the ensuing inflationary consequences, then the Madrid conditions had been fundamentally compromised. As Thatcher did not deny the story, Lawson's position was once more being undermined just as he was completing the paper on competing currencies, which stated that sterling would become a member of a 'hard' ERM.[10]

Matters deteriorated further, when on 18 October the *Financial Times* published extracts from an article by Walters due for publication in an American academic journal, in which he stated that the ERM was 'half baked' and that the arguments for entry 'have never attained even a minimum level of plausibility'.[11] Since at the beginning of October the Labour Party had fully committed itself to early ERM entry, it was in a stronger position than ever before to exploit the differences between Lawson and Walters. On 19 October, charging that the credibility of Britain's exchange rate policy was 'being fatally undermined', the

Labour front bench called for Thatcher to distance herself from Walters's stance.[12] After Thatcher remained silent, Lawson concluded that with 'Number 10 constantly giving the impression that it was indifferent to the depreciation in sterling', his job was 'impossible'.[13] Ironically, on 25 October Lawson successfully secured Thatcher's agreement to join the ERM when the Madrid conditions, as Lawson understood and defined them, were satisfied as part of his competing currencies proposal.[14] But the day after this somewhat Pyrrhic victory, he told Thatcher that he could no longer continue as Chancellor so long as Walters remained in his position. After Thatcher refused to sack Walters, Lawson resigned, declaring in his resignation letter:

> The successful conduct of economic policy is possible only if there is *and is seen to be* full agreement between the Prime Minister and the Chancellor of the Exchequer. Recent events have confirmed that this essential requirement cannot be satisfied so long as Alan Walters remains your personal economic adviser.[15]

In the short time left for trading that day, sterling plummeted by 7 pfennigs against the Deutschmark, despite repeated intervention from the Bank of England and Walters's own resignation.

After Lawson

Whilst Howe vainly pleaded that it was essential the government quickly reaffirmed the Madrid conditions in order to maintain the confidence of its EC partners, Lawson's departure once more removed ERM membership from the ministerial agenda.[16] Although John Major, the new Chancellor, did publicly back the conditions on 31 October, neither he nor Douglas Hurd, the new Foreign Secretary, showed any signs of wanting to push the issue as their predecessors had.[17] Indeed Major's position could at best be described as agnostic: 'I don't think Mr Major was ever pro-ERM, in the sense that he came with a strong conviction that that was the way we should run our affairs.'[18]

Unthreatened by Major and Hurd, Thatcher felt free to express herself publicly in an interview with Brian Walden:

> The various countries in that particular exchange rate play by different rules. That is nonsense. When you join any system, you must all play by the same rules ... You just simply can't have a system with a currency like sterling, which is a big currency, which has London as the most open market, freest

market in the world, playing under that higgeldy-piggeldy set of rules.[19]

Asked by Walden if it was true that 'Britain shall not be going into the ERM for quite some time', Thatcher replied: 'That depends on them, on the gap between what they say and do.'[20]

In terms of immediate policy, Thatcher and Major abandoned the pursuit of exchange rate stability and inflation convergence, as prescribed by the Madrid conditions. Despite the slump in sterling in the aftermath of Lawson's resignation, Major neither raised interest rates nor ordered Bank intervention. After stabilizing at the start of November, sterling started to fall again in mid-November, and was trading below DM2.80 by the end of the month. Thatcher's response was to retort that 15 per cent interest rates were not there to defend sterling. When Major was asked in the House of Commons about his attitude to sterling's sharp fall, he refused to respond, and simply warned that inflation might now rise and that there was 'much to be done' on ERM membership.[21]

Monetary policy had effectively been detached from the exchange rate once again. Evidently, Thatcher and Major neither wanted further damaging rises in mortgage rates nor to increase the risk of a recession with an election drawing closer.[22] But, paradoxically, ERM membership would have offered them the interest rate reductions they desired. Outside the ERM they were not reaping the full counter-inflationary benefit of high interest rates because there was not a credible floor for sterling. In contrast, the ERM states were enjoying exchange rate stability for a lower rate of interest. As Figure 5.4 shows, British nominal interest rates were significantly higher than in the ERM states with the exception of Spain, where to reduce inflation the government was using its wide ERM margins to keep interest rates deliberately, and unnecessarily, high. Nevertheless, with inflation higher in Britain than in all the ERM states, a reduction in interest rates would have to have been accompanied by the kind of counter-inflationary measures categorically ruled out by Thatcher and Major.

The problem for Thatcher and Major was that their existing policy embraced the risk both of increased inflation through a depreciation in sterling and of a recession through tight monetary policy. If it had a rationale, this policy was based on two premises. First, that the means by which inflation was reduced was more important than reducing inflation itself. Thus, high inflation could remain until 15 per cent interest rates started to reduce it, and there would once again be no trade-off between interest rates and tax increases. Second, the policy assumed that with 15 per cent interest rates, sterling could not come under indefinite downward pressure; ultimately sterling must rise and act as a counter-inflationary force on the economy.

But whilst Thatcher and Major were abandoning the Madrid conditions, because of sterling's increased volatility the pressure from business to enter the ERM mounted. A poll published on 18 November showed that company directors remained overwhelmingly in favour of membership.[23] In the same month the CBI expressed its fear that unless Britain joined the ERM by July 1990 it could not seriously participate in the monetary union debate.[24] Responding to such anxiety, Conservative back-bench restlessness grew. Most significantly, Michael Heseltine raised his profile on the issue.[25] On 20 November he told a meeting of the European League of Economic Co-operation: 'Britain's absence from the ERM makes less likely a positive response by our partners to our more Atlanticist, free-trade objectives. The more we

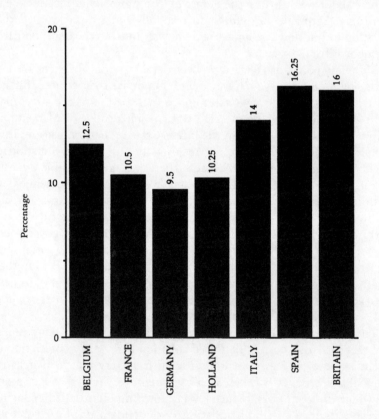

Figure 5.4: Comparative Nominal Interest Rates November 1989
(Source: Economist Economic and Financial Indicators, November 4, 1989)

have prevaricated, the longer we have denied ourselves a leading and influential role.'

The limits on Thatcher's and Major's freedom of manoeuvre were intensified by the fact that they were implicitly repudiating the Madrid conditions just as another EC summit loomed in Strasbourg, where the agenda would be dominated by discussions about whether to hold an IGC on monetary union. Clearly, some common ground did exist between Britain and other member states on monetary matters. On 1 November Britain and Germany had joined forces to impose changes on the Commission's proposals about how policy should be co-ordinated during Stage One of monetary union.[26] But on the most fundamental issues, Britain's non-membership of the ERM deterred other states from allying themselves with the Thatcher government.

If Thatcher's and Hurd's aim at Strasbourg was to avoid the creation of an IGC, then Germany was its most promising ally. Facing the prospect of absorbing 17 million East Germans into its state and economy, Germany was now less sanguine about the prospect of monetary union, and the Bundesbank was pressurizing Kohl to oppose an IGC. Yet only the now-marginalized Geoffrey Howe made any attempt to exploit the development, when on 1 December he avowed that there was a 'real possibility' that sterling would enter the ERM before the next general election.[27] Unmoved by Howe, Thatcher and Hurd appeared to go to Strasbourg simply hoping for the best. When the summit opened on 7 December it was clear that Thatcher was not going to find an ally in Kohl. The following day the heads of government agreed to set up two IGCs on monetary union and political union respectively to begin in Rome in December 1990, despite Thatcher's opposition. Casually dismissed by the other Community states, Thatcher was simply left to confirm that Britain would attend the conferences.[28]

Having remained passive on the ERM issue since his arrival at the Foreign Office, after the Strasbourg summit, Douglas Hurd now began to assert himself. Believing that it would be impossible for Britain to influence the IGC outside the ERM, he quickly persuaded Thatcher and Major to modify at least the presentation of their stance.[29] On 12 December the *Financial Times* published an interview with Thatcher and reported:

> It was possible to detect a change of nuance, perhaps an
> important one. For the Prime Minister would not give way on
> which if any of her well known conditions had to be met, to
> what extent and by when. 'There'll be no difficulty, for example,
> in France getting rid of her controls on foreign exchange', she
> said . . . 'We are obligated to join the ERM', she said, adding for

a 'when', when the terms and conditions laid down at Madrid were 'broadly met'. She went on, . . . 'I'm not looking at it as taking a whole page of graph paper and making a dot in each little square. Life isn't like that.' Was it her view that the ERM would break down with the end of exchange controls? 'No, she didn't think so'.[30]

On the same day Major told the Conservative back-bench finance committee that he was persuaded that Britain would benefit from ERM membership, but now was not the right time for entry.[31]

However, the change in public words masked not only the absence of any sincere commitment on behalf of either the Prime Minister or the Chancellor but ever-growing difficulties about how ERM entry could be reasonably achieved in economic terms. Whilst Thatcher professed that the Madrid conditions obliged Britain to join the ERM, her Chancellor's economic policy was not designed to achieve inflation convergence. Moreover, if the economics of membership were eventually to be sacrificed to the case for entering the system before the start of the IGC, serious problems would result. In this context on 13 December Robin Leigh-Pemberton warned that 'premature' entry into the ERM would damage both the British economy and the system itself. Although Britain had much to gain from membership, the Governor cautioned, there would be considerable economic risks if entry occurred before British inflation and interest rates were more in line with those prevailing in the ERM states.[32] Nonetheless, if 1989 seemed to end with European politics and economic policy pulling the ERM debate in different directions, the irony would be that during the next year Thatcher would finally do a *volte-face* for reasons to do with the latter rather than the former.

A PUBLIC CONCESSION: JANUARY – APRIL 1990

For the first few months of 1990 Thatcher appeared to believe that events were moving in her direction. Within Community politics, Germany, preoccupied with reunification, seemed to be procrastinating on monetary union. In March Germany blocked a Franco-Italian attempt to bring forward the IGC by several months. In the same month the Commission published its plan for monetary union, recommending 'binding procedures' on member states' budget deficits rather than the centrally set rules prescribed by the Delors Report. At an ECOFIN meeting on 31 March – 1 April Germany – supported by Holland – opposed the plan, and made it clear that their support for monetary union was conditional on it taking place on terms acceptable to the Bundesbank.[33] Meanwhile at home in the first weeks of 1990 sterling had finally stabilized without any increase in interest rates, and by February, it was again trading between DM2.80 and DM2.90.

Yet any hope Thatcher had that the ERM issue could now be laid to rest were soon shaken on both fronts. In April Kohl, without the Bundesbank's knowledge, promised the French government that Germany would no longer prevaricate on monetary union. On 22 April Kohl and Mitterrand issued a joint communiqué calling for the start of the process of both monetary and political union to take effect from 1 January 1993.[34] Whilst Thatcher dismissed their words as 'premature and esoteric', the Franco-German initiative unambiguously restored the onus for Britain to join the ERM before the start of the IGC in December 1990.[35]

In economic terms, Thatcher's optimism was dashed in March 1990 by another fall in sterling. In the first two weeks of the month it lost more than 4 per cent on its trade-weighted index. With Major taking no action to defend the currency, he and Thatcher evidently hoped that his impending budget would stabilize sterling, but then on 20 March he delivered very little save the creation of a new Tax Exempt Special Savings Accounts (TESSA). In the words of *The Economist*, 'when the City looked at the gap where macro-economic policy should have been, it took fright; sterling slumped'.[36] With Nigel Lawson returning to the public offensive to warn that sterling would remain weak so long as ERM entry was delayed, sterling then fell further in the wake of the poll tax riots of 31 March.[37]

Sterling's weakness left Thatcher and Major confronting deep problems to which their approach to economic management offered few, if any, solutions. Even after the currency had stabilized during the previous two months, inflationary pressure in the economy had endured, in part from the impending introduction of the poll tax in England and Wales from April. Now, despite 15 per cent interest rates, inflation was likely to rise further, at the same time as unemployment was increasing for the first time since 1986. In this context immediate ERM entry still offered Thatcher and Major the benefit of lower nominal interest rates for maintaining exchange rate stability. As Figure 5.5 shows, whilst the strongest ERM states were able to maintain a rate differential with Germany of less than 1 per cent, British nominal rates were 5.5 per cent higher, albeit that there was less differential in real rates. Similarly, Britain suffered from high long-term government bond rates in comparison to the majority of the ERM states. But, as in previous years, the cost of membership would be that with lower interest rates alternative counter-inflationary policies would need to be used to sustain sterling in the medium term; although Spain continued to use high interest rates they were used to compliment its overall counter-inflationary stance. At the same time, after a final balance of payments deficit of £23.9 billion for 1989, the question remained of how Britain could sustain a sterling parity given the deficit, and how the deficit could be alleviated within the constraints of the ERM.

By contrast, a credible commitment to join the ERM in the foreseeable future offered Thatcher and Major overwhelming monetary benefits. Indeed, since they were unwilling to raise interest rates or turn to alternative policies, pledging themselves to membership to strengthen sterling was effectively their sole counter-inflationary option. If the foreign exchange markets believed that they were committed to entry and hence a floor for sterling, then in all probability they would buy sterling to take advantage of high British interest rates. The Prime Minister and Chancellor would then be delivered an appreciating exchange rate to bear down on inflation, and could possibly enter the ERM when inflation was reduced in line with the Madrid conditions. At the same time, unless they were willing to sacrifice inflation, a public

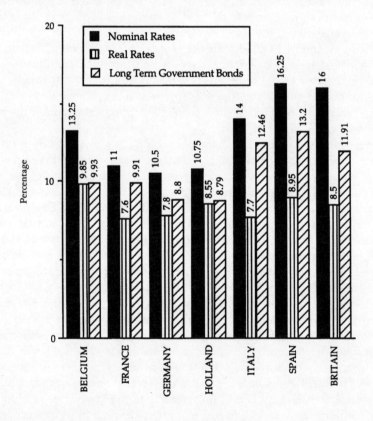

Figure 5.5: Comparative Interest Rates March 1990
(Source: Economist Economic and Financial Indicators, March 24, 1990)

commitment to membership was the only means for Thatcher and Major to eventually reduce interest rates and lessen the risk of a recession. Once a floor for sterling was established, then it could probably be defended with lower interest rates as prevailed in the ERM states. In sum, to all intents and purposes Thatcher and Major now possessed no means of achieving their macro-economic objectives without a genuine commitment to place sterling inside the ERM within the foreseeable future.

The Hurd-Major Axis

These economic and Community developments proved fertile territory for Douglas Hurd to work in. Although in the words of one official he 'never felt as strongly about it [the ERM] as Geoffrey Howe – I think he just believed in the inevitability of it', in the first months of 1990 Hurd had set out to convince Major of the value of entry before the start of the IGC[38]. Over a serious of informal bilateral meetings, Hurd converted Major to his cause, re-establishing the old Treasury-Foreign Office axis on the issue.[39] According to one senior Treasury official, mixed motives lay behind Major's reversal: 'He took a look at the position we were in and more or less decided we couldn't go on living this way. I think he was every bit as impressed by the politics as by the economics.'[40] But for his own part, Major was keen to stress the economic justification of his new position:

> The more I realised, day after day, that the most priceless gift
> you could offer British business over the medium term was a
> stable exchange rate and a stable inflation rate. And what was
> the best mechanism to achieve this, or the best and most proven
> mechanism to achieve it over the years would be the ERM.[41]

By March Hurd and Major were publicly expressing their support for membership. Hurd declared that there were strong foreign policy reasons for entering and 'of course, it is conceivable that a decision could be taken during the present parliament'.[42] In the budget, Major stated that entry was now a question of 'when' and not 'if'.[43] Five days later Major reinstated the Madrid conditions, noting that 'encouraging' progress towards their fulfilment was being made. He then redefined the inflation convergence condition, declaring that it was necessary for British inflation to be 'proximate' to the inflation rates of the ERM states.[44] On the same day Howe reminded his audience that the other ERM states were fulfilling their side of the Madrid conditions.[45] But given economic conditions, this renewed round of ministerial enthusiasm to join the ERM was given a cold reception at the Treasury and the Bank of England. Whilst officials feared that outside the ERM

Britain would be in a weak position in the IGC, throughout the first half of 1990 they were deeply worried that the economy was not sufficiently responding to high interest rates. Since ERM entry would have placed an onus on interest rate cuts, they judged, it should be delayed until a sizeable reduction in interest rates could be justified on counter-inflationary grounds, which on the Treasury's own calculation would be at the earliest 1991.[46]

Of course, the crucial question was what impact Major and Hurd could now have on Thatcher. Although he would have had over-whelming support within the Cabinet, Major opted to operate on a low-key bilateral basis, no doubt recalling the events of 1985. Moreover, Major was in a significantly stronger position than Lawson and Howe had been in June 1989. The Conservatives were now trailing Labour by over 20 per cent in the opinion polls, and could not offer voters more of the same on the economy just as the first poll tax bills were arriving. At the same time Thatcher's own position within the Conservative Party was weaker after having been challenged for the leadership in the autumn of 1989. Press and back-bench speculation was now growing of a serious second challenge later in the year, which this time would involve Michael Heseltine. With back-bench Conservative dissent on European issues generally, and ERM membership in particular, coalescing to create a new Positive Europe group, Thatcher could ill afford to lose another Chancellor or Foreign Secretary over the issue.[47] Neither was Thatcher herself likely to be immune to the argument that Labour's advocacy of ERM membership put the government at a direct dis-advantage on the issue. First, it gave Labour credibility in the City at a time when the financial markets were showing little faith in the Conservative government. Second, it allowed Labour to claim that it could make cuts in interest rates that the government could not.

Amidst these circumstances Major exacted at least some concessions from Thatcher in March – April 1990; the question is just what exactly did she agree to. In her memoirs, Thatcher denies any development took place at all, stating simply, 'when I saw him [Major] on the morning of Thursday 29 March I said that I did not believe that the conditions for our membership had yet been met'.[48] According to David Smith, Thatcher finally conceded defeat and accepted that sterling could join the ERM 'at the earliest possible opportunity', presumably before the IGC began.[49] However, the evidence is far more convincing, particularly in view of just how entry was finally accomplished, that Major per-suaded Thatcher only that they should at least *act* as if entry would take place by the end of 1990. This would assure an appreciation in sterling and make interest rate cuts possible, and convince the ERM states that Britain wanted to be a full-time player at the IGC. One Foreign Office official recalled that Thatcher did not actually change her mind until far later in the year:

> I think that the Prime Minister was only convinced quite late, when it appeared that joining the ERM would allow us to control inflation at lower interest rates at a time when the government's economic policies were under attack.[50]

Similarly, according to a Thatcher confidant, her private position did not change until September 1990.[51] Viewed as whole, it appears that Thatcher was prepared to economically exploit a commitment to join the ERM without making any firm commitment to Major or Hurd to actually do so.

JOINING THE ERM: MAY–OCTOBER 1990

Once Thatcher and Major had agreed to publicly commit themselves to ERM entry, their problem was how to make their words credible given that British inflation was again rising counter to the prescription of the Madrid conditions. Unsurprisingly, their solution was to redefine the conditions. At the Scottish Conservative Party conference on 12 May, Norman Lamont, the Chief Secretary to the Treasury, asserted that if British inflation was measured on a properly comparative basis to other states, it was only 1.5 per cent above the EC average.[52] The following day Thatcher pronounced that her conditions for membership were near to being fulfilled, and insisted that inflation convergence was taking place: 'If we calculated our inflation as they do in most countries in Europe, it would be almost 3 percentage points lower. So, if you compare like with like, we are not so far above Europe's average for inflation.'[53] In the same week Major told the IMF that British inflation would significantly fall by the beginning of 1991, and pointedly remarked that this would narrow the inflation gap between Britain and the ERM states.[54] On 17 May Major assured the *Wall Street Journal* that 'anyone who thinks we are playing with this as a gesture is wrong'.[55] The same day he told the CBI that 'I am sure we will benefit from joining the ERM and join it we most certainly will when our conditions are met'.[56] In a similar vein, a week later Peter Lilley, the Financial Secretary to the Treasury, argued that membership would serve as a useful anti-inflationary discipline.[57]

At the same time ministers sought to recover the initiative on the issue from Labour, presenting themselves as the only ones who were tough and credible enough to manage membership successfully. On 13 May Thatcher declared that Labour lacked the financial discipline to make membership work: 'The ERM is no soft option. You agree to keep your exchange rate within well defined limits. If it fails you have no choice but to raise interest rates, which is precisely what Labour attack us for doing.'[58] Shortly afterwards Howe returned to the same theme:

> I detect an expedient advocacy by Labour of the ERM as a
> substitute to a counter-inflationary policy, not a complement to
> it. Labour believes that the ERM will bring Britain an economic
> margin for manoeuvre that can be used to finance higher
> government spending and lower interest rates and so fend off
> the need for tax increases [under its policies][59]

Very quickly the new policy produced the desired effect. After Major's comments on 17 May, sterling rose by 3 pfennigs against the Deutschmark.[60] On 23 May sterling initially fell on poor trade figures, but then recovered on speculation that membership was imminent.[61] As Thatcher and Major hoped, the foreign exchange markets believed that the supposed commitment to membership provided a floor for sterling, and, therefore, wanted to take advantage of high British interest rates. On 12 June Major told the press that Britain was looking to enter the ERM in either September or October, and sterling soared to a four-month high.[62] All in all, from the budget to the end of June, sterling rose by more than 6 per cent against the Deutschmark.[63]

Although at the Dublin summit in July Thatcher nearly condemned the policy when she attacked the 'folly' of a fixed exchange rate system[64], through the summer Major successfully used carefully timed statements on the ERM to sustain sterling's appreciation.[65] By the end of August, sterling was trading above DM3.00. The problem was that, despite sterling's performance, inflation continued to rise, reaching 10.6 per cent in August in the wake of increased pay settlements and a surge in the price of oil after Iraq's invasion of Kuwait. Even measured at the underlying level, British inflation was still clearly moving away from the ERM average.

To make matters worse, during the third quarter of 1990 the economy fell into recession. From July to September: GDP fell by 1.4 per cent; manufacturing output by 1.6 per cent; private sector investment by 7 per cent; retail sales by almost 1 per cent; and unemployment rose by approximately 20,000 a month. With bank lending falling and corporate profits tumbling, business confidence was shattered. But the onset of the recession appeared to take Thatcher and Major by surprise, particularly given the advice they were being given by the Treasury about rising inflation. In the words of one Bank of England official:

> I remember going down to a monthly meeting in the Treasury
> in May 1990 and finding our Treasury hosts saying, 'Well look,
> we still can't see much evidence of the end and this boom
> actually turning down. Inflation is looking set for continuing
> acceleration. Have we really got policy tight enough?' I think in

saying that they knew perfectly well that whatever they might recommend, their political masters wouldn't contemplate tightening policy, so it was a free option. But we found ourselves saying, 'Well for heaven's sake there must be one hell of a lot in the pipeline, surely it can't be right to be doing anymore now.' And of course in a couple of months, as we know, the whole thing had fallen off a cliff.[66]

According to one banker ministers were simply caught unaware of what was happening:

As a clearing bank, we told the Bank of England to tell the Treasury that bad debts that started in an onslaught in the summer of 1990 were a bad omen, because normally bad debts don't get really going until the end of a recession. It was perfectly clear that something serious was happening, but the Treasury didn't see it. They really didn't see it. The Bank probably did. The Bank got us into recession by design, the Treasury by accident ... The Bank felt they were put in an impossibly compromised position by the inflationary boom ... And now even though it was going to be very costly – they no doubt had a clear understanding of the costs – believed that we must sweat it out this time.[67]

In the face of the failure to reduce inflation and the onset of the recession, Thatcher and Major had run out of time to make their policy work; they were left denying the reality of what was happening, as much as anything because their desire to reduce inflation through an appreciation in sterling left them unable to reduce interest rates.

Meanwhile the post-March public commitment to ERM entry had yielded virtually no rewards in terms of British credentials before the monetary union IGC. During these months Major or one of his senior officials visited the finance ministers of all the other Community states to impress on them that Britain wished to participate constructively in the debate.[68] Although the diplomatic offensive earned Major a significant amount of personal goodwill, feelings elsewhere in the Community towards the 'British problem' were changing. Some ERM states now believed that sterling's participation would simply impose costs on them, given the problems of the British economy.[69] On 31 May Pöhl reflected: 'Under the present circumstances, I don't believe Britain can be a member of the ERM with its inflation rate and large balance of payments problem.'[70] Similarly, one Commission official privately remonstrated: 'What makes the British think they will be doing the ERM such a favour by agreeing to join it?'[71] In terms of monetary union, other Community governments increasingly believed that Britain's non-membership of the ERM need not hinder progress.[72]

Rather understandably the new tone on the ERM issue could not dent the impression that Britain was not a full-time player in European monetary matters. This was all too evident when Major published a new British alternative to the Delors plan on 20 June – the 'Hard Ecu' approach. The scheme was originally the idea of Michael Butler from the City European committee. Under the blueprint the Ecu basket currency used in the ERM would be hardened into an international currency backed by a new European Monetary Fund. The Hard Ecu would exist as a parallel currency alongside the existing EC currencies, and would never depreciate against them. If a market for the currency grew, then in the long term it could become a common currency for Europe, and ultimately a single currency if governments so chose. The Fund would manage the Hard Ecu, co-ordinating member states' interventions against the dollar and the yen, and eventually setting interest rates for the currency.[73]

Although, unlike the competing currencies proposal, the scheme included the creation of a new independent monetary institution in the Community, it was received no more enthusiastically. The Italian and Dutch Finance Ministers immediately denounced the plan as inferior to the Delors Report.[74] Meanwhile Pöhl dismissed the proposals as impractical, and alleged that they would not achieve a monetary union.[75] Unsurprisingly, having invested so much political capital in achieving a single currency, France and Germany were not prepared to see it reduced to a possibility rather than a certainty. Even in tactical terms the Hard Ecu offered potential allies very little: by consigning a central bank to an unspecified future, it did not address the French desire to reduce the influence of the Bundesbank; and Germany was unlikely to warm to the idea given the Bundesbank's well-known anti-inflationary dislike of parallel currencies.[76]

If these difficulties were not enough, Major's and Hurd's ability to sell the Hard Ecu was further undermined from within the government itself. On 21 June Thatcher dismissed suggestions in the House of Commons that the Ecu could eventually replace sterling, saying: 'It does not mean that we have approved a single European currency, it says specifically we have not.'[77] Shortly afterwards Nicholas Ridley, the Trade and Industry Secretary, in a notorious interview with the *Spectator* magazine condemned monetary union as:

An all-German racket, designed to take over the whole of Europe. It has to be thwarted. This rushed take-over by the Germans on the worst possible basis with the French behaving like poodles, is absolutely intolerable ... If Britain was going to give up sovereignty to 17 un-elected reject politicians we might just as well give it to Adolf Hitler frankly.[78]

166

Despite Ridley's resignation, many assumed that Thatcher basically shared her former colleague's view, particularly when, a month later, she remarked that the substance, if not the style, of some of Ridley's remarks were in tune with people's feelings.[79]

With the economic policy rationale of the ERM commitment foiled and the European policy logic deficient, it would seem reasonable to presume that Thatcher and Major spent the summer doing some soul-searching about which way to turn next. But there is little evidence that any kind of strategic thinking took place on the issue during these months. In her memoirs, Thatcher alleges that she told Major on 13 June that she would not resist sterling joining the ERM, 'but the timing was for debate'.[80] By contrast, David Smith states that Major 'flirted briefly' with entry in July 1990 to coincide with the start of Stage One, but Thatcher rejected the option. Then in the following weeks, according to Smith, Major and officials decided that entry would take place during the first weekend of October prior to the Conservative Party conference.[81]

Evidence from officials, however, suggests not only that no timetable for membership was established over the summer but that Thatcher's willingness to accept membership at all was still open to question. One Bank of England official admitted to his confusion as to what was happening:

> I am not quite sure what was going on in 1990. I don't think there was a great deal of actual debate about ERM membership or the basis of ERM membership, though it is quite clear that the markets in 1990 were getting hold of the idea that the ERM was something we were clearly about to join ... There were no set pieces that I could recall involving the official machine. Obviously, in all the institutions with an interest in the subject, including our own, we were doing our best to assemble our ideas ... But we were not, as it were, concerting on a game plan such as would have produced this pretty blatant talking up of expectations of membership and thereby of the exchange rate as at the other end of town. We got to know it was happening. But it was not something that I was ever involved in discussing – whether it should be done, how it should be done, or whatever.[82]

At the heart of the strategic gap was the continuing tension between Thatcher and Major on the issue:

> There were really rather deep divisions within government, which actually inhibited the proper process of open debate within the government and the official family that would desirably happen. Because those who wanted to move in this

[ERM] direction did not want to show too much head above the parapet for her next door to sort of slide back. I suspect that was the position, and so that made it rather difficult to get very close to what was going on.[83]

The result was, in the view of another Bank official, the absence of any clear policy:

I get the impression, for example, the Spaniards when they entered the ERM had more of a strategy, in the sense that they talked the exchange rate down. One could almost see them leading up to it and there was a fairly clear indication of when in the year they were proposing to go. They stage-managed it in a way we did not.[84]

Yet, clearly, different people within government were thinking independently about the terms on which ERM entry could or could not be achieved. During June senior Treasury officials reverted to supporting entry by the end of 1990, believing that it was crucially important for sterling to be inside the ERM before the IGC began, and that wide 6 per cent bands could avert 'premature' interest rate cuts. Indeed, with wide margins sterling holders would face a substantial downward risk, which could justify a substantial interest rate differential over other ERM states as Spain had accomplished.[85] In terms of a central rate for sterling, the Treasury believed that this would have to be around the prevailing market rate at the time of entry, but judged that an 'appropriate' central rate would be around DM2.95, given that this was the average rate over the previous ten years.[86]

Meanwhile senior Bank of England officials remained sceptical as to whether there had been sufficient convergence with the ERM states, particularly in terms of inflation, to justify entry. In the view of one sceptic at the Bank: 'If we were going to go in, it should be on the basis that going in was going to provide a strong anti-inflationary discipline.'[87] Consequently, if sterling was shortly to join the system, the Bank believed, there should be a high central rate of around DM3.20 and wide margins to avoid interest rate cuts.[88]

Of course, the crucial sceptic was still Thatcher herself. Without having made any promises to Major, she was certainly open enough to the idea of membership to give some consideration to how it might operate. In the House of Commons on 1 May, she made clear her preference for flexibility: 'It is one thing to join an exchange rate mechanism with certain quite wide margins within which the currency can fluctuate, as has been necessary. It would be much more unwise to go to locked exchange rates.'[89] After the June Dublin summit, Thatcher again emphasized that there would have to be room for manoeuvre for sterling: 'You could have one of those weekend sessions when you altered the valuation of your currency. So there is no locking at all . . . and it would not work if there was.'[90] Apparently, Thatcher imagined that wide margins would be a way of operating a *de facto* floating exchange rate, but from which interest rate cuts could accrue.

Unsurprisingly, these musings over the summer yielded few constructive options in dealing with the economic crisis that confronted Thatcher and Major in September 1990. A policy which had been based on convincing the foreign exchange markets of something which was far from true now fell to pieces. With inflation having risen above 10 per cent in August, Major was forced to redefine the Madrid conditions to bolster sterling. On 7 September he insisted that entry could take place when British inflation was 'proximate to that of its European partners'. But the foreign exchange markets were now unresponsive to his words, and, despite earlier speculation that membership was only days away, sterling fell on Major's comments.[91] Within the next week even the alleged commitment to membership was thrown into doubt. On 19 September Pöhl suggested that British entry was unlikely in view of rising inflation, and sterling fell in response.[92] Five days later, on a visit to Switzerland, Thatcher was quoted as saying that inflation would have to fall several points further before sterling could enter the ERM.[93] With her alleged remarks increasing the pressure on sterling, and desperate not to raise interest rates, Major resorted to dropping the Madrid conditions. In a speech to the IMF on 26 September, he affirmed that the key factors in the decision were the prospective rates of inflation between Britain and its EC partners.[94] But such words now fell on deaf ears, and it took concerted intervention from the Bank of England, the Bundesbank and the US Federal Reserve to stop sterling going into freefall.[95] Only ERM entry itself could now convince the markets of the government's intentions and provide a floor for sterling.

Consequently, by the start of October, ERM entry offered Thatcher and Major overwhelming immediate counter-inflationary monetary benefits. It alone could stabilize sterling and allow interest rates to be reduced. Unlike Britain, after March 1990, most ERM states had been able to reduce interest rates further towards the German rate, and in Holland's case below it. As Figure 5.6 shows, British nominal rates were now 3 per cent higher than Italy's compared to 2 per cent in March, and 5.5 per cent higher than French rates compared to 5 per cent in March. British real rates, which were lower than those in Spain, Holland and Belgium in March 1990, were now higher than in any ERM state. Nevertheless, Britain would still be entering a fixed exchange rate system with inflation rising. Although Spain had entered the system in a similar situation, it had adopted the kind of counter-inflationary policies which Conservative ministers had renounced. The absence of such policies would be particularly pertinent in terms of wage increases, which were growing at around 10–11 per cent for the year. Only if the recession quickly dampened wage claims, and the preceding tight monetary policy and appreciation in sterling swiftly fed through into a lower inflation rate in 1991, would Thatcher and Major be able to avoid a broader reversal in policy.

In terms of the recession, immediate ERM entry offered short-term benefits but long-term problems. Since Thatcher and Major showed no willingness to sacrifice their low inflation objective, they would not have been able to cut interest rates quickly to respond to the recession outside the ERM. But by joining the system they would be tying monetary policy to the exchange rate at the same time as the consequences of high interest rates for the real economy were rising. ERM membership would make the ability to cut interest rates beyond the immediate future dependent on sterling's relationship with the

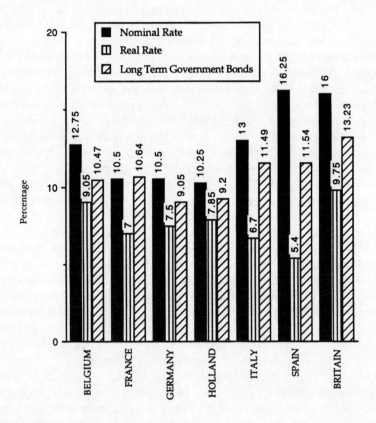

Figure 5.6: Comparative Interest Rates October 1990
(Source: Economist Economic and Financial Indicators, October 6, 1990)

Deutschmark. Whilst the recession would demand a reduction in British interest rates, German interest rates were likely to continue to rise, and make cuts impossible. Just as crucially, entry at the prevailing market rate between DM2.90 and DM3.00 was likely to cause serious difficulties, particularly given the size of the external deficit. Sterling's appreciation in the previous months had already further damaged the competitiveness of British companies, and hence contributed to the fall in output in the third quarter of 1990. By the end of 1990, the manufacturing trade deficit would stand at nearly £18 billion and the overall balance of payments deficit at £13.8 billion.[96] With the foreign exchange markets likely to judge that ultimately a devaluation would occur, there was a high risk that interest rates would have to be higher than German economic conditions would already impose.

Amdist the gloomy economic prognosis of September 1990, Thatcher and Major could take little more comfort from EC politics. Certainly, in a general sense ERM membership perhaps offered more reward than earlier in the year. At an ECOFIN meeting in September in Rome the Franco-German axis on monetary union was again fractured with only France, Belgium, Denmark and Italy still wanting a treaty commitment to move to Stage Two from January 1993. Indeed the Spanish Finance Minister presented a scheme for Stage Two to start in 1994 that incorporated some aspects of the Hard Ecu plan and interested some other states.[97] But ERM entry offered very little in terms of any axis with Germany of the kind which might end the drive towards monetary union. Whilst on 24 September, Pierre Bérégovoy, the French Finance Minister, reiterated the French desire for Britain to join the ERM as 'soon as possible', the Bundesbank still did not want sterling inside the system until inflation convergence had been achieved.[98]

In terms of ministers' capital accumulation priorities, the case for joining the ERM remained reasonably strong. The City was still overwhelmingly in favour of entry, not simply for its long-standing reasons, but as an immediate stimulus to activity. By October 1990 banks, building societies, stockbrokers, fund managers and insurers were all being squeezed by high interest rates and stagnant markets, and faced cuts in capital spending and jobs. With ERM membership offering lower interest rates and likely to buoy up the stock market, financial analysts believed it could breathe new life into those businesses driven by sentiment.[99]

Industrial opinion remained similarly disposed towards the ERM. But although manufacturing firms would obviously benefit from exchange rate stability and a quick reduction in interest rates, entry at the prevailing market rate was likely to hurt those in the competitive international sector. These companies would face the combination of falling domestic demand and competing abroad at a permanently difficult exchange rate, at the same time as unit costs were still rising faster than elsewhere in the EC. In October output was falling faster in services than in the manufacturing sector, but the risk of joining the ERM would be that exporters would reduce labour and investment and drag manufacturing industry further into recession.[100] As relatively small exporters, the service sector would be less directly affected by ERM membership. Nevertheless, although cuts in interest rates would be beneficial, the high rate for sterling would be likely to have a damaging knock–on effect on the services' performance. With output falling quickly in the service sector, it was looking to manufacturing industry to provide an upturn in domestic demand. If joining the ERM dragged manufacturing industry further into recession, then new demand for services would not be forthcoming.

Entry at Thatcher's whim

Against this background a decision that Britain would join the ERM was finally made in October 1990. At the start of the month Major, backed by Hurd, the Treasury and the Foreign Office, decided to push Thatcher for entry before the IGC began. In part, as sceptical Bank of England officials recognized, the Prime Minister and Chancellor had become victims of the expectations of membership they had created for a quite different purpose:

> We suddenly found ourselves in the autumn of the year with the reality of a decision. Either you go in and validate those expectations. And if you go in, you go in at about the present exchange rate. Or you invalidate the expectations, because if you don't do it, prior to December, given the political focus of the IGC, no one is going to expect it to happen for quite some time. You will get an enormous let-down in the markets. All that premium will once again be demanded, and in so far as the appreciating exchange rate has helped you on the road towards getting your inflation back under control, so that will be lost. And that really was an unappetizing choice for those of us who still retained some misgivings as to whether this was a timely thing to be doing.[101]

On 4 October Major, senior Treasury officials and Eddie George, Deputy Governor at the Bank, went to Thatcher anxious to persuade her to accept entry sometime before the end of the year.[102] One senior Treasury official described the meeting:

> We went to the Prime Minister for an informal discussion about this – she was going out to dinner somewhere; she had to get into a long dress, so the whole thing was punctuated by this

changing – with a view to joining later in the year. The party conference was coming up, and none of us wanted to join close to the party conference. I'm totally allergic to doing things close to party conferences – interest rate changes or anything. It was a Thursday night when we went to see her.

She said: 'All right, do you think it will be all right?'

'It will certainly be alright for the next six to seven months.'

The Prime Minister said: 'Could you bring down interest rates at the same time?'

We said 'yes' because we wanted to bring down interest rates anyway.

She then said: 'Well, can you do it [join ERM] tomorrow?'

'Well that would be extremely difficult.'

So we then adjourned to see when we could assemble the monetary committee and we said, 'No, we can't do it tomorrow, but we can have it done by the weekend.'

And she said: 'Goodness knows how we are joining at 2.95.'[103]

This suggestion that Thatcher took her decision almost on the spur of the moment is hinted at in other accounts. According to a Thatcher confidant, Thatcher privately reversed her position in mid-September during the time she was preparing for the party conference:

It came as the result of a lot of things: the state of the economy, the fact that inflation was going up. She was very keen to start getting interest rates down, and sensed it was a trade-off between her and John Major and interest rates. If he would announce virtually simultaneously, she would accept that it was sensible to join ERM providing we did so at a sensible parity ... I think that one of the reasons *why no decision was taken until the very last minute* is because a decision is in itself a highly market – sensitive thing [my emphasis].[104]

In the words of one Bank of England official:

Discussions most immediately associated with the decision itself were very closely focused on a short period of time. There had been quite a lot of fairly general discussion about it in the run-up. But then suddenly when things started to coalesce, [and] move very fast, it was really a *very* short period of discussions about things like [the] appropriate rate and [the] precise moment.[105]

Similarly, a Foreign Office official recalled: 'the Prime Minister's view on ERM entry changed only *very* shortly before we joined in October 1990'.[106]

In this manner on 5 October at 4.00 p.m. Major announced that sterling would join the ERM on 8 October at a central rate of DM2.95 with 6 per cent margins, accompanied by a reduction in interest rates from 15 per cent to 14 per cent. No doubt as hoped, Major's announcement squeezed the end of Labour's successful party conference off the early evening news and from the weekend press coverage. More crucially, Thatcher's insistence on entry at such short notice had rendered any strategic discussion about the details or presentation of the decision almost impossible. She apparently left the question of a central parity to the Treasury, who believed that entry would have to be around the prevailing market rate of DM2.93 at the end of trading on 4 October.[107] However, whether this was a correct assessment of what was possible is open to dispute. Asked whether it would have been possible to go in 10 per cent below the prevailing rate, one former Bank of England official remarked:

> It would have been very difficult politically to do that, but it is possible to do so. You call a meeting. You call around on a Friday afternoon – say we want to come in. We spend the whole night in Brussels and everybody argues and you probably wouldn't be allowed the 10 per cent. But since everyone thought the rate was high, I think they would have allowed it.[108]

But clearly 'everyone' did not include the Treasury themselves, for whom the timing of Thatcher's decision was almost impeccable. Even after Black Wednesday, a senior official affirmed: 'I was pretty confident it was a reasonable rate'.[109] According to a City economist with close links to Whitehall: 'The Treasury, Terry Burns, was very confident he had got the right rate'.[110]

Neither did Thatcher's decision allow for much discussion of the appropriateness of simultaneously cutting interest rates. Leigh-Pemberton, who was absent from the 4 October meeting, and other senior Bank officials were mortified when they learned of what had occurred. At one stroke the decision undermined the Bank's hope that wide margins could be used to maintain the interest rate differential with the ERM states. With rising wage settlements, the Bank was far less confident than the Treasury that inflation would soon fall as the lagged result of the previous two years' policies. At the same time it believed that for membership to be successful, it was necessary for ministers to send a clear signal to the markets that they understood membership to be a counter-inflationary discipline. Only when some credibility had been earned inside the ERM, in the Bank's view, could a cut in interest rates be justified.[111] In the words of one former Bank official who had long supported membership:

They snatched at the interest rate cut. They could have had the interest rate cut if they had waited a few weeks. But to do it at the time made the whole thing vulnerable. They got themselves off on a very bad start. It could not have been a worsely [sic] handled decision.[112]

Showing just how frustrated he was, in television interviews over the weekend, Leigh-Pemberton rebuked the interest rate cut as 'politically motivated'.[113]

Meanwhile, since Thatcher had been forced to accept that actual ERM membership could not begin until Monday 7 October, it is reasonable to surmise that she insisted that the announcement took place on 5 October. With no time for the EC monetary committee to be convened, Thatcher succeeded in precluding any consultation with the ERM states about the decision. As one Thatcher confidant described her attitude: 'I am afraid the attitude would have been "stuff them". There was no need for it [consultation]. It was our decision.'[114] But Thatcher's scorn for her Community partners left Hurd and the Foreign Office in no position to exploit the development. On hearing the news, the ERM states were quick to welcome it, and were genuinely relieved that Britain's isolation was over. The German government described it as 'extraordinarily positive', and the French as 'good news for Europe'.[115] But in private the other states were angry that the announcement pre-empted what should have been confidential negotiations in the monetary committee, particularly about a central rate. Since the ERM represented a collective responsibility to defend currency parities, they believed that a central rate should be arrived at by a mutual agreement. Moreover, some member states and central banks, led by the Bundesbank, believed that the DM2.95 parity that had been chosen was too high, particularly in view of Britain's external deficit.[116] One former Bank of England official reacted furiously to the absence of consultation:

Typical. After waiting after all these years, they just told them. If they had actually had a meeting, had a whole weekend, and said in any kind of an open sense: 'Look, we are thinking of this kind of rate'. I'm sure they would have heard from the others, at least privately, if not in open committee: 'Are you sure about this rate?' ... It was an extraordinary thing to do.[117]

The response of business groups was rather more fulsome. Immediately, the Chairman of Barclays Bank, John Quinton, responded: 'Thank goodness, I've been advocating this for five years or more'.[118] For its part, the CBI issued a statement saying that it was 'delighted': 'It gives a clear indication of the commitment of the British government to greater monetary union. Both ERM membership and lower interest rates will help to sustain business confidence in a difficult economic climate.'[119] Only the IoD was more cautious, reflecting that high inflation would make membership quite difficult.[120]

Nevertheless, within both the City and manufacturing industry, principled enthusiasm was fused with wariness that DM2.95 was too high a rate for sterling, given the problem of British competitiveness. Whilst sceptics in the City did not want to give rise to market jitters, manufacturing companies were more open in their dissent.[121] One spokesperson for a large exporting company commented:

> We would have preferred a rate of DM2.65. The current rate is far too high. The internationally tradeable sector will have a very tough time; there could be two years of sub-optimal growth, investment will be cut and I expect a sharp rise in unemployment.[122]

With some prescience one senior executive in another top manufacturing company denounced the rate decision as 'an unmitigated disaster'.[123]

To conclude, after Thatcher defeated her Chancellor and Foreign Secretary on a timetable for ERM entry at the Madrid summit, the Lawson-Howe axis was quickly broken. Thatcher was able to sack Howe from his position, essentially over the very issue on which the axis was based, without Lawson offering Howe any support. Then Thatcher used Walters to undermine Lawson to the point when he concluded that he could no longer continue in office, without Howe backing Lawson. With Lawson departed and Howe marginalized, Thatcher apparently hoped that the ERM issue could be laid to rest. But this outcome proved impossible beyond the short term, since Thatcher was neither willing nor able to influence the ultimate imperatives for entry in terms of either the government's economic or EC policy. Until the government readdressed the issue of ERM membership in 1990, it could not use the exchange rate as any kind of policy tool, and without this tool ministers would have left themselves with no means to pursue their macro-economic goals. Similarly, after the government announced that it would attend the IGC on monetary union and Germany indicated its continued support for the conference, there would have been little chance for Britain to make any kind of effective contribution on the issue either by itself or in alliance with other states outside the ERM.

During the second and third quarters of 1990 Thatcher was prepared to accept that her new Chancellor and Foreign Secretary should create and then exploit the expectation that entry was imminent. In so doing, she increased the premium for actual membership within the government's own economic terms of reference, since not fulfilling those expectations would impose new and immediate costs. The problem for the government was that this strategy meant that it entered the ERM at a time and on terms likely to involve significant short- to medium-term costs. At the same time those costs, and the precise circumstances of entry, undermined the possibility that membership could be used to strengthen the Conservatives' European policy.

NOTES

1 For a discussion of the process of capital liberalization, see K. Dyson, (1994) *Elusive Union: The Process of Economic and Monetary Union in Europe*, Harlow: Longman, Chapter 5,

2 *Guardian*, 15 April 1991.

3 N. Lawson, (1992) *The View from No. 11: Memoirs of a Tory Radical*, London: Bantam, p. 939.

4 *Financial Times*, 30 June 1989; *Times*, 30 June 1989.

5 *Financial Times*, 3 November 1989.

6 *Ibid.*, 20 November 1989.

7 Non-attributable interview.

8 *Financial Times*, 4 July 1989; 13 October 1989.

9 *Ibid.*, 19 October 1989.

10 Lawson, *Memoirs*, p. 943.

11 *Ibid.*, p. 955.

12 *Financial Times*, 19 October 1989.

13 Lawson, *Memoirs*, p. 957.

14 Lawson, *Memoirs*, p. 943.

15 *Financial Times*, 27 October 1989.

16 *Financial Times*, 30 October 1989.

17 E. Pearce, (1991) *The Quiet Rise of John Major*, London: Weidenfeld & Nicolson, p. 113; *Financial Times*, 27 October 1989; *Times*, 30 October 1989; *Financial Times*, 1 November 1989; 3 November 1989.

18 Non-attributable interview with Treasury official.

19 *Financial Times*, 30 October 1989; *Times*, 30 October 1989.

20 *Ibid.*

21 *Financial Times*, 29 November 1989.

22 C. Goodhart, (1991) 'The Conduct of Monetary Policy', in G. Wood, (ed.) *The State of the Economy*, London: Institute of Economic Affairs, p. 69; D. Smith, (1992) *From Boom to Bust: Trial and Error in British Economic Policy*, Harmondsworth: Penguin, p. 158.

23 *Times*, 18 November 1989.

24 *Ibid.*, 11 November 1989.

25 *Financial Times*, 29 November 1989; *Times*, 21 November 1989; 2 December 1989.

26 *Financial Times*, 1 November 1989; 2 November 1989.

27 *Times*, 2 December 1989.

28 Smith, *Boom to Bust*, p. 166; *Financial Times*, 9 December 1989; *Times*, 9 December 1989.

29 *Financial Times*, 13 December 1989.

30 *Ibid.*, 12 December 1989.

31 *Ibid.*, 13 December 1989.

32 *Ibid.*, 14 December 1989.

33 D. Marsh, (1992) *The Bundesbank: The Bank that Rules Europe*, London: Mandarin, p. 246; *Economist*, 24 March 1990, pp. 61–62, 122; *Financial Times*, 2 April 1990.

34 *Financial Times*, 23 April 1990.

35 *Economist*, 28 April 1990, p. 57.

36 *Ibid.*, 24 March 1990, p. 29.

37 Smith, *Boom to Bust*, p. 166; *Financial Times*, 27 March 1990.

38 Non-attributable interview.

39 Smith, *Boom to Bust*, p. 166; A. Watkins, (1991) *A Conservative Coup: The Fall of Margaret Thatcher*, London: Duckworth, p. 132; *Guardian*, 1 June 1992.

40 Non-attributable interview with Treasury official.

41 W. Ellis, (1991) *John Major*, London: MacDonald, p. 258.

42 *Financial Times*, 26 March 1990.

43 Smith, *Boom to Bust*, p. 168.

44 *Financial Times*, 26 March 1990.

45 *Ibid.*

46 Smith, *Boom to Bust*, pp. 184, 187; *Financial Times*, 10 April 1990; 14 May 1990; 21 May 1990; *Observer*, 7 October 1940.

47 *Financial Times*, 22 January 1990.

48 M. Thatcher, (1993) *The Downing Street Years*, London: HarperCollins, p. 719.

49 Smith, *Boom to Bust*, p. 167.

50 Non-attributable interview with Foreign Office official.

51 Non-attributable interview.

52 *Times*, 14 May 1990.

53 *Financial Times*, 14 May 1990; *Times*, 14 May 1990.

54 *Economist*, 19 May 1990, p. 29.

55 *Financial Times*, 18 May 1990; *Times*, 18 May 1990.

56 *Ibid.*

57 *Financial Times*, 25 May 1990.

58 *Times*, 14 May 1990.

59 *Ibid*, 20 July 1990.

60 *Financial Times*, 18 May 1990.

61 *Times*, 24, May 1990.

62 *Financial Times*, 13 June 1990.

63 *Bank of England Quarterly Bulletin*, August 1990, p. 332.

64 *Financial Times*, 2 July 1990.

65 Smith, *Boom to Bust*, p. 169; *Financial Times*, 11 July 1990; 20 July 1990; 26 July 1990; 28 July 1990; *Times*, 10 July 1990; 22 September 1990; *Economist*, 15 September 1990, p. 34.

66 Non-attributable interview with Bank of England official.

67 Non-attributable interview with banker.

68 Smith, *Boom to Bust*, p. 167.

69 *Financial Times*, 14 May 1990.

70 *Ibid.*, 1 June 1990.

71 *Ibid.*, 14 May 1990.

72 *Ibid.*, 22 June 1990; *Times*, 22 June 1990.

73 *Financial Times*, 22 June 1990.

74 *Ibid.*, 21 June 1990.

75 *Ibid.*, 22 June 1990.

76 *Ibid.*, 21 May 1990.

77 *Ibid.*, 22 June 1990.

78 *Economist*, 14 July 1990, p. 35.

79 *Times*, 16 July 1990; 1 August 1990.

80 Thatcher, *Downing Street Years*, p. 722.

81 Smith, *Boom to Bust*, p. 169.

82 Non-attributable interview with Bank of England official.

83 Non-attributable interview with Bank of England official.

84 Non-attributable interview with Bank of England official.

85 *Financial Times*, 12 June 1990; 14 June 1990; 20 June 1990; 13 August 1990.

86 Non-attributable interview with Treasury official.

87 Non-attributable interview with Bank of England official.

88 Smith, *Boom to Bust*, p. 184; non-attributable interviews with Bank of England officials.

89 *Financial Times*, 2 May 1990.

90 *Ibid.*, 2 July 1990.

91 *Ibid.*, 8 September 1990.

92 *Ibid.*, 20 September 1990.

93 *Economist*, 29 September 1990, p. 11.

94 *Financial Times*, 27 September 1990.

95 *Ibid.*

96 D. McKie, (ed.) (1992), *The Election: A Voter's Guide*, London: Fourth Estate, p. 103.

97 *Economist*, 15 September 1990, p. 57.

98 *Financial Times*, 20 September 1990; 25 September 1990.

99 *Ibid.*, 8 October 1990.

100 Smith, *Boom to Bust*, p. 177; *Financial Times*, 6, October 1990; 8, October 1990.

101 Non-attributable interview with Bank of England official.

102 Non-attributable interview with Treasury official.

103 Non-attributable interview with Treasury official.

104 Non-attributable interview.

105 Non-attributable interview with Bank of England official.

106 Non-attributable interview with Foreign Office official.

107 Non-attributable interviews with Treasury official and Cabinet Office official.

108 Non-attributable interview with Bank of England official.

109 Non-attributable interview with Treasury official.
110 Non-attributable interview with City economist.
111 Smith, *Boom to Bust*, p. 172.
112 Non-attributable interview with former Bank of England official.
113 *Financial Times*, 8, October 1990; 9, October 1990; *Times*, 9, October 1990.
114 Non-attributable interview.
115 *Financial Times*, 8, October 1990.
116 *Ibid.*
117 Non-attributable interview with former Bank of England official.
118 *Financial Times*, 6 October 1990.
119 *Times*, 6 October 1990.
120 *Ibid.*
121 Non-attributable interviews with City officials.
122 *Financial Times*, 6 October 1990.
123 *Times*, 6 October 1990.

6

The More Things Change: 1990–1994

I conclude, therefore, that as fortune is changeable whereas men are obstinate in their ways, men prosper so long as fortune and policy are in accord, and when there is a clash they fail. Machiavelli, *The Prince*

But you must know that we are all in agreement, whatever we say.
Turba Philosophorum

THE ROAD TO MAASTRICHT: OCTOBER 1990–DECEMBER 1991

Having stubbornly opposed ERM membership for a decade, Thatcher was to preside over only seven weeks of sterling's participation in the system, unwilling to use her U-turn to advantage on the monetary union issue. Determined to push forward towards a single currency, the Italian government, which was holding the EC presidency, called an extra European Council meeting in Rome for 27–28 October. There it hoped to set a timetable for Stage Two to begin in January 1993 before the content of that stage had been agreed, and to secure a formal commitment to achieving a single currency. For her part, backed by Douglas Hurd, Thatcher could see no rationale either to the imminent summit, or for taking any early decisions. But once again the Thatcher government lacked allies in the Community. In now characteristic fashion, at the Rome summit all the heads of governments, except Thatcher, issued a communiqué announcing that they would proceed to Stage Two by January 1994, and committing themselves to the irrevocable fixing of exchange rates but not to a single currency. Outflanked again, Thatcher retorted that the agreement was 'cloud cuckoo land'[1] and insisted that she would block things that were not in Britain's interests.[2]

Yet the reality was that, as Thatcher had already discovered, 'blocking things' was not particularly easy – the cost of isolationism was a marginalization the price of which Conservative ministers consistently baulked at. In this context once home, Thatcher, under pressure from other ministers, appeared to revert to a more conciliatory negotiating position. On 30 October Thatcher told the House of Commons, in a prepared statement, that Britain would press for the Hard Ecu at the

IGC, as a potentially evolutionary path to monetary union. If people and governments so chose, Thatcher stressed, the Hard Ecu could one day evolve into a single currency. But in answering subsequent questions, Thatcher proceeded to give full rein to her instinctive horror of the whole idea: people would not want to use the Hard Ecu, she proclaimed, and the opposition parties who enthused after a single currency were preparing to betray British democracy to foreigners. Writhing at her performance, Geoffrey Howe concluded that since Thatcher was making it impossible for Britain to negotiate effectively in the Community, he could no longer remain within the Cabinet. Two days later Howe resigned, and ignited all the anxieties of those Conservative MPs worried not only about European isolation but the Prime Minister's style of leadership. On 13 November Howe delivered his stinging resignation speech to the Commons, charging that Thatcher's behaviour on monetary union was risking the 'future of the nation'.[3] With Howe's speech precipitating a challenge from Michael Heseltine to Thatcher for the Conservative Party leadership, Thatcher fell to a party who now believed that she was an electoral liability, and on 27 November John Major became Prime Minister.[4]

By the time Major assumed the premiership and Norman Lamont arrived in Number 11 Downing Street as Chancellor, ERM membership was already posing difficulties for the government, with sterling trading below its central parity. Sterling appeared to lack credibility, in part because the interest rate cut which had accompanied entry had created uncertainty in the markets about just how committed Conservative ministers were to their new policy stance. At the same time the recession was deepening. During the final quarter of 1990 GDP fell by 0.8 per cent and manufacturing output by 3.3. per cent. Yet with Major and Lamont more than ever needing the interest rate cuts which Thatcher had presumed membership would deliver, sterling's weakness did not allow for any further loosening of monetary policy. Unable to respond with monetary policy and unwilling to use any other means, Lamont was left denying that the economy was in recession at all, and talking optimistically of a mild downturn.[5]

To make matters worse, on 31 January 1991 the Bundesbank raised its interest rates by 0.5 per cent, and in the aftermath sterling fell to become the weakest currency within the ERM. Quickly, opposition to membership began to mount. On 13 February *The Times* published a letter from six monetarist economists, including Alan Walters, arguing that unless Britain either left the ERM, or devalued within it, 'real disaster' would strike the economy.[6] But on the same day fortune finally turned in Major's and Lamont's favour, when a cut in Spanish interest rates reduced the pressure on sterling – the peseta being temporarily the strongest currency within the system – and allowed the Chancellor to cut rates from 14 to 13.5 per cent. Thereafter, the Deutschmark started to weaken against all the ERM currencies, as the dollar rose and the problems of German reunification increased. These shifts sufficiently strengthened sterling for Lamont to cut interest rates in half-per cent stages to 10.5 per cent by the start of September 1991 without jeopardizing sterling.

By the first anniversary of sterling's entry into the ERM, Major could reflect that membership had delivered the specific economic ends that he and Thatcher had been seeking a year previously. During the year sterling never fell below 2.25 per cent of its central rate, allowing the interest rate differential between Britain and the ERM states to be removed. Similarly, inflation fell steadily to 3.7 per cent in October 1991, leaving it comparable to levels elsewhere in the Community. But the overriding problem for Major and Lamont was that the abstract benefit of the interest rate cuts did not produce the tangible economic outcomes which they desired. The 4.5 per cent cut had not stopped the recession deepening through the first three quarters of the year, or unemployment rising to 8.5 per cent. For her part, in June Thatcher felt dissatisfied enough to disown her own authorship of the decision to join the ERM: 'If you fix the exchange rate, then interest rates and domestic monetary conditions go where they will. And finance ministers are left like innocent bystanders at the scene of an accident.'[7]

The net result was that Major and Lamont faced two increasingly large problems. First, although interest rates were now within a fraction of German rates, they were still high in absolute terms, and German rates were a floor below which British rates could not fall. Whilst the Bundesbank was setting rates to manage rising German inflation, the recession left Britain at the opposite end of the economic cycle. With the Bundesbank likely to raise its rates further, Major and Lamont were going to find it exceedingly difficult to give the economy any further monetary stimulus. Second, the 4.5 per cent cut in rates which had taken place did not appear to have been particularly effective. The extraordinarily high levels of personal and corporate debt created by the prior credit boom left potential mortgage holders and companies unwilling to borrow any further, even when given the incentive of lower interest rates. As the American experience of loose monetary policy and continuing recession was already demonstrating, debt overhang was changing the dynamics of the macro-economy and the rules of economic recovery.

Yet if the ERM was rapidly becoming a trap, Major and Lamont imprisoned themselves and the economy further by the nature of their overall macro-economic approach. They were no more willing to use non-monetary means to stimulate the economy than Thatcher and Lawson had been to control inflation. In the 1991 budget Lamont explicitly ruled out using an expansionary fiscal policy to assist recovery. Indeed he actually tightened policy by £295 million for 1991–92. At the same time, and with the housing market dead, he abolished mortgage tax relief against the 40 per cent rate of tax. To compound the overall deflationary effect of the budget, Lamont increased VAT from 15 to 17.5 per cent to finance a general reduction in poll tax bills. Without a policy framework which extended beyond interest rates, Major and Lamont left themselves looking to sterling's membership of the ERM to deliver what was in the circumstances impossible.

Just as importantly, the balance of payments remained in significant deficit. Although exports to the EC grew strongly during the first year of membership, this change was largely due to manufacturers taking advantage of high German growth in the wake of reunification. After this particular and finite boost to Continental demand, most manufacturing exporters would in all probability confront obstacles of competitiveness. For the whole of 1991 the current account was £6 billion in deficit. Whilst this figure was low in comparison with 1988–90, it was a large deficit given that the economy was in recession. Even with home markets depressed and foreign markets expanding, British manufacturing industry evidently could not sufficiently provide for domestic demand. In this light the DM2.95 parity could only tighten the noose around the economy further and ultimately make it difficult for Major and Lamont to sustain their ERM policy.

If the first year of ERM membership offered at best an economic mixture, in European policy terms the rewards of the October 1990 decision were no less limited. On 8 January 1991 Lamont published a draft monetary union treaty, outlining details of how the Hard Ecu could be created and managed by a European Monetary Fund. But within only a few months ministers were forced to conclude that they could not build on the interest shown in the Hard Ecu in the previous autumn, and dropped the scheme as a negotiating tactic.[8] They now appeared to face a choice between vetoing any treaty on monetary union that emerged from the IGC, or committing themselves to a single currency with the other states. By choosing the former course, Britain's whole membership of the Community would have been hugely compromised, but to decide on the latter would have been contrary to ministers' own preferences, and have risked permanently splitting the Conservative Party.

Whilst Major had promised that his policy was for Britain to be at the heart of Europe, Britain was seemingly isolated again. Only in May 1991 did Jacques Delors suggest the basis of a compromise, proposing writing a special clause into the eventual treaty allowing Britain to postpone any final decision on joining a single currency until it was prepared to make such a commitment.[9] With a summit impending in

Luxembourg, Major and Lamont took up the idea enthusiastically, and stressed that they were not looking to use the British veto, or prepared to be sidelined in the talks. Nonetheless, they would not under any circumstances, Lamont insisted, accept 'any changes to the Treaty of Rome that would bind us to move to a single currency or a single monetary policy without a separate decision by the British Government and Parliament'.[10] Having adopted this new position, at the Luxembourg summit Major joined the other heads of government in agreeing to leave any firm commitments on both the monetary and political union treaties to the Maastricht summit in December.

Yet having found the basis of a compromise, the months leading up to Maastricht revealed the full weakness of the Major government's bargaining position across the Community policy spectrum. Clearly, if Britain had remained outside the ERM there would have been even less room for manoeuvre than had already been achieved. As one Bank of England official reflected on the advantage that membership gave:

> I think we were seen as a full-time professional player rather than an amateur, as it were ... It must have helped us I think gain some of the Britain-specific concessions that we secured. It didn't necessarily affect so much perhaps the overall shape of the Maastricht Treaty. Where there were other people we could associate ourselves with, we had perhaps much the same weight as they had because we were full-time players rather than part-time.[11]

But in accepting an opt-out British ministers were effectively licensing the possibility of a two-track Europe and the peripheralization of Britain within the Community. When the Dutch presidency published a draft treaty in autumn 1991, it proposed a clause that would allow any state to opt out of the third phase of monetary union. Of course, this suited Major's purposes perfectly, and he found an ally in the Danish government, who wanted to hold a referendum before moving to a single currency. But with the other states opposed to the draft because they did not want to give Germany the opportunity to wriggle out of monetary union, the generally pro-European Danish government eventually switched sides rather than side alone with the recalcitrant British.[12] Consequently, only Britain was eventually allowed to opt out of the third stage. Revealing just how deep was the lack of trust in the British government, the monetary union treaty, put to the heads of government at Maastricht, proposed majority voting in 1998 on whether to move to a single currency, specifically to avoid any possibility of Britain derailing the whole project.[13]

At the Maastricht summit of 9–10 December 1991 the monetary union part of the treaty proved to be the least problematic aspect of the negotiations. The treaty outlined three steps to the achievement of a single currency. During Stage Two, to begin on 1 January 1994, member states would seek to avoid 'excessive' budget deficits, and maintain their currencies within the narrow bands of the ERM without devaluations. Each member state would implement steps to make its central bank independent, if it was not so already. Stage Two would also see the creation of a European Monetary Institute (EMI) composed of central bank governors to strengthen the co-ordination of monetary policies, with a view to ensuring price stability and to monitoring the EMS. By 31 December 1995, the EMI would specify the framework for the establishment of the European System of Central Banks (ESCB), composed of a European central bank and the national central banks.

At the end of 1996 the heads of governments would decide by majority voting whether at least seven states had achieved the following set of convergence criteria:

- An average rate of inflation in the previous year of not more than 1.5 per cent higher than that of the three best performing member states.
- An annual budget deficit of no more than 3 per cent of GDP and a national debt below 60 per cent of GDP.
- No devaluation within the ERM for at least two years.
- An average nominal long-term interest rate no more than 2 per cent higher than those of the three best performing member states in terms of inflation.

If seven states had achieved such convergence, a date would be set for the start of Stage Three. If, by the end of 1997, the date for the beginning of Stage Three had not been set, it would start automatically on 1 January 1999, even if only five member states qualified. Other member states would then be able to enter on achieving the convergence conditions.[14]

At the start of Stage Three the currencies of the participating member states would be irrevocably fixed at a chosen set of rates. The Ecu would then be substituted for those currencies at these rates, and finally would become a single currency for those states under the auspices of the ESCB. The primary objective of the ESCB would be to maintain price stability with the European central bank and national central banks, independent from Community institutions and member state governments. In a protocol attached to the treaty, the 12 signatories agreed that whether they fulfilled the necessary conditions for the adoption of a single currency or not, they would respect the will of the Community to enter swiftly into Stage Three.[15]

At the same time the treaty recognized that Britain would not be obliged or committed to move to Stage Three without a separate decision to do so by its government and parliament, but at no stage and under no circumstances could Britain use a veto or any other instrument that might slow down the process. If Britain notified the Council that it would not move to Stage Three, then it would not have voting rights on deciding whether sufficient member states had achieved economic convergence. Nonetheless, at any time it would have the right to change its mind and move to Stage Three if it satisfied the convergence criteria. Significantly, Britain would participate in Stage Two as if it were preparing for Stage Three like any other state. What this was supposed to mean in practice, however, was unclear. The protocol was explicit only that Britain would seek to avoid excessive budget deficits, submit to a formal review of its monetary policy and be subject to rules on balance of payments problems.

Whilst Major and Hurd heralded a negotiating triumph, the final treaty once again exposed their lack of leverage. If monetary union had been essentially a German concession to the French, the German government had ensured that a single currency would only be achieved on its own terms, which effectively meant creating a European central bank modelled on the Bundesbank. Moreover, the tough convergence criteria were going to impose a very significant deflationary bias on the Community for the rest of the decade. Since Britain was neither opting out of Stage Two nor wishing to renounce the possibility of joining Stage Three, Major and Lamont were going to have accept costly restrictions on their macro-economic options simply to allow themselves room for manoeuvre for something neither of them apparently desired. By preserving an *opt-in* to a single currency they were guarding against isolation enveloping the City, and by presenting an *opt-out* they could keep the Conservative Party together; but ultimately the monetary union treaty reflected only how marginalized Britain was in Community monetary matters.

This monetary weakness is further evident in light of the negotiating possibilities exploited by Major and Hurd on the political union aspects of the Maastricht Treaty. The Treaty created three pillars of a European Union (EU): first, the European Community itself; second a common foreign and security policy; and third co-operation in the field of justice and home affairs. Most crucially, the second and third pillars were to operate outside the institutional framework of the Community and with no provision for majority voting. Whilst the overall three-pillar approach was largely a French design, the British government had effectively combined with Italy to thwart Franco-German aspirations for a more supra-national approach to foreign policy and defence, and with France against the German desire for a common immigration policy.[16] At the same time Britain had found allies to oppose any more than a very limited expansion of the European Parliament and qualified majority voting in the Council of Ministers.[17] With the treaty also enshrining the principle of subsidiarity – that decisions should only be taken at the Community level where a compelling case could be made that this was more appropriate than the national level – Major and Hurd could plausibly claim that they had played a significant role in producing a treaty which stressed inter-governmentalism more than most believed likely.

The most seemingly intractable issue at Maastricht was the social chapter, with Major insisting that he could accept only the most watered-down kind of common policy towards labour regulation. For a time it appeared that the failure to agree on this issue might bring the summit to a halt and unravel the whole treaty, because other states were simply not willing to allow Britain any kind of opt-out. But as time was running out Chancellor Kohl brokered an agreement achieving just that, whereby the social chapter was dropped from the draft treaty and replaced with a protocol in which the other 11 member states committed themselves to making progress towards a common social policy. Given that this second British 'opt-out' rather defied the whole rationale of a common approach by effectively giving Britain a competitive advantage, the protocol was a significant victory for Major. His problem was that in return for German support, Kohl extracted a very significant price, namely a reversal of British policy towards Yugoslavia. Whilst Major and Hurd had hitherto argued, along with the French, that the territorial integrity of Yugoslavia should be retained until there was an overall solution to the crisis, now the Prime Minister agreed to back Germany's long-standing wish to recognize the break-away republics of Slovenia and Croatia.[18]

As 1991 ended, it seemed that Major and Hurd had secured a treaty which the Conservative Party could accept but which stored up problems for the future especially on the monetary front. They could sell a line to the Conservative Euro-sceptics that Maastricht enshrined inter-governmentalism, and that where it did not Britain had opted out. But by not renouncing the possibility of a single currency, Major and Lamont were going to have to invent a new strategy for managing the economy to deliver the requisite electoral benefits. To stay on the monetary union track as long as possible meant not only that the ERM policy was going to have to be maintained just as its costs were inexorably rising but forsaking the opportunity to U-turn on fiscal policy to abet an economic recover. Once that was understood within the Conservative Party, the praise which was heaped on Major for his

Maastricht 'triumph' would inevitably become a very distant memory.

FROM MAASTRICHT TO BLACK WEDNESDAY: DECEMBER 1991–SEPTEMBER 1992

Very shortly after the Maastricht summit the latent problem of the credibility of sterling's ERM membership became graphically visible. On 19 December the Bundesbank raised its interest rates by 0.5 per cent, and the Deutschmark soared. With all the other ERM states raising their rates accordingly, Major and Lamont were trapped in a Catch-22. On the same day as the German action, they were having to announce that unemployment had risen above 2.5 million for the first time in almost four years. To raise interest rates, in these circumstances, would have risked plunging the economy yet further into recession. But by deciding to do nothing they were disregarding the informal ERM rules and putting sterling under new pressure. Unsurprisingly, by the end of the year sterling was only 6 pfennigs off its ERM floor at DM2.83. Although the Bank of England's intervention eventually stabilized the situation, it was difficult to see how this was going to prove anything more than a short-term respite.

By acting as they did in December 1991, Major and Lamont were demonstrating that there was a ceiling above which they were not prepared to raise interest rates until a recovery had begun to materialize. Their problem was that such an approach was very difficult to reconcile with sustaining the sterling parity. Indeed, the only grounds on which the policy mix was tenable was if the Prime Minister and Chancellor believed that an end to the German monetary squeeze would be quickly forthcoming. As one Bank of England official recalled:

My recollection of that period and the ensuing months is that
people kept on thinking that German monetary growth would
come under control soon. The need for the Bundesbank to go on
tightening would cease, and there was a hope that the
divergence in interest rates which was opening up would halt
and if only one could hang on rather than following the market
each time, one might get through.[19]

The situation hardly represented fertile territory for fighting the general election called by Major for 9 April 1992. High interest rates apart, the rising PSBR required to finance recession-level social security payments meant that there was no real room for manoeuvre on taxation. In his pre-election budget Lamont was only able to create a new 20 per cent tax band on the first £2000 of income, and promise that his objective for the next parliament was to reduce the basic rate from 25 to

20 per cent. But deteriorating public finances and the commitment to achieve the Maastricht convergence criteria did not stop the Conservatives focusing their election campaign almost exclusively on Labour's expenditure and taxation plans. Charging that a Labour government would deliver a 'double whammy' of £1000 a year on everybody's tax bills – impossible in a system of progressive taxation – and an annual increase in the PSBR of £37 billion, Major defied the pundits to return to office with a 21-seat majority.

Whatever the truth of their lucky escape and the ticking of the ERM time bomb, the Prime Minister and Chancellor appeared to believe that the Conservatives' election victory would in itself both stimulate an economic recovery and strengthen sterling without any change of policy. On 5 May Lamont was sufficiently confident about the latter to cut interest rates to 10 per cent, leaving British rates just 0.25 per cent higher than the German Lombard rate. But if Major and Lamont were looking for a new dawn, they were quickly to be bitterly disappointed, as the fault lines in their economic and European policy approaches became fatally exposed. On 2 June the Danes narrowly rejected the Maastricht treaty in their referendum. The next day President Mitterrand, believing that the likely 'yes' vote would add legitimacy to the now embattled treaty, announced that France too would hold a referendum on Maastricht. Sensing that the monetary union project might now die, the foreign exchange markets concluded that the ERM states would now have less incentive to hold their currency parities, and swiftly began buying Deutschmarks. As a result, the Deutschmark rose, pushing most of the other currencies, and particularly sterling and the lira, towards the bottom floor of their ERM bands.

Major and Lamont's response was emphatically to avouch that their commitment to the ERM parity was inviolable. On 10 July Lamont declared that if Britain left the ERM:

> The credibility of our anti-inflationary strategy would be in tatters ... We would have surrendered. The ERM is not an optional extra, an add-on to be jettisoned at the first hint of trouble. It is, and will remain, at the centre of our macro-economic strategy.[20]

Under no circumstances, the Prime Minister and Chancellor repeatedly pledged, would they devalue. In their view, there was no reason for sterling to be weak in terms of economic fundamentals; indeed, their aim was to deliver zero inflation, and to turn sterling into the hardest currency in the ERM. In this respect they floated the idea of cutting interest rates below German rates, on the basis that Germany was no longer the best performing counter-inflationary state and, therefore, it was no longer necessary for those rates to be the floor for other ERM states.[21]

On 16 July the situation deteriorated further, when the Bundesbank raised its discount rate by 0.75 per cent to 8.75 per cent. Alone among the ERM states Italy raised its rate in response. As a system, the ERM now faced its most serious crisis for years. German interest rates were set to squeeze inflation out of its post-unification economy, but many of the ERM states had lower inflation rates than Germany and needed to boost their economies and thwart the threat of recession. Even those states which were economically closest to Germany and had faithfully followed every move of the Bundesbank had finally baulked at the price. If the aim of the monetary union project had been to tame the power of the Bundesbank, it simply had not arrived quickly enough.

But for all Major's and Lamont's bravura in the face of the foreign exchange markets, the systemic crisis could not disguise the fact that sterling and the lira confronted unique difficulties in the ERM credibility stakes. For sterling there were two obdurate realities. First, whilst the other ERM economies were still tentatively growing, the British economy was mired in its longest post-war recession, with real interest rates stuck at around 7 per cent. Although there was some evidence that the recession might be at least bottoming out,[22] any 'green shoots' of recovery were too dependent on oil production, and without policy encouragement were likely to go the same way as those sprouts prematurely detected in autumn 1991. Whereas it was, therefore, possible for the foreign exchange markets to believe that in the final analysis other states would raise interest rates to defend their currencies, it just about defied belief that the British government could. Second, it was open to very serious question as to whether the DM2.95 parity for sterling was either judicious or sustainable.[23] Not only had a large deficit in the external account persisted through the recession but the fall in the dollar against all the ERM currencies, precipitated by the tightening of German monetary policy, had left sterling trading around the $2 mark. Given that Britain had the strongest trading links in the Community with the USA, and that it competed in many more of the same markets as American producers than other states, British exporters were effectively being squeezed by sterling on two fronts.[24]

It is both against these economic conditions and Community politics that the options open to Major and Lamont in the summer of 1992 have to be understood. If they sought to maintain the parity, they were going to have to maintain interest rates at their present levels until the Bundesbank loosened its policy. Neither, as Robin Leigh-Pemberton later articulated, was there much point in tightening monetary policy further to strengthen sterling's credibility:

I do believe that it was very difficult for us to establish credibility through an increase in interest rates ... There was a sort of dilemma for us because the credibility of interest rates turned enormously on the extent to which the markets would believe we could actually raise them enough and sustain them at that level long enough to choke off the speculation without the effect of those interest rates coming through into the real economy in a way which was, quite honestly, going to be unacceptable and unrealistic.[25]

If, therefore, monetary policy could not be used to reassure the markets of the government's counter-inflationary resolve, then some other tightening of policy was necessary to try to sustain the parity. In the circumstances this would have required either a more restrictive fiscal approach or some kind of formal wage restraint, both of which would have represented a departure from the entrenched stance of Conservative ministers since the early 1980s. Moreover, the status quo would have meant accepting the constraints imposed by the DM2.95 parity and sterling's rise against the dollar on the possibility of an export-led recovery, just as Major and Lamont might have to deny themselves the opportunity to use fiscal policy to stimulate domestic demand.

By contrast, to have left the ERM in the summer of 1992 would have meant venturing into less predictable economic territory. Certainly, there was a reasonable possibility that an exit might have allowed for a significant reduction in interest rates, but only so long as sterling did not go into complete free fall. But at the same floating would have meant sacrificing the credibility in the foreign exchange markets achieved by membership, and risked, in the medium to long term, a consistent interest rate premium over the ERM states, as had existed for much of the previous decade. Of course, the depreciation in sterling and the boost to competitiveness was likely to provide a desperately needed stimulus to the economy, and given the severity of the recession, the inflationary cost of any depreciation was likely to be far less than in other circumstances. Nonetheless, in view of the previous experience of broadly loose policy from 1986–88, floating sterling was likely to put an onus on keeping fiscal policy tight to reassure the markets of the government's counter-inflationary resolve.

The final option open to Major and Lamont was to seek a devaluation of sterling within the ERM. Unlike floating, this would not have provided direct monetary benefits because Germany set the floor for interest rates whatever the central parity. Instead, the primary profit would have been a boost in competitiveness to stimulate export-led growth. In the Treasury model, a 4 per cent depreciation in sterling was considered equivalent to a 1 per cent cut in interest rates in macro-economic effect. However, the benefit of a depreciation in sterling was likely to be less inside the ERM than through floating, since sterling was unlikely to fall against the dollar in the case of the former option. Again, whilst the recession would have mitigated against the usual inflationary price of devaluation, policy was likely to have to have been kept tight elsewhere to bolster sterling's credibility at the new parity.

The problem for Major and Lamont was that whilst these second two options offered short-term economic rewards, they could only be achieved at significant expense in terms of their European policy. First, a depreciation in sterling would have compromised the government's ability to achieve the Maastricht convergence criteria, particularly the conditions relating to exchange rates and interest rates, which ultimately depended on credibility. Second, to accept a unilateral devaluation in sterling, in whatever form, would have given lie to the idea that Britain was at the heart of Europe; given the political stakes attached to the ERM parities, both before and after Maastricht, the end of the sterling and lira parities would have relegated Britain and Italy to second-tier status behind Germany, France and the Benelux states. This contradictory set of imperatives was well reflected in the division of costs and benefits in regard to ministers' capital accumulation priorities. Neither the City nor the service sector, which needed to feed off manufacturing export growth, could welcome a recession prolonged by a high and unsustainable parity. But if protecting the position of the City was a central plank of the government's European policy and the monetary union 'opt-in', then a depreciation in sterling would have extracted significant costs in these terms.

In practice, opinion was divided about just what was feasible in the circumstances. At official level there were some who believed that the crisis would still blow over. In December 1992, after the policy had collapsed, one Treasury official reflected: 'From June onwards, we still thought we could get through. I think we could have done, but for an unfortunate few events'.[26] But the Bank was always more circumspect:

I think by July our horizons had effectively shortened to that
period after the French referendum ... which if it were to lead
to a no vote would plainly cause a rethink. In which
circumstances it seemed to us likely that there could be a more
satisfactory way to restore order than if we were attempt to
bring about a realignment by ourselves before it. But the one
thing that was absolutely certain was that the French would
absolutely not change their Deutschmark parity before that
referendum. That simply was not on.[27]

For Major, European policy was paramount, as Lamont later bemoaned:

Monetary policy should be simply about controlling inflation, not about fulfilling political aims. The government's desire to be 'at the heart of Europe', together with the Maastricht treaty, constituted a huge political obstacle to voluntary departure from the ERM.[28]

This attitude meant adopting a dual strategy. On the one hand, Major and Lamont tried to reassure the foreign exchange markets with ever more hardline rhetoric about the sanctity of the parity and the pursuit of zero inflation. Trying to dispel the scepticism at such talk in the face of the recession, the Prime Minister and Chancellor secured the Cabinet's agreement in July to a new system of fiscal control in which a Treasury planning total would be sacrosanct in all public expenditure negotations. On the other hand, Major and Lamont discreetly started to signal, via officials, their willingness to participate in a general realignment of all currencies against the Deutschmark, which would in all probability allow for a reduction in interest rates. But, they made clear, they were not prepared to countenance any devaluation in sterling if the franc parity remained in tact.[29] As one Bank of England official described: 'We would have no difficulty in joining in any such arrangement [realignment] which didn't have as its starting point that there would be no change in the franc–Deutschmark parity.'[30]

Its Community politics rationale apart, the policy contained an element of fantasy. Not only were French inflation and unit labour costs lower than those of Germany but the French current account was in surplus.[31] Whilst by most technical calculations the franc was perhaps undervalued, sterling was overvalued. Implicitly believing that the position of sterling and the franc were comparable, one Bank official reflected ruefully how events might have turned out otherwise:

There was I think a view that if there was a realignment, it would have to be a general realignment, and that a general realignment would not be possible because of the *franc fort*. I would love to know if there were similar arguments going on in La Treasure and the Banque de France that they might have thought that a general realignment was the only solution, but it was not possible because the British could not agree to it. I suspect that there was something of that process going on.[32]

For those advising Major and Lamont, sterling was vulnerable due to a systemic crisis and not the limitations of British membership of the ERM on existing terms. The DM2.95 parity itself was not the problem, in the view of the Bank:

I don't regard our exit in September [1992] as actually constituting evidence of any particular sense that the parity was wrong. I do attribute it much more to the disturbances from the German shock … I'm perfectly prepared to contemplate the possibility that our Deutschmark exchange rate could be back at 2.90 in the next couple of years, not necessarily that that would be the basis of a parity.[33]

Neither, according to the same official, could there be any resolution to the crisis without an end to the *franc fort*:

I think it was a mixture of two things. One was that if the franc–Deutschmark parity didn't change that was still another prospective obstacle to come … I think it also reflected our thinking that if we were to create circumstances in which the other necessity, that is to say an easing of internal monetary tightness in Germany to enable the relationship with the dollar to become more satisfactory could happen, we actually had to look for a significant appreciation of the Deutschmark against the generality of ERM currencies.[34]

By the end of August, Major and Lamont could realistically do no more than hope to get through to the French referendum through ever more dramatic rhetoric. On 25 August a poll was published showing a majority of French voters opposed to the Maastricht Treaty, and the weak ERM currencies, including sterling, sank further. Three days later Lamont secured a declaration from all the ERM governments that there would be no devaluations. But, as sterling fell through its divergent indicator and then the DM2.80 mark, Lamont instructed the Bank not to intervene to defend the currency.[35] Only on 3 September did he change course and take out a £10 billion Ecu loan to add to the exchange reserves.[36] This provided a temporary respite for sterling, leaving the lira as the weakest currency in the system. On the following day Italy was forced to raise its interest rates, and the Bundesbank supplied the Bank of Italy with billions of Deutschmarks to support the lira.[37]

With the French referendum looming on 20 September, an ECOFIN meeting was scheduled for 5 September in Bath. Before the meeting Italy told Germany that whilst it would not devalue alone, it would consider participating in a broader realignment of currencies. Theo Waigel, the German Finance Minister, and Helmut Schlesinger, the new Bundesbank chief, went to Bath hoping to persuade as many states as possible to join Italy in such a realignment in exchange for a cut in German interest rates. But Major and Lamont remained adamant that they would not support any realignment given the French refusal to devalue. As Chairman of the meeting, Lamont effectively ruled out any open discussion of the subject, and pointedly refused to admit to sterling's weakness. Instead, he made a vain plea to Schlesinger to cut

interest rates unconditionally.[38] After the meeting terminated in re-
criminations, the finance ministers issued a statement pledging, hope-
fully, that there would be no realignment.[39]

The Bundesbank was furious at the outcome of Bath, since it
remained obliged to defend currency parities that it judged unsustainable. On 8 September Schlesinger informed the press that the Bundesbank could not indefinitely support the lira. The same day, the Finnish
markka, which was informally shadowing the Deutschmark, was allowed to float by the Finnish government. The following day the
Swedish Riksbank raised its marginal lending rates to 75 per cent to try
to defend the krona's peg to the Ecu. By 11 September the lira's position
was beyond redemption. Accordingly, the Italian government requested
a full meeting of the EC monetary committee to resolve the situation,
but, not wishing to discuss the possibility of a broad realignment, Major
and Lamont joined the French and Spanish governments in refusing the
petition, and shut their ears to what Germany might offer.[40] Consequently, on 13 September Germany and Italy were forced to negotiate a
unilateral devaluation of the lira by 7.5 per cent between themselves. In
response the Bundesbank cut its key Lombard rate by 0.25 per cent and
its discount rate by 0.5 per cent.[41]

Such a small cut in German interest rates was never likely to increase
Major's and Lamont's room for manoeuvre. By the end of Tuesday 15
September, sterling was on its floor of DM2.78. That evening Lamont
held a meeting with officials to discuss a plan of action for the following
day. The first line of defence, they decided, would be overt intervention
by the Bank, followed by an increase in interest rates if necessary.[42]
However, within hours their task was made more difficult, when alleged
comments from Helmut Schlesinger that sterling needed to be devalued
were released by the German press.

By the time the financial markets reopened on 16 September the
Riksbank had raised its overnight marginal lending rate to 500 per
cent. When sterling came under immediate pressure Major was forced
to turn a meeting he was presiding over on the French referendum with
Lamont, Hurd, Kenneth Clarke, Michael Heseltine and Richard Ryder,
the Chief Whip, into a crisis summit. At 10.30 a.m. Lamont agreed to
a request from Leigh-Pemberton for a 2 per cent rise in interest rates.
But by lunchtime sterling was on its deathbed. At 12.45 p.m. Terence
Burns, Permanent Secretary at the Treasury, Leigh-Pemberton, Eddie
George, Deputy Governor at the Bank, Robin Butler, the Cabinet
Secretary, and Sarah Hogg, the Head of the Policy Unit, joined the crisis
summit. Leigh-Pemberton told the assembled group that the scale of
the selling was totally unprecedented and it was now impossible to hold
the line.[43] With the policy in tatters, a consensus was reached, later
shown to be erroneous, that it was necessary to defend the parity under

the obligations of ERM membership until the end of the day's trading.[44] Within an hour Lamont licensed Leigh-Pemberton's request for a further 3 per cent increase in interest rates to 15 per cent. But reserve intervention totalling £11 billion – amounting to half Britain's exchange reserves – and 15 per cent interest rates were powerless to stop the flood out of sterling.

The choice confronting the group Major had assembled was now whether to request a formal devaluation of sterling or to suspend Britain's membership of the ERM. It does not seem that much consideration was given to the former option. Whatever the cost of exit in European policy terms, the consensus was that there was no alternative in economic terms. Lamont later told the Treasury and Civil Service Select Committee:

> I suppose in theory on the day I might have done it [devalue], but I had also seen what had happened to the Italians. The Italians had devalued on the Monday and had been under intense pressure ever since, and frankly, the game was up by Wednesday and we had no option but to withdraw.[45]

In a similar vein a Bank of England official insisted:

> There was no way a sensible new parity could have been negotiated ... If in these circumstances [the low dollar] we had set about to arrive at a new ERM parity that was acceptable to our ERM partners as not putting them at a massive competitive disadvantage – i.e. not too much – but was also such as to satisfy the markets that sterling had sufficiently depreciated – supposed we got down from $2 to what shall we say, $1.80 – that scarcely would have done enough in market terms. There wasn't actually the remotest possibility of arriving at a new parity before the wider scope might exist for a realignment.[46]

So at 7.40 p.m. Lamont stepped out of the Treasury to announce the suspension of sterling's participation in the ERM and the withdrawal of the final 3 per cent increase in interest rates:

> Today has been an extremely difficult and turbulent day. Massive financial flows have continued to disrupt the functioning of the ERM ... The government has concluded that Britain's best interests are served by suspending our membership of the Exchange Rate Mechanism.[47]

The Chancellor next convened the EC monetary committee, where British officials unsuccessfully asked that the whole ERM be suspended until after the French referendum. Given the British decision to leave, the Italian government reluctantly decided that the lira, hovering at the bottom of its new bands, would also have to be withdrawn from the system. At the same time the monetary committee agreed to a devaluation of the Spanish peseta.

Suspending sterling's membership of the ERM left Major and Lamont facing an uncertain future in both economic and European policy terms. Just whether Britain was now going to be effectively relegated to a second tier in the EC was going to depend on the outcome of the French referendum the following Sunday. If a 'yes' French vote and the ejection of sterling and the lira from the system stabilized the ERM, then Major's 'heart of Europe' policy would be fatally compromised; the 'opt-in' to monetary union would be redundant if Britain was left behind in the convergence criteria stakes. But if the French voted 'no', or the currency turbulence continued anyway, then the whole Maastricht project might well be doomed. Meanwhile the future of the economy, and just what benefits could be gained from floating, would be conditional on how the foreign exchange markets responded to sterling.

THE ILLUSION OF LIBERATION: SEPTEMBER 1990–AUGUST 1993

Faced with the ruins of the ERM policy, Lamont returned interest rates to 10 per cent on 17 September. By the end of the week, sterling was trading at DM2.61, 6 per cent below its previous ERM floor. The most immediate question for Major and Lamont now was whether they wished to try to salvage the policy and look for a quick return to the ERM, or completely abandon ship. When Lamont quickly remarked that he was 'singing in the bath', and 'we will now have a British economic policy for the needs of the British economy', it was clear that he was not disposed to seeing life outside the ERM as anything other than a liberation.[48] Meanwhile the Cabinet heavyweights, Michael Heseltine and Kenneth Clarke, were forcefully telling the Prime Minister that sterling could not expect to survive long outside the ERM, and that the government needed to act to restore its Community credentials.[49] Before long, however, it was apparent that Major had decided that the best course was to make a virtue out of the Black Wednesday disaster, as he proclaimed 'a growth strategy is what the country wants and a growth strategy is what we are going to get'.[50]

Although this U-turn did not stop a string of pronouncements about the conditions on which Britain would return to the ERM, Major's and

Lamont's words progressively betrayed just how much had changed. Four days after Black Wednesday Lamont told the IMF:

> The United Kingdom will resume membership of the ERM as soon as conditions allow. But before sterling rejoins the ERM, we will need to reflect carefully on the lessons of the past two years, and in particular of the past few months.[51]

On 24 September Major informed the House of Commons that he could not see how sterling 'could readily return to the mechanism' until its 'fault lines' had been repaired.[52] The Chancellor went further and asserted three specific conditions for re-entry: first, that the foreign exchange markets stabilize; second, that there be a review of the whole intervention and co-operation procedures of the system; and third, that the Germany and British economies move into step with each other.[53] By 8 October Lamont was adding another condition, namely that the wide differential between interest rates in the USA and in Germany narrow.[54] On 16 November the prospect of an early ERM return receded yet further, as, in evidence to the Treasury Select Committee, Lamont stuck on a fifth condition–the complete end of the recession.[55]

But if the re-entry option was quickly ruled out, there was no unanimity between Major and Lamont as to what a new policy should be. Whilst Lamont told the IMF that monetary policy would be guided by 'a range of indicators', including the exchange rate, a series of remarks clearly exhibited a personal preference to return to the monetary targets of the early Thatcher years.[56] In evidence to the Treasury Select Committee on 12 October, Lamont revealingly remarked:

> We are going to have a target for narrow money ... Although M0 is not a leading or predictive indicator, it is in my opinion a very good guide to the current trend of money GDP. I personally believe, although many people outside dispute this, that it has an excellent and very good track record. I attach a lot of importance to M0.[57]

But in practice the core of the post-Black Wednesday policy was to allow sterling to float downwards and to cut interest rates aggressively to achieve a recovery as soon as possible. Between 17 September and 23 January 1993 the Chancellor cut interest rates from 10 to 6 per cent. At its lowest point, at the end of February 1993, sterling was trading around DM2.30, a 17 per cent depreciation of its value at the start of September 1992.

As a counter-inflationary anchor against this loosening of policy, Major and Lamont set in place a new monetary framework backed by a tight fiscal policy. In a letter to the Treasury Select Committee on 8 October and his Mansion House address on the 29 October, Lamont announced an inflation target of 1–4 per cent for the remainder of the Parliament, and for the long term of less than 2 per cent. To monitor this target, he was asking the Bank of England to produce quarterly inflation reports, which would not be subject to Treasury editing. Operationally, however, this meant that policy was to be based on the discretionary judgement of the Chancellor about the performance of the 'range of indicators' previously described.[58]

If the monetary policy now effectively mounted to 'trust Norman and the Bank', the reins of fiscal policy were drawn far more tightly as a counter-inflationary anchor. Although the 1992 autumn statement included a £4 billion recovery package aimed at industry, housing and capital investment, the new public expenditure control system was being rigorously enforced by the Chancellor. In order to meet the expenditure figure for 1992–93 set in the previous July, Lamont made significant cuts in defence and transport, and imposed a ceiling for increases in public sector pay of 1.5 per cent. By the start of 1993, the Treasury was predicting a PSBR of £50 billion for the year, putting further fiscal tightening firmly on the economic agenda. The problem was that tax increases now risked choking the tentative recovery that was starting to take place, whatever the anti-inflationary benefits. In this context the March 1993 budget introduced a package of indirect and direct tax increases to come into effect one year later. These taxes included: the imposition of VAT on fuel; an increase in National Insurance contributions and excise duties; and restrictions on mortgage tax relief and the married couple's allowance. The Chancellor also held out the prospect of a further fiscal squeeze later in the year in a new unified budget, in which expenditure and taxation decisions would be taken together.

Once again British policy was markedly different from those Community states who belonged to the ERM. The turbulence in the foreign exchange markets had not ended with sterling's and the lira's ejection from the ERM, but other ERM states either used interest rate increases to stabilize their currencies – most notably France on 23 September 1992 – or had devalued within the system. Between 17 September 1992 and the end of June 1993 Ireland devalued, as did Spain and Portugal twice. This left a hard core of ERM currency parities intact, but with everybody remaining chained by the level of German interest rates. In these circumstances, as Figure 6.1 shows, Britain now enjoyed significantly lower nominal and real interest rates than the ERM states. Given these monetary differentials, as Figure 6.2 indicates, it was not surprising that during 1993 a British economic recovery began just as the ERM states moved into recession. What low interest rates achieved was a consumer-led recovery, primarily by reducing the huge debt burden of households and firms. So by the second quarter of 1993, non-oil GDP was growing 0.4 per cent above the final quarter of 1992, unemployment was falling and Lamont could pronounce the recession dead.

But if ministers wanted to trumpet the benefits of floating, some awkward realities remained. Lower interest rates and the emerging economic recovery were not producing a political recovery for the Conservatives battered in the opinion polls by the recession, Black Wednesday and a widespread public revolt over proposed coalmine closures. On 6 May the Conservatives lost a by-election in Newbury to the Liberal Democrats on a swing of over 28 per cent, and suffered an ignominious loss of control of 15 councils in local elections. Meanwhile the Prime Minister-Chancellor axis had been fatally damaged by the events leading up to Black Wednesday. Apparently rebuffed over a return to monetarism, and having adopted a bunker mentality in the

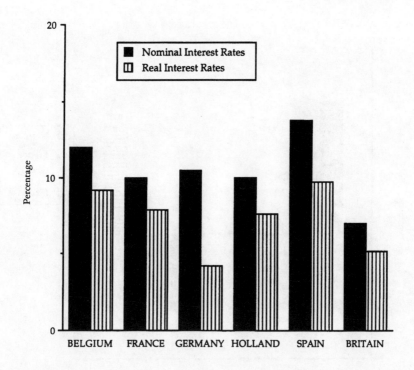

Figure 6.1: Comparative Nominal and Real Interest Rates March 1993
(Source: Economist Economic and Financial Indicators, March 27, 1993)

Treasury during the last months of 1992, Lamont now became an easy sacrificial victim for Major's desperate efforts to restore the government's credibility, and Kenneth Clarke was made Chancellor.[59]

Whilst in September 1992 Clarke had been one of the prime movers arguing for a quick return to the ERM, by the time he moved to 11 Downing Street, he appeared to have accepted the permanency of floating, at least for the medium term. Whether his personal preferences remained unaltered or not, any change in direction from the new Chancellor would have provoked uproar within certain quarters of the Cabinet and much of the back benches. As Andy McSmith comments: '[It had become] an article of faith on the party's right-wing that the economy had been in recession until 16 September but had recovered on that day and had been growing ever since.'[60] In one of his first television interviews after taking office, Clarke affirmed his commitment to the ERM in principle but ruled out a return to the system before the end of the existing Parliament.[61] Underlying his acceptance of the existing policy, Clarke told an ECOFIN meeting on 7 June that 'conditions in

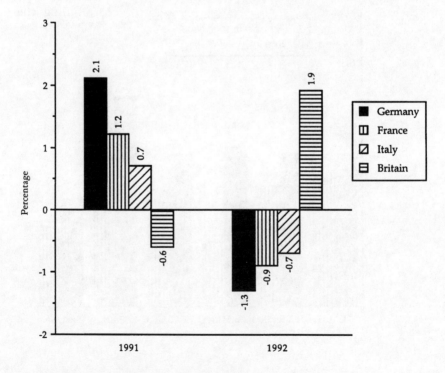

Figure 6.2: Comparative Growth 1992-1993
(Source: Economic Outlook)

Germany are so far out of line at the moment that the conditions are not there for anyone to talk about rejoining the ERM'.[62]

The Problem of Maastricht

The dramatic change in economic policy ushered in by Black Wednesday could not but raise questions about Britain's future 'at the heart of Europe'. In the immediate aftermath Major seemed prepared to take the U-turn to its logical conclusion and abandon the commitment to ratify the Maastricht Treaty. On 20 September Major told a television interviewer that Britain would ratify Maastricht only when 'popular concerns' about EC bureaucracy, the need to reform the ERM and the 'Danish problem' had been dealt with.[63] But after threats from the French and German governments that if Britain and Denmark prevaricated, a hard core would unilaterally go ahead in areas such as monetary union, Major swiftly promised his Community partners that Britain would press ahead with ratification later in the year.[64] But moving forward outside the ERM and sticking with Maastricht left a paradox at the centre of European policy. If the negotiations in December 1991 gave Major a potential 'opt-in' on monetary union, fulfilling the convergence criteria, without which the opt-in was redundant, was going to be practically impossible outside the ERM. Only if sterling were to rejoin the ERM by the end of 1994 would Britain have the realistic option of participating in any single currency which began in 1997.

This apparently incoherent approach could be rationalized on two assumptions. First, that the Maastricht project as it related to a single currency was unravelling. At the Edinburgh summit in December 1992 Denmark negotiated an 'opt-out' on monetary union, along with a common defence policy, until 1996. Meanwhile the ongoing turbulence in the foreign exchange markets and the series of devaluations that took place in late 1992 and the first half of 1993 provided reasons to believe that other currencies might ultimately go the way of sterling and the lira. Moreover, as the Bundesbank was proving so slow to cut interest rates and the monetary costs of defending the ERM parities took their toll in a Continental recession, so the other Community states would find their borrowing rising to levels incompatible with the convergence criteria. In December 1991, Major had told the House of Commons:

> Let there be no doubt: Britain is among those which will meet the strict convergence conditions. We took the lead in setting them and will continue to be involved at every stage leading up to the decision whether to launch a single currency.[65]

But on 4 November 1992 the Prime Minister proclaimed to MPs:

The timetable that was set at Maastricht was too ambitious. I think that it is becoming increasingly apparent to nations across Europe as week succeeds week. We were, therefore, right to have our special protocol. It is doubtful that the necessary degree of economic convergence will be there in the time scale set out in the treaty, and I have made that point to the House on many occasions.[66]

If monetary union then died its own death, in ministers' calculations, what would be left would be the three-pillared approach of Maastricht, sufficiently inter-governmental in emphasis to ensure than any re-negotiation was likely to be unfavourable to their interests.

Second, even if unilateralism in economic policy did compromise the desire to be at the 'heart of Europe', the imperatives of party manage-ment left no other option. Whilst back-bench opinion had started to turn against Maastricht in the aftermath of the Danish 'no', with 84 Conservative MPs signing an early day motion calling for a 'fresh start' on the treaty, after Black Wednesday opposition to all European monetary matters intensified.[67] On 4 November the government scraped through by three votes on a paving motion to reintroduce the Maastricht Bill into the House of Commons for its third reading. Moreover, even such a narrow victory was achieved only after Major succeeded in creating the impression that the issue was one of con-fidence, and with a last-minute concession that there would be no vote on the bill until after the outcome of the second Danish referendum. Although with Labour's abstention the government was able to secure relatively easily the ratification of the main Maastricht Treaty in 1993, a Labour amendment ensured that the final ratification was dependent on a separate vote on the social chapter protocol. With the Conservative Euro-rebels willing to join forces with the opposition parties and vote for Britain to be effectively reinstated into the social chapter, Major and his Cabinet were faced with a ticking timebomb. Despite intense pressure from the party whips, on 22 July the government was defeated on the substantive motion to accept the social chapter protocol. Major was forced to hold a vote of confidence the next day to secure ratification of the treaty, and his threat of a general election was sufficient to bring all but one of the rebels back into line.

What the Cabinet's battle to ratify Maastricht amply demonstrated was that for many Conservative MPs the ERM represented the scapegoat for all their political troubles. As one Euro-rebel described his view of the events of 1992–93 on the electorate:

Interest rates went up to a point where our PSBR was high . . . people were driven out of business, they lost their homes. Then we brought in huge tranches of taxation, including VAT on gas and fuel. I mean, it was a double reverse whammy; they're trapped in negative equity in their houses because of the ERM ... I don't blame them for being furious. I'd be furious. And why? All because of the absolutely blind stupid policy of staying in the ERM.[68]

To even think about returning to the ERM or monetary union, in this view, was absurd:

> I don't think anyone who thought we could go back into the ERM could possibly be other than consigned to a lunatic asylum ... There's no chance whatsoever of any ERM or EMU ever working. We'll end up with massive unemployment, the single currency will be under as much attack as the yen or the dollar, but more so because of the flight of capital ... It will be constantly open to speculation. There'll be high unemployment, riots in parts of Europe and the return of fascism ... It's pure madness.[69]

Whatever the incoherencies in the Cabinet's economic and European policy approaches, with a party in this mood and crucially a small Commons majority, there was simply very little room for manoeuvre.

Yet for all Major's problems with his party, in the summer of 1993 salvation seemed to beckon. Even after the devaluations of the punt, the peseta and the escudo, the ERM was now tottering on the edge of further crisis. With the Bundesbank still keeping German monetary policy tight, the ERM states were slipping ever deeper into recession. After French unemployment rose to a record 11.5 per cent, criticism of the *franc fort* mounted within the ranks of the governing Gaullist party. Increasingly desperate, on 21 June the French government cut short-term interest rates below German levels for the first time. Trumpeting France's now consistently low inflation performance on all indicators, French ministers began ruminating that the franc might replace the Deutschmark as the anchor currency of the ERM.[70] But when the French Finance Minister publicly called for co-ordinated interest rate cuts in Germany and France, the German government cancelled a top-level bilateral economic meeting.[71] As if nemesis for French presumption, by the end of the month, the franc had slipped towards the bottom of its ERM range.

Matters were made worse, when on 1 July the Bundesbank finally cut its discount rate by 0.5 per cent, but France could only shave 0.25 per cent off its relevant rates. With the franc under severe pressure, the Bundesbank became notably less firm in its willingness to defend the currency than it had been in 1992. Witnessing that France was trapped in the same recession-driven dilemma as Britain a year earlier, the markets concluded that France would not raise its rates again; the future of the French economy lay in the hands of the Bundesbank. French hopes were raised when the Bundesbank cut its repo rate twice in a week, yielding the expectation that the key discount rate would be cut at the next council meeting. But on 29 July the Bundesbank cut only its Lombard rate by 0.5 per cent and left the discount rate unchanged. During the next day and a half most of the ERM currencies, including the franc, crashed to the very bottom of their ranges. By the end of trading on Friday 3 August, it was obvious that most of the parities would not survive the inevitable onslaught of the next week. With the ERM on the brink of collapse, EC finance ministers met in crisis talks over the weekend, and, amidst some acrimony, agreed that all ERM currencies, except the Deutschmark and the guilder, would use new 15 per cent bands. The ERM as it had existed for 14 years was *de facto* suspended.

Major and Clarke were quick to herald the ERM crisis as proof of the 'fault lines' they had implored others to deal with and a vindication of their own growth strategy.[72] Envisaging that others would now seek to repeat the British experience outside the ERM, they saw no reason to believe that the monetary union project was anything other than dead, ensuring that they would not have to try to sell the impossible to their back-benchers. But amidst the triumphalist notes struck, even in the summer of 1993, there were some warning signs about the future for the Prime Minister and Chancellor if they chose to look. Whilst floating may have seemed a panacea in the circumstances, some hard facts remained. For all the freedom that non-membership seemed to give, in July 1993 French and German short-term interest rates were only 1.5 per cent above those in Britain.[73] More crucially, the Italian experience after Black Wednesday showed just how containing the costs of floating was dependent on fortune in the foreign exchange markets. Unlike the British government, Italy had been looking for a quick return to the ERM and eschewed a swift reduction in interest rates until fiscal tightness had reduced inflationary pressure further. Nonetheless, Italian short-term interest rates remained volatile, and the lira was perpetually weak through the first half of 1993. Clearly, credibility could not be straightforwardly bought outside the ERM.

Even leaving aside the danger that the markets might suddenly turn on sterling, floating had put an onus for Major and Clarke on fiscal tightness as a counter-inflationary anchor which entailed significant costs in terms of economic strategy. Having won three elections helped by the taxation issue, the Conservative government was having to impose serious tax increases on the electorate. At the same time keeping public expenditure under control had embroiled ministers in a public sector pay policy, which though not conceived as a wage policy ultimately risked opening the vexed question of wages in the private sector. Black Wednesday may have seemed like liberation, but it had taken Conservative ministers into territory their predecessors had spent over a decade trying to by-pass.

OLD GHOSTS: SEPTEMBER 1993–DECEMBER 1994

At least some of these notes of caution were indeed reflected in Clarke's approach and rhetoric in the last months of 1993. On 25 November he observed to the House of Commons, 'the argument that the recovery started because we left the ERM is a mythology'.[74] He carried on: 'I'm surprised that I keep being asked about economic and monetary union. I made my first speech in the House of Commons in favour of it in 1971 or 1972 and have not changed my view.'[75]

In the first unified budget in the same month Clarke tightened fiscal policy dramatically. On the revenue side this amounted to: freezing the income tax allowance and the basic rate limit from April 1994; increasing excise duties again; further restricting mortgage tax relief and the married couple's allowance from April 1995; and introducing two new taxes on air travel and insurance premiums. The combined tax increases of the two budgets represented the biggest post-war increase in taxes, taking the equivalent of 3 per cent GDP out of the economy. At the same time Clarke announced a cut of 1.3 per cent in real public expenditure for 1994–95 and then smaller increases in 1995–96 and 1996–97 from that lower base, which would be achieved in part through a public sector pay freeze. The rationale for such fiscal restrictiveness, Clarke explained, was to reduce the PSBR, which he predicted would fall to £38 billion for 1994–95 and be eliminated by the end of decade.

But what was most significant was left unsaid by the Chancellor, namely that he had produced a budget which reduced the PSBR to only 2.75 per cent of GDP in 1996–97 to be within the Maastricht convergence criteria. Explaining himself to the Treasury Select Committee, Clarke replied rather disingenuously: 'I did not do it deliberately ... It is a happy coincidence, although given I was in favour of Maastricht, and given the budget opinions I was in favour of as well, it is not surprising that the two roughly coincide.'[76]

Meanwhile the first signs that sterling might ultimately find floating a volatile and risky experience were starting to become evident. In October 1993 sterling started to fall during the Conservative Party conference, as the publication of Margaret Thatcher's memoirs both gave full rein to the former Prime Minister's antipathy towards her successor and rise to speculation of a challenge to Major for the party leadership. Whilst Major surmounted his autumn tribulations and sterling recovered, clearly continuing political uncertainty had all the potential to make exchange rate management difficult again.

Yet if Major was backing Clarke to direct economic policy to keep the government's long-term options open, he was prepared to adopt a much more cavalier approach within the EU, as if there was nothing to lose. In spring 1994 the impending enlargement of the Union to embrace Sweden, Austria, Finland and Norway[77] made it necessary to reconsider qualified majority voting arrangements in the Council of Ministers. The easiest solution, supported by most EU governments, was to increase the votes required to block legislative proposals from 23 to 27, as a consistent 30 per cent of the total vote. But, bent on showing his back-benchers that he was tough in Europe, Major braced himself for a showdown. On 22 March Major promised the House of Commons that Britain would 'fight its corner hard', to keep the blocking vote at 23, and would veto enlargement until the other states accepted the British view.[78] Yet within a week, bereft of allies, Major was forced to back down and accept the new voting procedures, succeeding only in putting both his leadership and sterling under renewed pressure.

In futilely allowing party management to dictate policy in this way, Major was acting as if the 1993 ERM crisis had liberated the government from any constraints in EU politics. However, this stance betrayed an ignorance of the perceived interests and emerging perspectives of other EU governments. In the wake of the summer of 1993, the remaining ERM states had only cut interest rates gradually, in line with the Bundesbank, and had maintained policies to stabilize their currencies. During December 1993 the franc had risen above its old ERM floor, and, by March 1994, most currencies were trading either within their old narrow or wide 6 per cent bands.[79] With the ERM back by stealth, some EU governments were now concluding that the Maastricht monetary union timetable was feasible after all. On 9–10 April central bank governors had thwarted the desire of some – most notably the Danish government – to formally resurrect the narrow bands.[80] But as Alexander Lamfalussy – head of the fledgling EMI that had begun life in January 1994 as part of Stage Two – observed a few weeks later, monetary union could progress without the narrow bands so long as currency stability was maintained.[81]

Far from Maastricht being dead, future integration within the Union was up for debate again. On 15 April Alain Lamassoure, the French European Affairs Minister, asserted that

when the decision is made to pass to monetary union certain European countries, including France and Germany, should propose the status of the 'new founding members for Europe' for

the largest possible number of countries applying all the
[Union] policies in the monetary, security and social fields.[82]

Lamassoure's words reflected a growing French view that, given both
the British and Danish Maastricht opt-outs and impending enlargement, the hard-core Union around the Franco-German axis should act
to protect their integrationist interests. If countries like Britain wanted
the 'variable geometry' of Maastricht, France insisted, then they had to
pay the price in terms of shaping the future of the Union.

As some of these realities started to dawn on British ministers, all the
old tensions within the Cabinet and the Conservative Party rose to the
surface. At the start of May Michael Portillo, Chief Secretary to the
Treasury and standard-bearer of the Euro-rebel Right, broke from the
official Cabinet agnostic line to proclaim that 'political or monetary
union would mean giving up the government of this country'.[83] Major
was now in the position of desperately trying to convince voters during
the Euro-election campaign that his Cabinet was united, just as it was
quite clear that the British government was out of step with its EU
partners on the matter. On 27 May Major claimed that 'I do not see a
single currency for a very long time; I'm not sure it will happen'.[84] On
the same day Chancellor Kohl told a BBC interviewer that he was firmly
in favour of a single currency, and that 'it will come, I have no doubt at
all'.[85]

With a war of words between Clarke and Portillo continuing into
June, Major and Hurd hit upon a three-pronged strategy over the next
few months to try to refocus the government's European policy. First,
they admonished ministers that no one should depart from the officially
stated policy that the government would decide about a single currency
only if and when the occasion made it necessary. Second, in order to
fortify their credentials with the Euro-rebels, Major and Hurd agreed to
draw another line in the sand, this time over the Franco-German wish to
appoint the Belgian 'Euro-federalist' Jean-Luc Dehaene to the Commission presidency. At the Corfu summit at the end of June Major
accordingly vetoed Dehaene's nomination. If the eventual appointment
of Jacques Santer, another federalist, indicated the shallowness of the
British victory, at least there was no repeat performance of Major
marching his troops back down the hill on qualified majority voting.
Third, the Prime Minister and Foreign Secretary started to look for
means of averting the risk of a hard-core Union emerging, from which
Britain was permanently excluded. On 31 May Major used a European
election rally to sketch out his vision of a 'multi-track, multi-speed' EU,
in which on different issues member states could move at different
paces. Unlike Lamassoure, however, Major did not intend that a hard
core would set the rules of the entire integration game.[86] By July, in the

spirit of wanting to deal with individual issues on their merits, Hurd was trumpeting British support for a stronger common foreign and security policy.[87] Joined by their experience as 'peacekeepers' in the former Yugoslavia, the British and French governments were already in advanced discussions about closer military co-operation, and making the West European Union operationally effective.[88] For their part Major and Hurd clearly believed that there was a basis for a long-lasting Anglo-French axis in this policy area.

In the same context the Prime Minister was backing Clarke in ensuring that they had room for manoeuvre on monetary union. At an ECOFIN meeting on 10–11 September Clarke agreed that the Commission could publish precise macro-economic convergence objectives for the British economy. Whilst those targets were unbinding, by October, the Chancellor had effectively accepted them as the framework for his impending budget, commenting:

> I think the Commission's advice is very sound and certainly in
> line with my own speeches and . . . my own policies . . . I want
> Britain to have a healthy economy so that we are one of the ones
> invited to join [the single currency.][89]

Prior to the budget itself Clarke reiterated his determination to keep British options open, warning:

> We shall have to ask ourselves about the dangers that could be
> involved in assuming a marginal role in Europe. It would be a
> serious mistake to exclude Britain from the major decisions
> concerning European economic and monetary union.[90]

In the 30 November budget, Clarke made £24 billion of cuts in public expenditure for 1994–95, allowing the PSBR to fall to 2.25 per cent in 1996–97, and reducing the overall debt to a level inside the convergence criteria.

But for all ministers' efforts to refocus European policy, profound problems remained, at the heart of which lay the vexed question of the ERM. Whilst Clarke was renouncing 'feel good' cuts in income tax to try to maintain the 'opt-in', the convergence criteria on exchange rates, and quite probably interest rates, could not be met so long as sterling remained outside the ERM. In straightforward economic terms, as one Bank of England official recognised, non-membership might not ultimately present an insurmountable obstacle to participation in Stage Three: 'If sterling was as stable outside the ERM as one of the currencies inside the ERM, why should Britain be debarred . . . We'll have to see how politicians grapple with that question.'[91] However, in October 1993 the German Constitutional Court had given the Bundestag 'the right to make its own evaluation regarding the transition to the third stage of economic and monetary union and to resist any weakening of the stability criteria'.[92] Given sterling's chequered history in the EU, it is difficult to see that the British government would be likely to be given the benefit of the doubt, even in the somewhat unlikely event of exchange rate stability having been achieved.

At the same time, by autumn 1994, the effective rebirth of the ERM was starting to change the contours of Major's and Clarke's macro-economic landscape. The economic recovery had continued into 1994 without igniting inflation or inducing any deterioration in the external account. At the same time Clarke had acted to strengthen the government's long-term counter-inflationary credentials by giving the Bank of England the right to decide on the timing of interest rate movements, and publishing the minutes of meetings between the Governor and himself. But creating a more autonomous role for the Bank in monetary decision-making did not have the effect on the markets that Clarke might have hoped. As soon as it became clear that a narrow band ERM was in *de facto* operation again, and the drive towards monetary union was alive and well, Britain started to pay a significant premium over the leading ERM states on long-term government bonds. As Figure 6.3 shows, whilst the differential between British and German and French rates in January 1994 was 0.71 and 0.73 per cent respectively, by May 1994 this had risen to 1.47 and 0.93 per cent. With long-term government bonds encapsulating the inflationary expectations of the financial markets, clearly the anti-inflationary credibility of a likely member of monetary union was now higher than those of perceived outsiders.

On 12 September 1994 Clarke, vociferously backed by Eddie George (the new Governor of the Bank of England), increased rates by 0.5 per cent; he was determined to make a pre-emptive strike against any inflationary pressure in the economy. Whilst Clarke's public justification for the move did not mention either the problem of long-term government bonds, or the risk that the bond premium might turn into a sterling crisis, the minutes of the Chancellor-Governor meeting reveal their growing anxieties in this direction.[93] Moreover, the interest rate increase left British prime rates just 1.25 and 0.75 per cent below French and German rates respectively. Once more the prospect beckoned of Britain having to pay a short-term interest rate premium for staying outside the ERM.

Whatever Major's and Hurd's hopes for a multi-track Europe, by autumn 1994, it seemed that the ERM and credentials on monetary union were already beginning to define a hard-core Union. On 30 August Edouard Balladur, the French Prime Minister, floated the idea of an EU of 'concentric circles', in which an inner core of states would move towards further pooling of sovereignty including a single currency, with an outer circle maintaining the existing common decision-making arrangements.[94] Two days later a German Christian Democratic policy paper was leaked, envisaging a hard core of EU states, led by Germany and France and implicitly without Britain, pushing ahead to a new phase of integration. Other states could join the hard core, the authors suggested, only when they were 'willing and able', to meet the requirements of integration.[95] Forced onto the defensive, Major used a speech at Leiden university in The Hague to try to stand up to the emerging Franco-German agenda. Declaring that an EU dominated by an exclusive hard core of states was unacceptable, Major again called for a Union in which integration was multi-speed but where states could pick and choose the individual areas in which they wished to participate in common policies.[96] But Major's plea for a 'Europe à la carte' fell

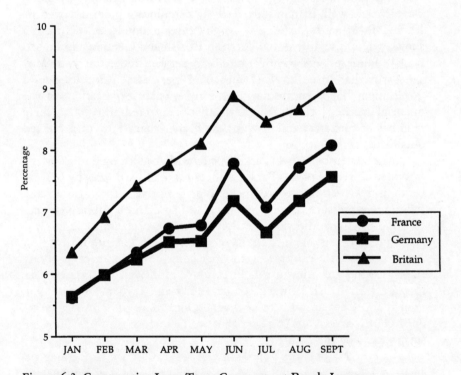

Figure 6.3: Comparative Long Term Government Bonds January-September 1994
(Source: Economist Economic and Financial Indicators, January-September 1994)

largely on deaf ears; for France and Germany, and their allies, integration was indivisible. In the words of Karl Lamers, the foreign policy spokesperson of the Christian Democrat parliamentary group: 'Any country that opposes monetary union can also be held to oppose political union and vice versa. Any country that comes out against either of these clearly has no interest in the success of the 1996 IGC.'[97] In this light procrastinating on monetary union and staying outside of the ERM could only be a route to more general isolation within the Union for British ministers.

However, even if the Continental economies were now recovering, sterling was trading at a value where the external deficit was being reduced, and the interest rates differential with the ERM states was small, rejoining the ERM was out of the question because of the problems of party management. With the government facing a dwindling majority as by-elections were lost, the Conservative Euro-rebels simply could not be ignored. Indeed, despite the efforts to appease them in 1994, their fury, particularly with the Chancellor, was mounting not diminishing. Slamming Clarke's desire to achieve the borrowing convergence criteria, one Euro-rebel fumed:

> It's why I'm so critical of Kenneth Clarke today. He's
> complaining about the lack of a feel-good factor. It's because
> he's hung up on the convergence criteria ... If you read what he
> said in the *House* magazine in January 1993 when he was Home
> Secretary, he said he had similar views to those of Hugh Dykes,
> Roy Jenkins, John Smith and Giles Radice about Europe ...
> How in God's name did he get the job [Chancellor] in the first
> place if he had those views in January 1993. You don't hand
> over the running of your economy to a person who has the same
> views as Roy Jenkins.[98]

At the end of November Major was forced to turn a vote on an EU Finances Bill, which increased British contributions to the Union, into a vote of confidence. But although the government was victorious on 28 November, eight Conservative MPs abstained on one or other of the votes that took place. The next day Major stripped the rebels of the party whip, and with one other MP resigning the whip too, the government lost its official majority in the Commons.

All the problems facing the Prime Minister, Chancellor and the Foreign Secretary were encapsulated in three days in December 1994. On 5 December the EU finance ministers issued a statement which effectively, if convolutedly, pronounced that the 15 per cent ERM fluctuations were 'normal' for the purposes of the Maastricht Treaty.[99] Indicatively, the British government was paying a political price for achieving half the convergence criteria whilst as likely excluding itself from meeting the rest. The following day the government was defeated in the House of Commons on a Labour amendment to stop the imposition of 17.5 per cent VAT on fuel, with eight of the whipless Euro-rebels rebelling again. Defeated on a plank of his budgetary strategy, the next day Clarke raised interest rates by 0.5 per cent to 6.25 per cent to try to avert a crisis of confidence in the markets. Leaving British rates just 0.25 per cent lower than German rates, and 0.7 per cent below French, the benefits of floating were diminishing. Major and Clarke were left presiding over an economic policy which had destroyed Conservative credibility on Black Wednesday, imposed bitterly resented fiscal austerity, helped create civil war on their back benches and, all in all, presented Labour with a record 39 per cent opinion-poll lead.

Major's response to the crisis was to open the door to the possibility of a referendum on monetary union. On 7 December he told a television interviewer that participating in a single currency would 'represent a very significant decision', and 'I have not ruled out a referendum but it is a long way away'.[100] But if his words were designed to tempt the Euro-rebels back into the fold, they were cold comfort to the Chancellor, who had been anxiously pressing him to offer no such thing. Whilst the distant hope of a referendum might have seemed to Major the only way out of his problems of party management, it only took him back into well-trodden territory. As 1994 ended, there loomed the prospect of a Prime Minister and Chancellor drifting slowly apart from each other in their inability to agree on sterling's future in Europe, and with it the sterling crises and interest rates premiums over the ERM states which had dogged the last half of the Thatcher years.

NOTES

1 H. Young, (1993) *One of Us*, London: Pan, p. 570.
2 *Ibid.* For a discussion of the Rome summit, see K. Dyson, (1994) *Elusive Union: The Process of Economic and Monetary Union in Europe*, Harlow: Longman, pp. 142–44.
3 Young, *One of Us*, p. 582.
4 For a discussion of Thatcher's downfall, see Young, *One of Us*; A. Watkins, (1991) *A Conservative Coup: The Fall of Margaret Thatcher*, London: Duckworth; E. Pearce, (1991) *The Quiet Rise of John Major*, London: Weidenfeld & Nicolson.
5 D. Smith, (1992) *From Boom to Bust: Trial and Error in Economic Policy*, Harmondsworth: Penguin, p. 188.

6 *Ibid.*, pp. 188–89.

7 *Guardian*, 21 June, 1991.

8 *Financial Times*, 9 January, 1991; N. Lawson, *The View from No. 11: Memoirs of a Tory Radical*, London: Bantam, p. 944.

9 S. George, (1994) *An Awkward Partner: Britain in the European Community*, 2nd edn., Oxford: Oxford University Press, p. 240.

10 N. Lamont, (1991) 'British Objectives for Monetary Integration in Europe', in Association for the Monetary Union of Europe, *European Monetary Union in a Turbulent World Economy*, London: Association for the Monetary Union of Europe, p. 26.

11 Non-attributable interview with Bank of England official.

12 *Economist*, 7 December, 1991, p. 112.

13 *Ibid.*, p. 118.

14 Conference of the Representatives of the Governments of the Member States, (1992) *Treaty on European Union*, Brussels.

15 *Ibid.*

16 George, *Awkward Partner*, p. 253; *Economist*, 7 December 1991, p. 58.

17 *Economist*, 7 December 1991, p. 58.

18 *Ibid.*, 18 January 1992, p. 49.

19 Non-attributable interview with Bank of England official.

20 *Guardian*, 11 July 1992.

21 *Ibid.*, 14 July 1992; 20 July 1992; 4 August 1992.

22 *Economic Outlook*, June 1992, p. 82.

23 For a full discussion of the economics of the parity, see R. Barrell, A. Britton and N. Pain (1994) 'When the Time was Right: The UK Experience of the ERM', in D. Cobham, (ed.) *European Monetary Upheavals*, Manchester: Manchester University Press; C. Johnson, (1994) 'The UK and the Exchange Rate Mechanism', in C. Johnson and S. Collignon, (eds.) *The Monetary Economics of Europe: Causes of the EMS Crisis*, London: Pinter; P. Gilibert, (1994) 'Living Dangerously: The Lira and the Pound in a Floating World', in A. Steinherr, (ed.) *Thirty Years of European Monetary Integration: From the Werner Plan to EMU*, Harlow: Longman.

24 Barrell *et al.*, 'When the Time was Right?', pp. 126–27.

25 House of Commons, (1992) *Select Committee on the Treasury and the Civil Service, First Report: Minutes of Evidence*, London: HMSO, pp. 30–31.

26 *Sunday Times*, 6 December 1992.

27 Non-attributable interview with Bank of England official.

28 N. Lamont, (1992) 'The Day I Almost Quit', *Times*, 16 September.

29 *Guardian*, 30 November 1992; 1 December 1992; 2 December 1992.

30 Non-attributable interview with Bank of England official.

31 R. Portes, (1993) 'EMS and EMU After the Fall', *World Economy*, 16 (1), pp. 5–6.

32 Non-attributable interview with Bank of England official.

33 Non-attributable interview with Bank of England official.

34 *Ibid.*

35 *Guardian*, 30 November 1992.

36 *Ibid.*

37 *Ibid.*

38 *Ibid.*
39 *Ibid.*
40 *Ibid.*, 1 December 1992.
41 *Ibid.*, 1 December 1992.
42 *Independent on Sunday*, 20 September 1992.
43 *Ibid.*
44 Non-attributable interview with Bank of England official.
45 House of Commons, *First Report: Minutes of Evidence*, p. 6.
46 Non-attributable interview with Bank of England official.
47 *Financial Times*, 17 September 1992.
48 *Guardian*, 31 December 1992.
49 M. Balen, (1994) *Kenneth Clarke*, London: Fourth Estate, p. 250.
50 *Guardian*, 31 December 1992.
51 *Financial Times*, 21 September 1992.
52 *Ibid.*, 25 September 1992.
53 *Ibid.*
54 House of Commons, (1992) *Select Committee on the Treasury and the Civil Service, First Report*, London: HMSO, p. xvi.
55 *Ibid.*, p. xvii.
56 *Financial Times*, 21 September 1992.
57 House of Commons, *First Report: Minutes of Evidence*, p. 8.
58 *Ibid.*, letter from Norman Lamont, p. 2.
59 Balen, *Kenneth Clarke*, p. 246.
60 A. McSmith, (1994) *Kenneth Clarke: A Political Biography*, London: Verso, p. 229.
61 Balen, *Kenneth Clarke*, p. 236.
62 McSmith, *Kenneth Clarke*, p. 221.
63 *Economist*, 19 December 1992, p. 18.
64 *Ibid.*
65 House of Commons, *Appendices to First Report: Minutes of Evidence, p. 142.*
66 *Ibid.*
67 See D. Baker, A. Gamble and S. Ludlam, (1993) '1846 ... 1906 ... 1996: Conservative Splits and European Integration', *Political Quarterly*, 64 (4), pp. 420–34.
68 Non-attributable interview with Conservative MP.
69 Non-attributable interview with Conservative MP.
70 *Economist*, 17 July 1993, p. 71.
71 *Ibid.*
72 McSmith, *Kenneth Clarke*, p. 222.
73 Johnson, 'The UK and the Exchange Rate Mechanism', p. 95.
74 *Hansard*, 25 November 1993, p. 607.
75 *Ibid.*
76 House of Commons, (1994) *Select Committee on the Treasury and the Civil Service, Second Report: 'The November 1993 budget'*, London: HMSO, pp. 87–88.
77 Norway's proposed membership of the EU was eventually rejected in a referendum.
78 *Economist*, 2 April 1994, p. 28.

79 D. Cobham, (1994) 'Introduction: Diversion or Dead End', in D. Cobham (ed.) *European Monetary Upheavals*, Manchester: Manchester University Press, p. 10; *Guardian*, 9 March 1993.

80 *Financial Times*, 15 February 1994; 11 April 1994.

81 *Ibid.*, 27 April 1994.

82 *Financial Times*, 16 April 1994.

83 *Ibid.*, 2 May 1994.

84 *Ibid.*, 28 May 1994.

85 *Ibid.*

86 *Ibid.*, 1 June 1994.

87 *Ibid.*, 19 July 1994.

88 *Guardian*, 19 July 1994.

89 *Ibid.* 11 October 1994.

90 *Financial Times*, 19 November 1994.

91 Non-attributable interview with Bank of England official.

92 The German Constitutional Court (1994) 'Appendix 3' in Steinherr, *Thirty Years of European Monetary Integration*, p. 252.

93 The Treasury, (1994) *Minutes of Monthly Monetary Meeting: 7 September 1994*, London: HMSO.

94 *Financial Times*, 31 August 1994.

95 *Ibid.*, 2 September 1994.

96 *Ibid.*, 8 September 1994.

97 *Ibid.*, 7 November 1994.

98 Non-attributable interview with Conservative MP.

99 *Guardian*, 6 December 1994.

100 *Financial Times*, 8 December 1994.

Conclusions

Vladimir: We could start all over again perhaps.
Estragon: That should be easy.
Vladimir: It's the start that's difficult.
Samuel Beckett, *Waiting for Godot*

The great belief in the Treasury, which I guess it still holds, is that
unless your economy is reasonably well-aligned, there is no point
joining an ERM. Because although you get an external discipline from
doing that, it isn't one you can live with.
Former Treasury official, 1992

In many ways this narrative has been the story of mishaps, mistakes and
misjudgements. The British Conservative government, under two different Prime Ministers, found it extremely difficult to formulate and
pursue a consistently rational approach to the ERM of the kind
conceptualized in the introduction to this book. Not infrequently,
decisions were made which offered minimal benefits, lacked any substantial level of consistency, or indeed were simply self-destructive.
Viewed as a whole, the British government missed out on the possible
benefits that ERM membership offered during the 1980s in terms of
interest rates and exchange rate stability, whilst incurring the costs that
the system imposed in the early 1990s. For most of the period from
1981 to 1989 the ERM offered a relatively effective means of achieving
exchange rate stability and lower interest rates for a given rate of
inflation. By October 1990 membership was certainly the only means
by which the government could immediately achieve either end, but
any sound assessment of the prospects of the British economy and the
likely behaviour of the Bundesbank could have predicted just how
quickly the situation would be reversed. In a recession as deep as the one
then facing Britain, exchange rate stability was an unnecessary counter-
inflationary discipline, and interest rates were far higher than might
have been possible outside the system, given the diametrically opposed
positions of the German and British economies. Monetarily, the government ended up imposing high interest rates and exchange rate instability on itself outside the ERM, and high interest rates and a non-credible
stability for sterling inside the ERM.

Within the government itself the protagonists on all sides of the argument were distinguished by the incoherence and inconsistencies of their positions. Those, like Lawson, who supported ERM membership never addressed the incompatibility of their support for entry with their view that inflation was only a monetary phenomenon. When Lawson made his first bid for entry as Chancellor, the inflation problem lay dormant. But outside the ERM from 1986 to 1990 Lawson and his successor both pursued policies which were directly inflationary and ignored inflationary pressures in the wage market. By the second half of 1988, rising inflation made it difficult to sustain sterling without high interest rates, and by the second half of 1989 and 1990 to sustain sterling at all. Yet neither Lawson nor Major adjusted their position to the changing economic conditions produced by their own policies.

At the same time they turned a blind eye to the relationship between the balance of payments and ERM membership. Although in 1985 the overall current account remained in surplus, underlying problems of competitiveness in the manufacturing sector were already emerging. Believing that it could easily be financed given the level of international capital flows, Lawson simply did not accept that the prospective external deficit constituted a potential problem. Between 1986 and the second quarter of 1989 his view was to some extent vindicated with the deficit only producing short episodes of sterling weakness in September 1986, May to June 1988 and November 1988, respectively. However, from May 1989 onwards the deficit became a manifest constraint on the ability of the government to pursue exchange rate stability as a policy. Yet despite this evidence, Lawson, followed by Major, did not seek a depreciation in sterling, or take action to tackle the structural aspect of the deficit by trying to re-create a broader manufacturing economic base. Ultimately, Major simply secured Thatcher's agreement to join the ERM without anyone examining just how membership was supposed to work.

In the same way, Thatcher's opposition to ERM membership flew in the face of the manifest failure of the monetary targets and her own acceptance of the costs of practising benign neglect towards sterling. The pursuit of exchange rate stability offered Thatcher a counter-inflationary framework centred around interest rates and was consistent with her rejection of policies assuming a causal relationship between costs and inflation. More importantly, whatever disadvantages Thatcher saw in membership, it was in the 1980s the most attractive means to pursue exchange rate stability because it offered lower interest rates for a given rate of inflation. By trying to pursue exchange rate stability outside the ERM, Thatcher left a perennially open question: if the British government was serious about currency stability and was not prepared to allow sterling to depreciate, why was it not a member of the

ERM? In effect, Thatcher was acting as if the costs of the public airing of divisions over ERM membership did not exist. For in the specific sense that the Thatcher government, once the money supply targets were discredited, wished to control inflation by a *monetary* counter-inflationary policy, ERM membership was always an inevitable outcome. If Thatcher ever wanted to do more than delay membership, she would have had to construct a counter-inflationary framework outside the vestiges of the MTFS. Like Lawson and Major, Thatcher ended up willing an end whilst renouncing the means to achieve it.

If these problems were not enough for any government to impose on itself, they were compounded by a propensity for high melodrama; Thatcher could not simply feud with her Chancellor about exchange rate management, she had to treat questions on sterling almost as an act of existentialist definition. Then, having stayed outside the ERM for over ten years, Thatcher took the decision to join in October 1990, no doubt to the bemusement of Major and his senior Treasury officials, suddenly and without systematic consideration as she dressed for dinner. Just less than two years later Norman Lamont was standing on the steps of the Treasury telling the world that at the end of a day when he had raised interest rates by 5 per cent in the depth of a recession, Britain was leaving the ERM. Certainly no one could accuse the British government of dullness on this matter.

Why then from a broad historical perspective did the Conservative government struggle so much with the ERM question? Undoubtedly, the issue was never likely to be particularly easy to handle. Managing sterling within the context of overall British foreign policy has posed serious problems to virtually all British governments since the end of the First World War. From the collapse of the Labour government in 1931, to Dalton's enveloping illness as the convertibility date beckoned in 1947, to Healey's about-turn at the airport in 1976, problems with sterling have been the high drama of British politics both in appearance and substance. Neither in 1979 was there any reason to believe that floating would ultimately prove a panacea to reconcile the problems of the domestic economy with a declining currency. Whilst the USA could do as it wished with the dollar, other states, as the establishment of the ERM testified to, were caught trying to balance a concern for both price stability and competitiveness in the face of the unpredictability of the foreign exchange markets. For Britain the prospects at the end of the 1970s were particularly unpromising. Those states which were always likely to be best able to cope with the new international monetary volatility were those able to sell high-quality goods abroad and where there were consensual economic institutions regularly delivering low inflation. With these assets states were likely to pay both a less high price for controlling inflation via the exchange rate and in terms of competitiveness from any appreciation of their currency.[1] In this context Britain's performance on both the inflation and competitiveness scores could hardly raise confidence that sterling would not continue to be a very awkward constraint for British governments. Whilst the international monetary environment was effectively rewarding the benefits of corporatism, the 1960s and 1970s in Britain had essentially been the story of the failure of a modernizing corporatist experiment, particularly as it related to orchestrating the kind of social consensus that could contain wage increases.[2]

For the first Thatcher government the likely difficulty of managing sterling was compounded by its own political perspective on Britain's economic problems. As Jim Bulpitt has persuasively argued, Thatcher and her colleagues entered office in 1979 seeking to recreate a governing competence for the Conservative Party that drew a line under the political catastrophe of the Heath government and its efforts to modernize the British economy.[3] Unwilling to tackle those economic problems which, everything else being equal, made sterling a generally weak currency, Thatcher and Howe could only attempt to manage Britain's economic decline, whilst trying to reassert the country's political position in world affairs. They, therefore, gave priority to controlling inflation via monetary means over not only growth and competitiveness but over reducing non-monetary sources of inflationary pressure as well. Their policies from 1979–80 represented an effort to manage the British economy as if floating exchange rates were a cost-less exercise, and the ERM at best unnecessary and at worse an attack on national economic autonomy.

However, by 1981, Thatcher and Howe found themselves mired in the problems of floating sterling, as the British economy could not stand the cost. From this point onwards the ERM hung like the sword of Damocles over the Conservative government, heralding danger if sterling were outside or inside its reach. After the failure of the monetary targets, ERM membership did offer the prospect of greater exchange rate stability and lower interest rates for a given rate of inflation, and at times, as in October 1992, it presented Conservative ministers with the only means to achieve these objectives given their overall political perspective. But, at the same time, for good or for ill, Britain did continue to enjoy at least short-term economic autonomy in fiscal policy and in financing high levels of consumption outside the system from which the Conservative government could make significant electoral capital. Moreover, the government's complete withdrawal from any attempt to modernize the British economy, in terms of producing low inflation without a high monetary cost or of rebuilding manufacturing competitiveness, meant that sterling was always going to face a very rough ride in the post-1983 ERM. If for other European states the ERM became a means of trying to ensure that the foreign exchange markets did not compromise their domestic counter-inflationary discipline, for the British Conservative government it offered itself as an alibi for politicians who did not know how else to control inflation.

From 1988 onwards the ERM problem was, of course, further compounded by the politics of the EC. Whilst some have been quick to portray the Community as marking a fault line within modern Conservatism between, to use Andrew Gamble's phrase, the free economy and the strong state, the British government's problems in this regard were not primarily of an ideological nature.[4] A party which has over the last century been free trade and protectionist, free-market liberal and collectivist and committed to appeasement and imperialism would not have a problem *per se* in being the party of Europe, the conscience-stricken objections of a small minority of back-benchers notwithstanding. Instead, the European problems which confronted the Thatcher and Major governments have essentially stemmed from the same divergence in economic structures and approach which made the ERM question so troublesome in straightforward economic terms. Other European states wished to use the Community to increase their ability to make national economic policy choices given the constraints of the international monetary environment, and, for concessions elsewhere, Germany was prepared to let them. But, outside the ERM and with a different set of economic problems, the British government did not share the same national agenda. Thatcher was, therefore, left straggling along in the monetary union debate and making vague pledges to join the ERM, preoccupied, despite her rhetoric, with trying to avoid both relegation to the second tier of a Community which her government could not do without, and plunging the City into an unpromising future.

Meanwhile, in 1989, the autonomy which the government had enjoyed in the foreign exchange markets came to an end, as, amidst substantial inflationary pressure, sterling's underlying weakness was exposed. Since Thatcher and her successive Chancellors would not contemplate any serious alternative or complement to monetary discipline as a counter-inflationary control, ERM entry with a relatively high parity for sterling became an accident waiting to happen. Not only was sterling fixed against the currencies of states with whom there had been no long-term convergence of structural and institutional economic patterns, but it was done after the respective macro-economic cycles had significantly diverged. In this context sterling's involuntary ejection from the ERM on Black Wednesday 1992 was hardly surprising. Damned inside the ERM by the absence of convergence and damned outside by Community politics and the roller-coaster of the foreign exchange markets, Major and Lamont were simply left to wait for time to run out. Whatever retrospective plausibility the suspension of the narrow bands in August 1993 appeared to lend to Conservative ministers, the reality remained that the seeds of the failure of Britain's participation in the ERM were sown by the terms of membership decreed by Thatcher in October 1990.

In 1993 and 1994 the Major government did manage to live a somewhat charmed life outside the ERM. Whilst the EU generally divided between hard-core and weak currencies, with the latter characteristic of those states where low inflation had been bought in the previous decade through an overvalued exchange rate, sterling's resilient performance proved a notable exception. Having enjoyed the good fortune of fiscal autonomy in the mid-1980s, and taken full political advantage of staying outside the ERM, the Conservative government now savoured a new-found freedom of manoeuvre from the Bundesbank. Nonetheless, the difficulties which originally gave rise to the ERM problem remained in place and seem likely to characterize the development of British policy towards the probable European monetary union if the Conservatives survive in office. The rise in long-term government bonds, the Chancellor's early tightening of interest rates in 1994 and a depreciation in sterling in the first months of 1995 all indicated that Britain still lacks counter-inflationary credibility. Whilst the 1990–93 recession did eventually squeeze wage increases, the reality remains that without major reform of the kind the Conservative government has set its stall against, costly deflationary policies are the only available means to even dampen wage inflation.[5] At the same time, despite an improved export performance after Black Wednesday and reduced consumption through fiscal austerity, the British economy is by no means strong enough to withstand either using monetary means to squeeze inflation, or to sustain much growth without the probability of currency depreciation. Lacking either of the assets which give states long-term advantage in the foreign exchange markets, a British government is likely to be damned both inside and outside a monetary union. It could not expect to match the long-term inflation performance of the strongest EU states within a monetary union, as necessary to sustain competitiveness. But continuing to float sterling aside from the Franco-German bloc would in all probability re-establish the monetary premium which existed for most of the 1980s, and leave Britain in the second tier of the EU. Not only would exclusion from a hard-core Europe have potentially damaging consequences for the British economy, especially the City, but there can be no assumption that a Conservative government has, or would have, any alternative forum to regularly manage those of its domestic policy choices constrained by state economic interdependence. In the end the development of British policy towards European monetary integration is the story of fifteen years of Conservative government. By repudiating any effort to create the social market economic structures which characterize Europe's most successful economies and would have led them to seek to advance the same kind of national policy choices as other northern EU states, the Thatcher and Major governments left themselves with no virtuous road to take.

NOTES

1 For a fuller and more general discussion of this argument, see P. Hirst and G. Thompson, (1992) 'The Problem of "Globalization": International Economic Relations, National Economic Management and the Formation of Trading Blocs', *Economy and Society*, 21 (4), pp. 357–96.

2 For a discussion of the political pitfalls of economic intervention in Britain in the 1960s and the 1970s, see D. Marquand, (1988) *The Unprincipled Society: New Demands and Old Politics*, London: Jonathan Cape, Chapter 2. For a discussion of Britain's problems of competitiveness, see M. Porter, (1994) *The Competitive Advantage of Nations*, London: Macmillan.

3 J. Bulpitt, (1986) 'The Discipline of the New Democracy: Mrs Thatcher's Domestic Statecraft', *Political Studies*, 34 (1), pp. 19–39.

4 See A. Gamble, (1990) 'The Great Divide', *Marxism Today*, October, pp. 34–37.

5 For a discussion of the importance of corporatist institutions to control wage increases, and the problem of their absence in Britain, see W. Hutton, (1995) *The State We're In*, London: Jonathan Cape, Chapter 4; and F. Scharpf, (1991) *Crisis and Choice in European Social Democracy*, Ithaca: Cornell University Press.

Bibliography

Aaronovitch, S. (1961) *The Ruling Class: A Study of British Finance Capital*, London: Lawrence & Wishart.

Allison, G. (1971) *The Essence of Decision: Explaining the Cuban Missile Crisis*, Boston: Little, Brown.

Alt, J. and Chrystal, K. (1983) *Political Economics*, Brighton: Wheatsheaf Books.

Anderson, B. (1991) *John Major: The Making of the Prime Minister*, London: Fourth Estate.

Anderson, P. (1964) 'The Origins of the Present Crisis', *New Left Review*, 23, pp 26–53.

Artis, M. and Miller, M. (1986) 'On Joining the EMS', *Midland Bank Review*, Winter, pp 11–20.

Association for the Monetary Union of Europe (1991) *European Monetary Union in a Turbulent World Economy*, London: Association for the Monetary Union of Europe.

Bachtler, J. and Davies, P. (1989) 'Economic Restructuring and Services Policy', in Gibbs, D. (ed.) *Government Policy and Industrial Change*, London: Routledge, pp 154–75.

Baker, D., Gamble, A. and Ludlam, S. (1993) '1846 ... 1906 ... 1996: Conservative Splits and European Integration', *Political Quarterly*, 64 (4), pp 420–34.

Baker, D., Gamble, A. and Ludlam, S. (1993) 'Whips or Scorpions? The Maastricht Vote and the Conservative Party', *Parliamentary Affairs*, 46 (1), pp 151–66.

Baker, D., Gamble, A. and Ludlam, S. (1995) 'Backbench Conservative Attitudes to European Integration', *Political Quarterly*, 65 (2), pp 221–32.

Balen, M. (1994) *Kenneth Clarke*, London: Fourth Estate.

Bank of England (1989) 'The Single European Market Survey of the UK Financial Services Industry', *Bank of England Quarterly Bulletin*, 29 (3), pp 409–12.

Barber, J. (1976) *Who Makes British Foreign Policy?* Milton Keynes: Open University Press.

Barnet, J. (1982) *Inside the Treasury*, London: Deutsch.

Barrell, R. (1992) *Economic Convergence and Monetary Union in Europe*, London: Sage.

Barrell, R. (1992) *Macro-Economic Policy Co-ordination in Europe: The ERM and Monetary Union*, London: Sage.

Barrell, R., Britton, A. and Pain, N. (1994) 'When the Time was Right: The UK Experience of the ERM', in Cobham, D. (ed.) *European Monetary Upheavals*, Manchester: Manchester University Press, pp 114–37.

Bempt, P. van den (1987) *The European Monetary System: Towards More Convergence and Closer Integration*, Louven: Acco.

Brittan, S. (1969) *Steering the Economy: The Rise of the Treasury*, London: Secker and Warburg.

Brittan, S. (1989) 'The Thatcher Government's Economic Policy' in Kavanagh, D. and Seldon, A. (eds.) *The Thatcher Effect*, Oxford: Oxford University Press, pp 1–36.

Britton, A. (1991) *Macro-Economic Policy in Britain 1974–1987*, Cambridge: Cambridge University Press.

Britton, A. and Mayes, D. (1992) *Achieving Monetary Union in Europe*, London: Sage.

Brivati, B. and Jones, H. (1993) *From Reconstruction to Integration: Britain and Europe Since 1945*, London: Leicester University Press.

Browning, P. (1986) *The Treasury and Economic Policy 1964–1985*, London: Longman.

Bruce-Gardyne, J. (1984) *Mrs Thatcher's First Administration: The Prophets Confounded*, London: Macmillan.

Bruce-Gardyne, J. (1986) *Ministers and Mandarins: Inside the Whitehall Village*, London: Sidgwick & Jackson.

Bruce-Gardyne, J. and Lawson, N. (1970) *The Power Game: An Examination of Decision-Making in Government*, London: Macmillan.

Bruno, M. and Sachs, J. (1985) *The Economics of Worldwide Stagflation*, Cambridge: Harvard University Press.

Buiter, W. and Marston, R. (eds.) (1985) *International Economic Policy Co-ordination*, Cambridge: Cambridge University Press.

Bulmer, S. (1983) 'Domestic Politics and European Community Policy-Making', *Journal of Common Market Studies*, 21(4), pp. 349–63.

Bulmer, S. and Patterson, W. (1987) *The Federal Republic of Germany and the European Community*, London: Allen & Unwin.

Bulmer, S. and Wessels, W. (1987) *The European Council: Decision-Making in European Politics*, London: Macmillan.

Bulpitt, J. (1986) 'The Discipline of the New Democracy: Mrs Thatcher's Domestic Statecraft', *Political Studies*, 34(1), pp. 19–39.

Bulpitt, J. (1988) 'Rational Politicians and Conservative Statecraft in the Open Polity', in Byrd, P. (ed.) *British Foreign Policy Under Thatcher*, Oxford: Philip Allan, pp. 180–203.

Bulpitt, J. (1991) *The Conservative Party in Britain: A Preliminary Paradoxical Portrait*, paper presented to the Political Studies Association.

Bulpitt, J. (1992) 'Conservative Leaders and the "Euro-Ratchet". Five Doses of Scepticism', *Political Quarterly*, 63(3), pp. 258–75.

Bundesbank, (1989) *The Deutsche Bundesbank: Its Monetary Policy Instruments and Functions*, Frankfurt: Bundesbank.

Burgen, M. and Lee, A. (1990) 'The UK', in Lodge, J. (ed.) *The 1989 Election of the European Parliament*, London: Macmillan.

Busch, A. (1994) 'Crisis in the EMS', *Government and Opposition*, 29 (2), pp. 80–96.

Busch, A. (1994) 'Central Bank Independence and the Westminster Model', *West European Politics*, 17(1), pp. 53–72.

Butler, D. and Kavanagh, D. (1988) *The British General Election of 1987*, London: Macmillan.

Buxton, T., Chapman, P. and Temple, P. (1994) *Britain's Economic Performance*, London: Routledge.

Calleo, D. (1994) 'America's Federal Nation State: A Crisis of Post-Imperial Viability', *Political Studies*, 42 (Special Issue), pp. 16–33.

Carlsnaes, W. and Smith, S. (eds.) (1994) *European Foreign Policy: The EC and Changing Perspectives on Europe*, London: Sage.

Castles, F. (ed.) (1982) *The Impact of Parties: Politics and Policies in Democratic Capitalist States*, London: Sage.

Castles, F. (1982) 'The Impact of Parties on Public Expenditure', in Castles, F. (ed.) *The Impact of Parties: Politics and Policies in Democratic Capitalist States*, London: Sage, pp 21–96.

Clark, A. (1989) 'Europe 1992: Regulatory Implications', *Banking World*, 7 (9), pp 35–36.

Coakley, J. and Harris, L. (1983) *The City of Capital: London's Role as a Financial Centre*, Oxford: Blackwell.

Coates, D. (1980) *Labour in Power*, London: Longman.

Coates, D. (1984) *The Context of British Politics*, London: Hutchinson.

Coates, D. and Hillard, J. (eds.) (1987) *The Economic Revival of Modern Britain: The Debate Between Left and Right*, Aldershot: Edward Elgar.

Cobham, D. (1989) 'Strategies for Monetary Integration Revisited', *Journal of Common Market Studies*, 27 (1), pp 203–18.

Cobham, D. (ed.) (1994) *European Monetary Upheavals*, Manchester: Manchester University Press.

Cockett, R. (1994) *Thinking the Unthinkable: Think-Tanks and the Economic Counter-Revolution, 1981–1983*, London: HarperCollins.

Collignon, S., Bofinger, P., Johnson, C. and de Maigret, B. (1994) *Europe's Monetary Future*, London: Pinter.

Commission of the European Communities (1992) *European Economy: One Market, One Money*, Luxembourg: Office for Official Publications of the European Communities.

Committee for the Study of Economic and Monetary Union (1989) *Report on Economic and Monetary Union in the European Community (The Delors*

Report), Luxembourg: Office for Official Publications of the European Communities.

Conference of the Representatives of the Governments of the Member States (1992) *Treaty on European Union*, Brussels.

Congdon, T. (1992) *Reflections on Monetarism: Britain's Vain Search for a Successful Economic Strategy*, Aldershot: Edward Elgar.

Conservative Party (1987) *The Conservative Campaign Guide 1987*, London: Conservative and Unionist Central Office.

Cowart, A. (1978) 'The Economic Policies of European Governments', *British Journal of Political Science*, 8, pp 238–311, 425–34.

Crawford, M. (1982) 'No EMS for Britain', *Banker*, 132(4), pp 51–56.

Culp, C. and James, H. (1989) *Joining the EMS: For and Against*, London: Centre for Policy Studies.

Davies, G. (1989) *Britain and the European Monetary Question*, London: Institute of Public Policy Research.

De Grawe, P. (1992) *The Economics of Monetary Integration*, Oxford: Oxford University Press.

Dell, E. (1993) 'The Report of the Three Wise Men', *Contemporary European History*, 2(1), pp 35–68.

Dell, E. (1994) 'Britain and the Origins of the European Monetary System', *Contemporary European History*, 3(4), pp 1–60.

Donoughue, B. (1985) 'The Conduct of Economic Policy', in King, A. (ed.) *The British Prime Minister*, London: Macmillan, pp 47–71.

Dowd, K. and Lewis, M. (eds.) (1992) *Current Issues in Financial and Monetary Economics*, London: Macmillan.

Dowding, K. (1991) *Rational Choice and Political Power*, Aldershot: Edward Elgar.

Dunleavy, P. (1991) *Democracy, Bureaucracy and Public Choice: Economic Explanations in Political Science*, Brighton: Harvester Wheatsheaf.

Dunleavy, P., Gamble, A., Holliday, I. and Peele, G. (1993) *Developments in British Politics 4*, London: Macmillan.

Dunleavy, P. and Husbands, C. (1985) *British Democracy at the Crossroads: Voting and Party Competition in the 1980s*, London: Allen & Unwin.

Dunleavy, P. and Rhodes, R. (1990) 'Core Executive Studies in Britain', *Public Administration*, 68 (Spring), pp 3–28.

Dunn, J. (ed.) (1990) *The Economic Limits to Modern Politics*, Cambridge: Cambridge University Press.

Dunn, J. (1994) 'Introduction: A Crisis of the Nation-State', *Political Studies*, 42 (Special Issue), pp 3–15.

Dunning, J. (1986) *Japanese Participation in UK Industry*, London: Croom Helm.

Dyson, K. (1994) *Elusive Union: The Process of Economic and Monetary Union in Europe*, Harlow: Longman.

Edwards, G. (1992) 'Central Government', in George, S. (ed.) *Britain and the European Community: The Politics of Semi-Detachment*, Oxford: Clarendon Press, pp. 64–90.

El-Agraa, A. (1983) *Britain within the European Community: The Way Forward*, London: Macmillan.

Elgie, R. (1993) *The Role of the Prime Minister in France 1981–1991*, London: Macmillan.

Ellis, W. (1991) *John Major*, London: MacDonald.

Emerson, M. (1979) 'The United Kingdom and the European Monetary System', in Major, R. (ed.) *Britain's Trade and Exchange Rate Policy*, London: Heinemann, pp. 66–95.

Emerson, M. and Huhne, C. (1991) *The Ecu Report*, London: Pan.

Emerson, M., Gros, D., Italianer, A., Pisani-Ferry, J. and Reichen Dach, H. (1992) *One Market, One Money*, Oxford: Oxford University Press.

Evans, P., Rueschmeger, D. and Skocpol, T. (eds.) (1985) Bringing the State Back In, Cambridge: Cambridge University Press.

Ferri, P. (ed.) (1990) *Prospects for the European Monetary System*, London: Macmillan.

Fockerts, D. and Mathicin, D. (1989) *The European Monetary System in the Context of the Integration of European Financial Markets*, Washington: IMF.

Freedman, L. (1986) 'The Case of Westland and the Bias to Europe', *International Affairs*, 63(1), pp 1–19.

Frieden, J. (1991) 'Invested Interests: The Politics of National Economic Policies in a World of Global Finance', *International Organization*, 45(4), pp 425–51.

Funabashi, Y. (1988) *Managing the Dollar: From the Plaza to the Louvre*, Washington: Institute for International Economics.

Galbraith, J. (1987) *A History of Economics: The Past as Present*, London: Hamish Hamilton.

Galbraith, J. (1992) *The Culture of Contentment*, London: Sinclair-Stevenson.

Gamble, A. (1974) *The Conservative Nation*, London: Routledge & Kegan Paul.

Gamble, A. (1988) *The Free Economy and Strong State*, London: Macmillan.

Gamble, A. (1990) 'The Great Divide', *Marxism Today*, October, pp. 34–37.

Gamble, A. (1990) *Britain in Decline: Economic Policy, Political Strategy and the British State*, 3rd edn., London: Macmillan.

Gamble, A. and Walkland, S. (1984) *The British Party System and Economic Policy 1945–1983: Studies in Adversarial Politics*, Oxford: Clarendon Press.

Geddes, A. (1993) *Britain in the European Community*, Manchester: Baseline.

George, S. (1991) *Politics and Policy in the European Community*, 2nd edn., Oxford: Oxford University Press.

George, S. (ed.) (1992) *Britain and the EC: The Politics of Semi-Detachment*, Oxford: Clarendon Press.

George, S. (1994) *An Awkward Partner: Britain in the European Community*, 2nd edn., Oxford: Oxford University Press.

Giavazzi, F., Micossi, S. and M. Miller (eds.) (1988) *The European Monetary System*, Cambridge: Cambridge University Press.

Giavazzi, F. (1989) *The Exchange Rate Question in Europe*, Brussels: The European Commission.

Giavazzi, F. and Giovanni, A. (1989) *Limiting Exchange Rate Flexibility: The European Monetary System*, Cambridge: MIT Press.

Giavazzi, F. and Pagano, M. (1988) 'The Advantage of Tying One's Hands: EMS Discipline and Central Bank Credibility', *European Economic Review*, 32, pp. 1055–82.

Gibbs, D. (1989) 'Government and Industrial Change: An Overview', in Gibbs, D. (ed.) *Government Policy and Industrial Change*, London: Routledge.

Giddens, A. (1985) *The Nation-State and Violence: Volume Two of a Contemporary Critique of Historical Materialism*, Cambridge: Polity Press.

Giddens, A. (1994) *Beyond Left and Right*, Cambridge: Polity Press.

Gilibert, P. (1994) 'Living Dangerously: The Pound and the Lira in a Floating World', in Steinherr, A. (ed.) *Thirty Years of European Monetary Integration: From the Werner Plan to EMU*, Harlow: Longman, pp. 105–43.

Gill, S. and Law, D. (1988) *The Global Political Economy: Perspectives, Politics and Problems*, Hemel Hempstead: Harvester Wheatsheaf.

Gilmour, I. (1992) *Dancing with Dogma: Britain Under Thatcherism*, London: Simon & Schuster.

Gilpin, R. (1987) *The Political Economy of International Relations*, Princeton: Princeton University Press.

Goodhart, C. (1991) 'The Conduct of Monetary Policy', in Wood, G. (ed.) *The State of the Economy*, London: Institute of Economic Affairs.

Goodhart, C. and Bhansali, R. (1976) 'Political Economy', *Political Studies*, 18 (1), pp. 43–106.

Goodman, J. (1992) *Monetary Sovereignty: The Politics of Central Banking in Western Europe*, Ithaca: Cornell University Press.

Grahl, J. (1990) 'After ERM', *Marxism Today*, November, pp. 14–17.

Grant, W. and Nath, S. (1984) *The Politics of Economic Policymaking*, Oxford: Blackwell.

Grant, W. with Sargent, J. (1987) *Business and Politics in Britain*, London: Macmillan.

Greenway, J., Smith, S. and Street, J. (1992) *Deciding Factors in British Politics: A Case Study Approach*, London: Routledge.

Gregory, F. (1983) *Dilemmas of Government: Britain and the European Community*, Oxford: Martin Robertson.

Grier, K. (1991) 'On the Existence of a Political Monetary Cycle', *American Journal of Political Science*, 33, pp. 376–89.

Gros, D. (1989) 'Paradigms for the Monetary Union of Europe', *Journal of Common Market Studies*, 27 (1), pp. 219–30.

Gros, D. and Thygesen, N. (1992) *European Monetary Integration*, London: Longman.

Guitzan, M., Russo, M. and Tullio, G. (1988) *Policy Co-ordination in the European Monetary System*, Washington: IMF.

Hall, P. (1986) *Governing the Economy: The Politics of State Intervention in Britain and France*, Cambridge: Polity Press.

Hall, P. (ed.) (1987) *The Political Power of Economic Ideas*, Princeton: Princeton University Press.

Hall, S. and Jacques, M. (eds.) (1983) *The Politics of Thatcherism*, London: Lawrence & Wishart.

Ham, A. (1984) *Treasury Rules: Recurrent Themes in British Economic Policy*, London: Quartet.

Hancock, M. and Welsh, H. (eds.) (1994) *German Unification: Process and Outcomes*, Oxford: Westview.

Harris, R. (1990) *The Good and Faithful Servant: The Unauthorised Biography of Bernard Ingham*, London: Faber & Faber.

Healey, D. (1990) *The Time of My Life*, Harmondsworth: Penguin.

Heclo, H. and Wildavsky, A. (1977) *The Private Government of Public Money: Community and Policy Inside British Politics*, London: Macmillan.

Hennessy, P. (1986) *Cabinet*, Oxford: Blackwell.

Hennessy, P. (1989) *Whitehall*, London: Secker and Warburg.

Heseltine, M. (1989) *The Challenge of Europe*, London: Weidenfeld & Nicolson.

Hibbs, D. (1977) 'Political Parties and Macro-Economic Policy', *American Political Science Review*, 71, pp 1467–87.

Hirst, P. and Thompson, G. (1992) 'The Problem of "Globalization": International Economic Relations, National Economic Management and the Formation of Trading Blocs', *Economy and Society*, 21(4), pp 357–96.

HM Government, (1990) *Developments in the European Community July–December 1990*, HMSO: London.

Hodgeman, D. (1983) *The Political Economy of Monetary Policy*, proceedings of a conference held in Perugia, Italy, July 1983.

Holmes, M. (1982) *Political Pressure and Economic Policy: British Government 1970–74*, London: Butterworth Scientific.

Holmes, M. (1985) *The First Thatcher Government 1979–83: Contemporary Conservatism and Economic Change*, Brighton: Harvester Wheatsheaf.

Holmes, M. (1989) *Thatcherism: Scopes and Limits 1983–87*, London: Macmillan.

Holmes, M. (1989) *Britain and the EMS*, London: Bruges Group.

Holtham, G. and MacKinnon, N. (1990) *Controlling Inflation: Two Views*, London: Fabian Society.

House of Commons, (1978) *Select Committee on Expenditure, First Report*, London: HMSO.

House of Commons, (1978) *Select Committee on Expenditure, First Report: Minutes of Evidence*, London: HMSO.

House of Commons, (1985) *Select Committee on the Treasury and the Civil Service, 13th Report*, London: HMSO.

House of Commons, (1985) *Select Committee on the Treasury and the Civil Service, 13th Report: Minutes of Evidence*, London: HMSO.

House of Commons, (1987) *Select Committee on the Treasury and the Civil Service, Sixth Report*, London: HMSO.

House of Commons, (1992) *Select Committee on the Treasury and the Civil Service, First Report*, London: HMSO.

House of Commons, (1992) *Select Committee on the Treasury and the Civil Service, First Report: Minutes of Evidence*, London: HMSO.

House of Commons, (1994) *Select Committee on the Treasury and the Civil Service, Second Report: 'The November 1993 budget'*, London: HMSO.

House of Lords, (1990) *Select Committee on the European Communities, 27th Report: Minutes of Evidence*, London: HMSO.

Howe, G. (1994) *Conflict of Loyalty*, London: Macmillan.

Hutton, W. (1989) 'Put Simply, Money Matters', *New Statesman*, 23 June, pp 14–15.

Hutton, W. (1995) *The State We're In*, London: Jonathan Cape.

Ingham, G. (1984) *Capitalism Divided: The City and Industry in British Social Development*, London: Macmillan.

Jackson, P. (ed.) (1985) *Implementing Government Policy Initiatives: The Thatcher Administration 1979–1983*, London: Royal Institute of Public Administration.

Jenkins, R. (1984) 'The European Monetary System and Sterling', *Midland Bank Review*, Summer, pp 23–25.

Jenkins, R. (1989) *European Diary 1977–81*, London: Collins.

Jenkins, R. (1992) *A Life at the Centre*, London: Pan.

Jenkins, S. and Sloman, A. (1985) *With Respect Ambassador: An Inquiry into the Foreign Office*, London: BBC.

Jessop, B. (1983) 'The Capitalist State and the Role of Capital: Problems in the Analysis of Business Associations', *West European Politics*, (6) 2, pp 139–62.

Jessop, B. (1986) 'Thatcherism's Mid-Life Crisis', *New Socialist*, 36, 1986.

Jessop, B. (1990) *Conservative Regimes and the Transition to Post-Fordism: The Case of Great Britain and West Germany*, Essex: Working Paper.

Jessop, B., Bonnett, K., Bromley, S. and Ling, T. (1987) 'Popular Capitalism, Flexible Accumulation and Left Strategy', *New Left Review*, 165, pp 104–12.

Jessop, B., Bonnett, K., Bromley, S. and Ling, T. (1988) *Thatcherism*, Cambridge: Polity Press.

Johnson, C. (1991) *The Economy Under Mrs Thatcher, 1979–1990*, Harmondsworth: Penguin.

Johnson, C. (1994) 'The UK and the Exchange Rate Mechanism', in Johnson, C. and Collignon, S. (eds.) *The Monetary Economics of Europe: Causes of the ERM Crisis*, London: Pinter, pp 85–102.

Johnson, C. and Collignon, S. (eds.) (1994) *The Monetary Economics of Europe: Causes of the ERM Crisis*, London: Pinter.

Jordan, A. and Richardson, J. (1985) *Governing Under Pressure: Politics in a Post-Parliamentary Democracy*, Oxford: Blackwell.

Jordan, A. and Richardson, J. (1987) *British Politics and the Policy Process: An Arena Approach*, London: Unwin Hyman.

Jordan, A. and Richardson, J. (1991) *Government and Pressure Groups in Britain*, Oxford: Clarendon Press.

Jung-Christian, A. (1992) *European Monetary Systems*, Zurich: Verlag Rüegger AG.

Kaldor, Lord (1983) *The Economic Consequences of Mrs Thatcher*, London: Duckworth.

Katzenstein, P. (ed.) (1984) *Between Power and Plenty: Foreign Economic Policies of Advanced Industrial States*, Madison: University of Wisconsin Press.

Kavanagh, D. (1990) *Thatcherism and British Politics: The End of Consensus*, 2nd edn., Oxford: Oxford University Press.

Kavanagh, D. and Seldon, A. (1989) *The Thatcher Effect*, Oxford: Oxford University Press.

Keegan, W. (1984) *Mrs Thatcher's Economic Experiment*, Harmondsworth: Penguin.

Keegan, W. (1985) *Britain Without Oil*, Harmondsworth: Penguin.

Keegan, W. (1986) 'Towards a New Bretton Woods', *Royal Bank of Scotland Review*, 149 (6), pp. 3–10.

Keegan, W. (1989) *Mr Lawson's Gamble*, London: Hodder and Stoughton.

Keegan, W. (1993) *The Spectre of Capitalism: The Future of the World Economy After the Fall of Communism*, London: Vintage.

Keegan, W. and Pennant-Rea, R. (1979) *Who Runs the Economy: Control and Influence in British Economic Policy*, London: Maurice Temple-Smith.

Kennedy, E. (1991) *The Bundesbank: Germany's Central Bank in the International Monetary System*, London: Pinter.

Keohane, R. (1984) *After Hegemony: Co-operation and Discord in the World Political Economy*, Princeton: Princeton University Press.

Keohane, R. and Hoffman, S. (eds.) (1991) *The New European Community*, Boulder: Westview Press.

Kitson, M. and Mitchie, J. (1994) *Managing the Global Economy*, Oxford: Oxford University Press.

Kitzinger, U. (1968) *The Second Try: Labour and the EC*, Oxford: Pergamon.

Kitzinger, U. (1973) *Diplomacy and Persuasion: How Britain Joined the Common Market*, London: Thames and Hudson.

Kremen, J. (1989) *Gaining Policy Credibility in the EMS: The Case of Ireland*, Washington: IMF.

Kruse, D. (1980) *Monetary Integration in Western Europe: EMU, EMS and Beyond*, London: Butterworth.

Lamont, N. (1991) 'British Objectives for Monetary Integration in Europe', in Association for the Monetary Union of Europe, *European Monetary Union in a Turbulent World Economy*, London: Association for the Monetary Union of Europe.

Lawson, N. (1992) *The View from No. 11: Memoirs of a Tory Radical*, London: Bantam.

Leigh-Pemberton, R. (1989) 'Europe 1992 and the City', *Bank of England Quarterly Bulletin*, 29(2), pp 224–26.

Leigh-Pemberton, R. (1989) 'The Future of Monetary Arrangements in Europe', *Bank of England Quarterly Bulletin*, 29(3), pp 372–74.

Leys, C. (1985) 'Thatcherism and British Manufacturing: A Question of Hegemony', *New Left Review*, 151, pp 5–25.

Llewellyn, D. (1983) 'Monetary Arrangements: Britain's Strategy', in El-Agraa, A. (ed.) *Britain within EC*, London: Macmillan, pp 251–70.

Llewellyn, D. and Holmes, M. (1991) *Competition or Credit Controls*, London: Institute of Economic Affairs.

Lodge, J. (ed.) (1990) *The 1989 Election of the European Parliament*, London: Macmillan.

Lomax, D. (1987) 'The UK Case', in van den Bempt, P. (ed.) *The European Monetary System Towards More Convergence and Closer Integration*, Louven: Acco.

Longstreth, F. (1979) 'The City, Industry and the State', in Crouch, C. (ed.) *State and Economy in Contemporary Capitalism*, London: Croom Helm, pp. 157–90.

Louis, J. (1990) *From EMS to Monetary Union*, Luxembourg: Office for Official Publications of the European Communities.

Ludlow, P. (1982) *The Making of the EMS: A Case Study of the Politics of the EC*, London: Butterworth Scientific.

Major, R. (ed.) (1979) *Britain's Trade and Exchange Rate Policy*, London: Heinemann.

March, J. and Olson, J. (1989) *Rediscovering Institutions*, London: Macmillan.

Marquand, D. (1988) *The Unprincipled Society: New Demands and Old Politics* London: Jonathan Cape.

Marsh, D. (1992) *The Bundesbank: The Bank that Rules Europe*, London: Mandarin.

Maynard, G. (1988) *The Economy Under Mrs Thatcher*, Oxford: Blackwell.

McDonald, F. and Zis, G. (1989) 'The EMS: Towards 1992 and Beyond', *Journal of Common Market Studies*, 27 (3), pp 183–202.

McKie, D. (ed.) (1992) *The Election: A Voters' Guide*, London: Fourth Estate.

McSmith, A. (1994) *Kenneth Clarke: A Political Biography*, London: Verso.

Middlemas, K. (1990) *Power, Competition and the State*, Vol. 2, *Threats of the Postwar Settlement: Britain 1961–1974*, London: Macmillan.

Middlemas, K. (1991) *Power, Competition and the State*, Vol. 3, *The End of the Postwar Era: Britain Since 1974*, London: Macmillan.

Miller, W. and Mackie, M. (1973) 'The Electoral Cycle and the Asymmetry of Government and Opposition Popularity', *Political Studies*, 21(3), pp 263–79.

Milward, A. (1984) *The Reconstruction of Western Europe, 1945–1951*, London: Methuen.

Milward, A., Hynch, F., Ranieri, R., Romero, F. and Sørensen, V. (1992) *The Frontier of National Sovereignty: History and Theory, 1945–1992*, London: Routledge.

Milward, A. (1992) *The European Rescue of the Nation-State*, London: Routledge.

Milward, A. and Sørenson, V. (1992) 'Interdependence or Integration: A National Choice', in Milward, A. *et al.*, *The Frontier of National Sovereignty*, London: Routledge.

Minogue, K. and Biddis, M. (1987) *Thatcherism: Personality and Politics*, London: Macmillan.

Moran, M. (1981) 'Monetary Policy and the Machinery of Government', *Public Administration*, 59 (Spring), pp 47–61.

Moran, M. (1983) 'Power, Policy and the City of London', in King, R. (ed.) *Capital and Politics*, London: Routledge & Kegan Paul, pp 49–68.

Moran, M. (1986) *The Politics of Banking*, Oxford: Blackwell.

Moran, M. (1991) *The Politics of the Financial Services Revolution*, London: Macmillan.

Mosely, P. (1976) 'Towards a Satisficing Theory of Economic Policy', *Economic Journal*, 86, pp 59–72.

Mosely, P. (1984) *The Making of Economic Policy*, Brighton: Harvester Press.

Nairn, T. (1979) 'The Future of Britain's Crisis', *New Left Review*, 113, pp 43–69.

Nordhaus, W. (1975) 'The Political Business Cycle', *Review of Economic Studies*, 142(2), pp 169–98.

Nørgaard, O., Pederson, T. and Peterson, N. (eds.) (1993) *The European Community in World Politics*, London: Pinter.

Nugent, N. (1991) *The Government and Politics of the European Community*, 2nd edn., London: Pinter.

O'Brien, R. (1992) *Global Financial Integration: The End of Geography*, 2nd edn., London: Pinter.

Offe, C. (1984) *The Contradictions of the Welfare State*, London: Hutchinson.

Ohmae, K. (1990) *The Borderless World*, London: Harper.

Oppenheimer, P. (1973) 'The Problem of Monetary Union', in Evans, D. (ed.) *Britain in the EC*, London: Gollancz, pp 99–128.

Overbeck, H. (1990) *Global Capitalism and National Decline: The Thatcher Decade in Perspective*, London: Unwin Hyman.

Panic, M. (1982) 'Monetarism in an Open Economy', *Lloyds Bank Review*, 145, pp 36–47.

Panic, M. (1993) *European Monetary Union*, New York: St Martin's Press.

Parsons, W. (1989) *The Power of the Financial Press*, Aldershot: Edward Elgar.

Pearce, E. (1991) *The Quiet Rise of John Major*, London: Weidenfeld & Nicolson.

Pinder, J. (1991) *European Community: The Building of a Union*, Oxford: Oxford University Press.

Plender, J. (1987) 'Lawson's Big Bang in International Context', *International Affairs*, 63 (7), pp 39–48.

Pliatzky, L. (1989) *The Treasury Under Mrs Thatcher*, Oxford: Blackwell.

Pollard, S. (1982) *The Wasting of the British Economy: British Economic Policy 1945 to the Present*, London: Croom Helm.

Polsby, N. (1984) *Political Innovation in America: The Politics of Policy Initiation*, London: Yale University Press.

Porter, M. (1994) *The Competive Advantage of Nations*, London: Macmillan.

Portes, R. (1993) 'EMS and EMU After the Fall', *World Economy*, 16 (1), pp 1–16.

Reich, R. (1993) *The Work of Nations: Preparing Ourselves for 21st-Century Capitalism*, London: Simon & Schuster.

Reid, M. (1988) *All Change in the City*, London: Macmillan.

Riddell, P. (1984) *The Thatcher Government*, Oxford: Blackwell.

Riddell, P. (1989) *The Thatcher Decade: How Britain Changed During the 1980s*, Oxford: Blackwell.

Riddell, P. (1991) *The Thatcher Era and Its Legacy*, Oxford: Blackwell.

Ridley, N. (1991) *My Style of Government: The Thatcher Years*, London: Hutchinson.

Sanders, D. (1991) 'Government Popularity and the Next Election', *Political Quarterly*, 62, pp 235–61.

Sanders, D., Ward, H. and Marsh, D. (1987) 'Government Popularity and the Falklands War: A Reassessment', *British Journal of Political Science*, 17 (3), pp 281–314.

Sandholtz, W. (1993) 'Monetary Policy and Maastricht', *International Organization*, 47 (1), pp 1–40.

Sargent, J. (1986) 'The Effect of Legislation and Pressure Group Development: A Case Study of the British Bankers' Association', unpublished PhD, London: London School of Economics.

Sargent, J. (1983) 'British Finance and Industrial Capital and the European Communities', in Marsh, D. (ed.) *Capital and Politics in Western Europe*, London: Routledge, pp 14–35.

Sbragia, A. (ed.) (1992) *European Political Institutions after 1992*, Washington: Brookings.

Scharpf, F. (1991) *Crisis and Choice in European Social Democracy*, Ithaca: Cornell University Press.

Schmidt, M. (1982) 'The Role of Political Parties in Shaping Macro-Economic Policy', in Castles, F. (ed.) *The Impact of Parties: Politics and Policies in Democratic Capitalist States*, London: Sage, pp 97–176.

Shelton, J. (1994) *Money Meltdown: Restoring Order to the Global Currency Systems*, New York: The Free Press.

Smith, A. (1989) 'Europe 1992: A Truly International Securities Market', *Banking World*, 7 (5), pp 31–32.

Smith, D. (1987) *The Rise and Fall of Monetarism: The Theory and Politics of an Economic Experiment*, Harmondsworth: Penguin.

Smith, D. (1992) *From Boom to Bust: Trial and Error in British Economic Policy*, Harmondsworth: Penguin.

Statler, J. (1981) 'EMS: Cul-de-sac or Signpost on the Way to EMU?', in Hodges, M. and Wallace, W. (eds.) *Economic Divergence in the EC*, London: Allen & Unwin, pp 101–34.

Steinherr, A. (ed.) (1994) *Thirty Years of European Monetary Integration: From the Werner Plan to EMU*, Harlow: Longman.

Stones, R. (1990) 'Government-Finance Relations in Britain 1964–1967: A Tale of Three Cities', *Economy and Society*, 19 (1), pp 32–55.

Strange, S. (1971) *Sterling and British Policy*, Oxford: Oxford University Press.

Strange, S. (1988) *States and Markets: An Introduction to International Political Economy*, London: Pinter.

Stewart, M. (1977) *The Jekyll and Hyde Years*, London: Dent.

Summer, M. and Zis, G. (eds.) (1992) *European Monetary Union: Progress and Prospects*, New York: St Martin's Press.

Swann, D. (ed.) (1992) *The Single European Market and Beyond*, London: Routledge.

Taylor, M. and Artis, M. (1988) *What Has the European Monetary System Achieved*, London: Bank of England.

Temperton, P. (ed.) (1993) *The European Currency Crisis*, London: Probus Europe.

Thain, C. (1985) 'The Education of the Treasury: The Medium Term Financial Strategy', *Public Administration*, 63(3), pp 261–85.

Thatcher, M. (1993) *The Downing Street Years*, London: HarperCollins.

Thompson, G. (1986) *The Conservatives' Economic Policy*, London: Croom Helm.

Thompson, G. (1990) *The Political Economy of the New Right*, London: Pinter.

Thompson, G. (1992) 'Economic Autonomy and the Advanced Industrial States', in McGrew, A. and Lewis, P. (eds.) *Global Politics*, Cambridge: Polity Press, pp 197–215.

Thygesen, N. (1993) 'Towards Monetary Union in Europe: Reforms of the EMS in the Perspective of Monetary Union', *Journal of Common Market Studies*, 31(4), pp 447–72.

Tsoukalis, L. (1977) *The Politics and Economics of European Monetary Integration*, London: Allen & Unwin.

Tsoukalis, L. (1993) *The New European Economy: The Politics and Economics of Integration*, 2nd edn., Oxford: Oxford University Press.

Tufte, E. (1978) *Political Control of the Economy*, Princeton: Princeton University Press.

Tugwell, J. (1989) 'Europe 1992: Clearing Banks Face the Challenge', *Banking World*, 7(3), pp 27–28.

Ungerer, H., Hauvonen, J., Lopez-Claros, A. and Mayer, T. (1983) *The European Monetary System: The Experience 1979–1982*, Washington: IMF.

Ungerer, H., Hauvonen, J., Lopez-Claros, A. and Mayer, T. (1989) *The EMS: Developments and Perspectives*, Washington: IMF.

Vital, D. (1968) *The Making of British Foreign Policy*, London: Allen & Unwin.

Wallace, H. (1981) 'National Politics and Supranational Integration', in Cameron, D. (ed.) *Regionalism and Supranationalism*, London: Policy Studies Institute, pp 111–26.

Wallace, H. (1986) 'The British Presidency of the EC's Council of Ministers', *International Affairs*, 62, pp 583–99.

Wallace, H. (1990) 'Britain and Europe', in Dunleavy, P. *et al.*, *Developments in British Politics 3*, London: Macmillan, pp 150–172.

Wallace, H. (1993) 'European Governance in Turbulent Times', *Journal of Common Market Studies*, 31(3), pp 293–303.

Wallace, H. (1994) 'Britain out on a Limb', *Political Quarterly*, 66(1), pp 46–58.

Wallace, W. (1975) *The Foreign Policy Process in Britain*, London: Royal Institute of International Affairs.

Wallace, W. (1983) 'Backwards Towards Unity', in Wallace, W., Wallace, H. and Webb, C. (eds.) *Policy Making in the EC*, Chichester: Wiley & Sons.

Wallace, W. (1990) *The Dynamics of European Integration*, London: Pinter.

Wallace, W. (1994) 'Rescue or Retreat? The Nation – State in Western Europe, 1945–1993', *Political Studies*, 42 (Special Issue) pp 52–76.

Wallace, W. and Wallace, H. (1990) 'Strong State or Weak State in Foreign Policy: The Contradictions of Conservative Liberalism, 1979–1987', *Public Administration*, 68(1), pp 83–101.

Wallerstein, I. (1980) *The Politics of the World Economy*, Cambridge: Cambridge University Press.

Walsh, J. (1994) 'International Constraints and Domestic Choices: Economic Convergence and Exchange Rate Policy in France and Italy', *Political Studies*, 42(2), pp 243–58.

Walters, A. (1986) *Britain's Economic Renaissance*, Oxford: Oxford University Press.

Walters, A. (1990) *Sterling in Danger: The Economic Consequences of Fixed Exchange Rates*, London: Fontana.

Watkins, A. (1991) *A Conservative Coup: The Fall of Margaret Thatcher*, London: Duckworth.

Whitelaw, W. (1989) *The Whitelaw Memoirs*, London: Aurum.

Wilks, S. (1985) 'Conservative Industrial Policy 1979–1983', in Jackson, P. (ed.) *Implementing Government Policy Initiatives: The Thatcher Administration 1979–1983*, London: Royal Institute of Public Administration, pp 123–44.

Williams, K. Williams, J. and Hadam, C. (1990) 'The Hollowing Out of British Manufacturing and its Implications for Policy', *Economy and Society*, 19(4), pp 456–90.

Williamson, J. (1993) 'The Fall of the Hard EMS', *World Economy*, 3, pp 377–79.

Wincott, D. 'The European Central Bank: Constitutional Dimensions and Political Limits', *International Relations*, 11 (2), pp 111–26.

Woolley, J. (1984) *Monetary Politics: The Federal Reserve and the Politics of Monetary Policy*, New York: Cambridge University Press.

Woolley, J. (1992) '1992, Capital and the EMS: Policy Credibility and Political Institutions', in Sbragia, A. (ed.) *European Political Institutions after 1992*, Washington: Brookings, pp 157–90.

Woolley, J. (1994) 'The Politics of Monetary Policy: A Critical Review', *Journal of Public Policy*, 14 (1), pp 57–85.

Wölling, W. *Monetary Policy in Europe After Maastricht*, London: Macmillan.

Young, H. (1993) *One of Us*, London: Pan.

Young, H. and Sloman, A. (1989) *But, Chancellor*, London: BBC.

Ypersale, J. van (1985) *The European Monetary System: Origins, Operation and Outlook*, Cambridge: Woodbeau Falkner.

BROADCAST SOURCES

Channel Four (1993) *A Brief Economic History of Our Time.*

NEWSPAPER AND PERIODICAL SOURCES

Annual Abstract of Statistics
Daily Telegraph
Economic Outlook
The Economist
Financial Times
Guardian
Independent on Sunday
Observer Monthly Digest of Statistics
Observer
Sunday Times
The Times

Index